PUBLIC SPEAKING IN THE 21ST CENTURY

DAVIS W. HOUCK

Published by Flip Learning

Copyright © 2019 by Davis W. Houck

All rights reserved.

No part of this book may be reproduced, in any form,
without written permission from the publisher.

Request for permission to reproduce selections from this book should
be mailed to:
Flip Learning, 432 West Fairmount Avenue, State College, PA 16801.

FlipLearning.com

First Flip Learning bundle edition 2019

ISBN-13 978-1-7355940-7-1

For information about special discounts for bulk purchases,
please contact Flip Learning Sales at sales@fliplearning.com.

Printed in the United States of America

3 5 7 9 10 8 6 4 2

Contents

ONE   THE MAGIC OF SPEECH

    1.1 Preface to the 2018 Edition   1

    1.2 *Public Speaking in the 21ˢᵗ Century*: A User's Guide   5

    1.3 "The Only Thing We Have to Fear is Fear Itself"   9

    1.4 Authenticity vs. Artifice   11

    1.5 Public Speaking in a Digital Age   13

    1.6 The More Things Change, the More They Stay the Same   14

    1.7 The "Magical" Properties of Speech   16

    1.8 The Power of Speech   21

TWO   BODIES, NERVES, DELIVERY

    2.1 Doing the Technicolor Yawn: Performance Anxiety   23

    2.2 Communication Apprehension   26

2.3 Communication Apprehension and Delivery   29

2.4 "Practice? We're talking about practice."   32

2.5 Slow it Down   38

2.6 Avoiding the Body Snatchers   39

2.7 Delivery in a virtual world   43

THREE   LANGUAGE, STYLE, HUMOR

3.1 An Introduction to Language, Style, and Humor   47

3.2 Language and "Reality"   51

3.3 Language and Gender   55

3.4 Style   57

3.5 Humor   70

FOUR   SELECTING A TOPIC

4.1 We All Have Expertise   77

4.2 Integrating Personal and Audience Interests   80

4.3 Brainstorming Geography to Identify Speech Topics   83

4.4 Brainstorming Academic Interests   85

4.5 Brainstorming Professional Interests   89

4.6 Taboo Topics   91

4.7 Narrowing a Topic to a Specific Purpose   93

4.8 Developing a Central Idea   98

FIVE   AUDIENCE ANALYSIS

5.1 Epic Fail: Know Your Audience   103

5.2 The Ancient Greeks on Audience Analysis   107

5.3 The Perils of Generalization   112

5.4 Situational Audience Analysis   115

5.5 Speaking Style and Audience   120

    5.6 Constraints in the Speech Classroom   122

    5.7 Audience Surveys   125

SIX BEGINNINGS AND ENDINGS

    6.1 Memorable Bookends   131

    6.2 Why Great Beginnings and Endings Matter   136

    6.3 How to Begin Your Speech   138

    6.4 How to Organize Your Introduction   145

    6.5 How to Achieve Closure   149

SEVEN ORGANIZING THE BODY

    7.1 Getting Out of Order   155

    7.2 Creating Logical "Flow"   158

    7.3 Chronological Order   160

    7.4 Spatial Sequence   163

    7.5 Topical Approach   166

    7.6 Causal Organization   170

    7.7 Problem-Solution Order   173

    7.8 Refutative Design   176

    7.9 Using Connectives   179

EIGHT RESEARCH: GOING DEEP AND GETTING CLOSER

    8.1 Google. The End.   183

    8.2 Supporting Material, or Research   184

    8.3 Conducting Quality Research: Go Deep and Get Closer   188

    8.4 Getting Closer with Primary and Secondary Source Materials   192

- 8.5 Stepping Back: An "Aerial View" of Primary Research   197
- 8.6 Know Thyself and "Staying Woke"   204
- 8.7 Transforming Research into Supporting Material   209

NINE GODDESSES, COURTSHIP, PERSUASION

- 9.1 Social movements need faces. And voices.   217
- 9.2 The "Persuasion Economy"   220
- 9.3 Defining Persuasion   224
- 9.4 Ethos   232
- 9.5 Pathos   238
- 9.6 Logos   244
- 9.7 Five Types of Inference   252

TEN SEEING AND BELIEVING IN A VISUAL WORLD

- 10.1 Visual Aids and Crutches   261
- 10.2 Visual Aids and Strategic Rhetorical Effect   265
- 10.3 Types of Visual Aids   267
- 10.4 Visuals in a Digital Age   271
- 10.5 Common Mistakes   274

ELEVEN SPEAKING ON SPECIAL OCCASIONS

- 11.1 Speech, Meaningfulness, and Special Occasions   277
- 11.2 Speeches of Thanks/Acceptance   282
- 11.3 Speeches of Introduction   285
- 11.4 The Wedding Toast   288
- 11.5 The Eulogy   291

TWELVE SEEING AND HEARING THE MAGIC
    12.1 Models of Public Speaking Excellence   301
    12.2 Speech Samples   303

CREDITS

1 The Magic of Speech

1.1 Preface to the 2019 Edition

Context can be pretty much everything.

When my good friend and colleague, Christian Spielvogel, first asked me to write *Public Speaking in the 21st Century*, our country was smack in the middle of the 2012 presidential election, which pitted incumbent Barack Obama against Mitt Romney. As with all U.S. presidential campaigns, things got fairly heated, really interesting speeches were given, crucial debates were had, and partisan media had different interpretations.

And the election came.

Former president Barack Obama won fairly convincingly. I

used a good bit of the campaign's rhetoric and public speaking in this textbook. Why not? It was very current and illustrated our key principles quite well.

That event, now in our rear-view mirror by more than five years, seems like a lifetime ago, or at least as long as a Major League Baseball game.

Today we inhabit a different political universe—due in no small measure to the election of Donald Trump. One of the first questions I got asked as he was sworn into office was, "What does this mean for public speaking on my campus?" Lurking below the surface in that question was something a bit more difficult, something like, "As the nation's chief public speaker, I don't want my students imitating his rhetorical style—nor his content. What do I do?"

Rather than avoid that hard question, I want to meet it head on in this latest edition of *Public Speaking in the 21st Century*.

Let's start with your author. Me.

Over my adult civic life, I've voted for pretty much every political stripe: conservative, independent, and liberal. I've been a registered voter in all three recognized "parties." I'm not an ideologue for a simple reason: I like to be persuaded by good ideas and compelling evidence and nuanced reasoning. And, as we know, good ideas-evidence-reasoning can come from lots of different political persuasions. In this textbook you will find all kinds of different speakers and speeches; the point is that they are here because they illustrate a concept—not because I'm trying to score political points. That's dumb and really bad audience analysis (as you'll read in Chapter 5). Students (and faculty) of all political persuasions can find a home here; if they can't, I haven't done my job as a writer.

Pre-President Trump, public speaking authors (and teachers) often turned to the presidency to select exemplary rhetorical moments; as our nation's highest office in which skillful public speaking takes place pretty much every single day, the video examples are plentiful. And they are relatively easy to use, and are free of messy copyright matters. So you'll find eloquent examples in *Public Speaking in the 21st Century* selected from the presidencies of Franklin D. Roosevelt, Ronald Reagan and Barack Obama, to name a few. Presidential scholars Karlyn Kohrs Campbell and Kathleen Hall Jamieson argue that one of the things every single president has to do in their inaugural address is to "re-knit the country," to bind up the wounds that have been inflicted over the course of the campaign. Presidential campaigns get loud, in-the-face angry, and very personal. So whoever wins has a lot of rhetorical work to do straight off the bat.

President Trump never did that work. He doesn't even try. No, Trump's America is premised rhetorically on division, on precisely NOT binding up the nation's wounds and moving forward together as we confront our hard problems.

Please note, I'm not talking about policy here; I am talking about a public speaking style that loves to demonize—the "sonsofabitches" of the NFL—the news organizations that are loudly and repeatedly labeled "fake"—and the near-constant vilification of one's political opponents. None of our country's previous 44 presidents have engaged in that sort of near-daily practice. Not even close. True, they also didn't have a smartphone with a platform that allowed instant access to the entire country.

As I write this in June 2018, the *Washington Post* has documented more than 3,200 false or misleading claims that Trump has made in less than 500 days of office.[1] By my count, that's over 6 lies/half-truths a day, or one every 4 hours. Pinocchio's nose would look like a trans-Atlantic cable. It's far easier to persuade someone when

---

1   Visit link: https://goo.gl/Ay3EmR

you can make up the evidence. Or straight up lie about it. Should we believe the *Washington Post*? I do. Though I never do so blindly; newspapers get stuff wrong all the time. But to label an entire news organization—be it the *New York Times*, the *Washington Post*, CNN, whomever—as "fake" is to purposefully inflame the country, to sow division and discord. Abraham Lincoln spoke famously of "the better angels of our nature" as the Civil War loomed. Trump's rhetorical style moves in precisely the opposite direction. Several news organizations have done the polling: we've never been more ideologically divided as a country.[2]

In public speaking class, our aim is always to try and bring people together, not disparage and demean. That is ethical speech making. And sometimes when we try, we fail, but that's fine; at least we made the effort. Audience disagreement isn't a bad thing. The point is you tried to do it in a manner that appealed to your listener's best instincts, those "better angels."

You've heard the expression, perhaps, "if you get some lemons, make some lemonade." That's exactly what I propose to do with the example of our current president in *Public Speaking in the 21st Century*. In our chapter on persuasion, for example, I talk a good bit about logical reasoning. Let's take a hard look at some recent examples of the argument by analogy used by the administration. Let's examine the unstated logic (which Aristotle called the enthymeme). Similarly, in our chapter on evidence, what sources can we trust to be credible sources and which ones are janky? Is Breitbart always wrong? Is the *Post* always right? How would we know? Great questions; let's take a look. In our chapter on language, what does it mean when we label a 25-year old college student from Mexico a "DREAMer" rather than an "illegal immigrant." What are the obligations of naming ac-

---

2   Visit link: https://goo.gl/spMAUd

curately and thus ethically? Another great question.

In brief, our present political moment gives us a very unique opportunity to have a conversation about the "how" of public speaking. We shouldn't turn our back on that moment, but instead embrace it and talk about it.

As you'll notice very quickly as you dive into our textbook, politics is only one branch of public speaking. Far more importantly as far as we're concerned, is what's going on in your classroom, what's going on as you think hard about the speech you want to give, and the great evidence you want to employ to inform, inspire and persuade your listeners. That's what matters ultimately to you—and to us.

1.2 *Public Speaking in the 21st Century*: A User's Guide

Episode 1: Fear Itself [Flip Learning video series]
Speech day, a mad dash across campus, the voices of great speakers past... Welcome to *Public Speaking in the 21st Century*.

I never thought I'd write these words: public speaking has become kind of a thing in the twenty-first century. Sure, not quite a thing like Marvel Superheroes, small-batch bourbon, Queen Bey, and leggings, but still a thing.

Have you watched a recent episode of *Shark Tank*, for example? Yeah, those budding entrepreneurs are using persuasive speeches to sell themselves and their creations to the sharks. What about those highly produced TED (Technology, Entertainment and Design) Talks? Sure, the tightly produced and packaged 18-minutes-or-less speeches are really, really interesting. And bars/lounges/coffee shops sponsoring story-telling contests? Seriously? You bet, *The Moth* and NPR, among other groups, are putting the pub back in public speaking, the speak in speakeasy.[3]

Crazy, right?

NPR, Ted Talks, and Shark Tank (left to right)

Crazy because in our highly digitized, smartphone leave-me-alone world, the oldest human technology is sort of hip. We're talking about the human voice. Whatever is mediating that voice—your phone, a radio, the web—is beside the point: we're tuning in to public speaking in lots of different contexts.

We've created the digital platform that accompanies this print supplement to help you tap into your own public speaking excellence. We've also created it to engage you in all kinds of ways. In each chapter of the digital version, you'll find, for example, many web links that illustrate ideas and topics we're writing about. Some of the links

---

3   Visit link: https://goo.gl/JWtRu6

are really funny. Some are poignant. Others are inspiring. We hope all are instructive, at some level. We update them all the time since our world changes instant-by-instant through the spoken word.

You'll also find at the beginning of each digital chapter serialized short videos that follow several characters in their fictional public speaking classes. You'll meet Laura, Kaitlyn, and Calvin as they work through the stresses and strains of speechmaking. You'll also get to know Mallory and the inimical TA Robert, whose passion for public speaking and debate is, well, inspiring and just a bit manic. Each short offers valuable advice, we think, without the Heavy Hand of Authority or some teacher figure with a red pen. What you don't want, we've learned, is a series of boring how-to-give-a-speech videos, with hideous production values and no sense of humor. We feel your pain.

You'll also get a healthy dose of the ancients in the digital version, upon whose ample public speaking shoulders we stand. You'll get to know the ever-questioning Socrates and his suspicions about public speech; you'll meet the highly patriotic and nervous Isocrates, who trained generations of Athenian leaders; you'll get introduced to the Macedonian, Aristotle, who loved long and well-organized lists and flashy rings; you'll also encounter the badass baller from Sicily, Gorgias, who introduced rhymes to speechmaking and who no doubt had spinner rims on his tricked-out chariot.

You'll also encounter a lot of speechmaking from your peers. Included in nearly every digital chapter are examples from your college cohorts giving speeches before real audiences during real public speaking rounds. We debated including "staged" speeches, ones that were really good in class, but were re-shot to achieve higher production values. We decided against such re-shooting. Why? Because it would be staged before a camera—not delivered before an audience; it wouldn't be real in ways that a live, graded classroom speech is. And so we've included clips from many speeches that illustrate key points, clips that we don't want you to feel like you need to slavishly mimic, but rather that you can generate ideas from (the entire student speech archive is in Chapter 12 of the digital version). Know that each speech, each clip, came from The Real Thing, not multiple re-takes with fancy editing techniques and great lighting.

Many of you are taking this class because your major, your minor, or your university requires you to take it. At Florida State University, where I teach, every undergraduate student is required to take some version of public speaking. Not surprisingly, I get a lot of students who really don't want to be in my class—such is the fear and loathing so many have toward required courses, especially this one. Many students also think that speaking 3 or 4 times to their peers is just something they have to do to check yet another box to meet graduation requirements. Their speeches, in other words, don't really matter that much, if at all.

We would beg to differ with you. Your speeches can change the world—and in the best ways. Allow me (and my good friend, Carly) to prove it to you. Back in the fall of 2014 Carly was an undergraduate at FSU—and living the dream. Thriving in a competitive major, doing an important internship, enjoying a great social life, popular in her sorority, her life changed overnight. As her mentor, professor and friend, Carly later confided to me about what had happened. It was awful—and terribly unjust. As a fearless fighter, I asked Carly later that semester if she would come to my public speaking class and tell us about what had happened; her college peers needed to know her story. She eventually said yes, she would bare her soul before more than 200 of her peers. One of her peers that day, an aspiring documentary filmmaker, Kaitlyn, had no idea that Carly's devastation would soon change her world; after all, she was just attending lecture like she always did every Monday afternoon in spring semester 2015. But as Carly's emotion-filled words echoed in Health and Wellness room 2102, Kaitlyn knew that something life-changing was happening before her eyes and ears.

Meet Carly and Kaitlyn; they reunited with their old professor back in room 2102 this past spring. We feature them and their remarkable story here because they represent everything that's good about public speaking—how it changes speakers, how it changes listeners, how it can change laws. And yes, even how it changes professors.[4]

1.3 "The Only Thing We Have to Fear is Fear Itself"

Speech day, a mad dash across campus, the voices of great speakers past... Welcome to *Public Speaking in the 21st Century.*

We should begin a book about public speaking with candor: if you're like most beginning students in public speaking, you really don't want to be here; in fact, you'd rather be just about anywhere else. You might have even convinced yourself that you don't need this subject; you already know how to talk, so why waste time on something so elemental, so basic? Perhaps your attitude isn't much different from that of the (in)famous college basketball coach Bobby Knight, who, when he was coaching, liked to torture sportswriters by saying, "All of us learn to write in second grade. Most of us go on to greater things." Similarly, one of our earliest accomplishments is learning to talk, and at this point in your life talking is as natural as breathing. So why bother making a formal study of talking?

In our years teaching public speaking, we've encountered this attitude a lot. What we've discovered is that most students' hostility to speech, and this course specifically, is less about a skill they've already mastered than it is a rather dreadful fear. Whether it's made fun of by Jerry Seinfeld or documented in yet another "top 10 great-

---

4   Visit link: https://goo.gl/mMF9nV

est fears" poll, it's a given that most (all?) of us are afraid of giving a public speech.[5] "According to most studies, people's number one fear is public speaking," notes Seinfeld. "Number two is death. Death is number two. Does that sound right? This means to the average person, if you go to a funeral, you're better off in the casket, then doing the eulogy." The rationality is indeed puzzling. The symptoms of that fear are varied enough to fill a sizable hard drive, but their cause seems rather singular: we are terrified about being judged negatively by our audience.

We'll have a lot more to say about speech anxiety—the highbrow academic name for it is "communication apprehension"—and how to productively manage it, but for now let's just note a few things. First, with very few exceptions, your audience wants desperately for you to succeed. Ever been an audience member for a speech in which the speaker struggled? Yeah, us, too, and it was miserable; our bodies felt like they were turning inside out. Just like the solo singer struggling to remember the words of the National Anthem who ended up singing an impromptu and lovely duet, audience members want you to nail it—even if they might not agree with you.[6] We

---

5   Visit link: https://goo.gl/Hxen8h

6   Visit link: https://goo.gl/wfTZVY

love to watch great performances of all types, and never forget: a public speech is a very public performance. This leads naturally to more reassurance: the flip side of your terror is that you want to influence your audience's judgment in a positive direction—otherwise you wouldn't care. And caring, as any athlete, musician, actor, teacher, student, or fill-in-the-blank will tell you, is crucial to performing well. If you don't care, you're not nervous, period.

PRPSA [Flip Learning survey]

Public Speaking Anxiety [Flip Learning chat]

1.4 Authenticity vs. Artifice

Second, we have a sneaking hunch, too, that public speaking textbooks and teachers haven't exactly helped ease students' speech anxiety. Why? Aristotle, that Macedonian polymath who authored both the *War and Peace* and *Ulysses* of public speaking textbooks back in the fourth century BCE, offers some clues. In Book III of *On Rhetoric*, he offers a curious editorial on delivery, or the ability to perform a speech live before an audience. He says delivery is an altogether "vulgar matter," and in a very long book about all manner of public speaking skills, this most critical component gets two brief pages.[7] Part of Aristotle's disgust with delivery is that a pleasant sound and appearance often trump a well-reasoned argument. No doubt you've experienced the attractive person with a pleasing voice who seemed

---

7   Aristotle, *On Rhetoric*, transl. George A. Kennedy (New York: Oxford University Press, 1991), 218-19.

Marble bust of Aristotle ca. 330 BC

convinced of what s/he was saying. Whether this is vulgar or not, suffice it to say that Beyoncé Knowles, Angelina Jolie, and Jennifer Lawrence's deductive syllogisms and/or Morgan Freeman, George Clooney, and Denzel Washington's inductive inferences get trumped by other, less logical things. This Aristotle knew. And this he fretted about. What would happen to a world where appearances trumped reality, where falsehood, however pretty, could overwhelm truth?

Aristotle and "Natural" Speech

But the vulgarity of delivery for Aristotle was also related to the most pleasing sounds of speech; he labeled these sounds as "natural," or those that occur in everyday conversation. You know the sound; you can pick it out from miles away, just as you can the canned/fake/phony/contrived sound of the memorized or rehearsed speech. This sound is off-putting. Because it sounds rehearsed it's not genuine; and because it's not genuine, you're not buying. And yet here's what we usually tell students of public speaking: practice sounding natural!

If this isn't vulgar, or at least ironic, we're not sure what is. It might also induce just a bit of nervousness and anxiety. Why do we need to become Streep or Pitt to have just the right sound? Why can't we just be ourselves? So what if we sound a bit nervous; after all,

Know Your Greeks! Aristotle [Flip Learning animation series] Animations are used in this and later chapters to introduce you to the ideas of various Ancient Greek philosophers whose works greatly influenced the theory and practice of public speaking.

aren't we just being natural? Is this public speaking class, or Acting 101? Great questions. You've entered Aristotle's world, and we promise to give this vexing topic more than a mere two pages.

1.5 Public Speaking in a Digital Age

Since we're on the topic of candor and also talking about some of our esteemed colleagues who've preceded us in this endeavor, we should say a word or two about our own motives in authoring a book on speaking in public. As students and academics we find ourselves in a fascinating moment of transition: in the not-too-distant future, books that we once held in our hands will be largely a thing of the past; instead, we'll retrieve their content on e-readers, tablets, laptops, computers, and smart phones and surely a few new devices that haven't even been dreamed up yet.

Presently and for the foreseeable future many fine books on public speaking will be retrofitted for this new media environment; books that were designed in and for the twentieth century and have educated generations of public speaking students will be shoehorned into these new platforms. There will be a great deal lost in translation; perhaps more important, as students in our digital world you've cut your teeth on technologies and mobile devices that allow you to do several things in several "places" at once—and do it now.

College Students in a Digital Age

Many of the consequences of our present digital revolution are still largely unknown, but several scientists are in agreement about one thing: the devices we use and how we use them (dare we say, how they use us) are literally rewiring our brains; as such, you are very different public speaking students than your twentieth-century peers. You learn differently, you think differently, you interact differently, you have very different educational expectations—and you do it all a lot faster.

We realize this Brave New World sounds just a bit frightening, but instead of grafting old technology and older knowledge onto the new, we've opted to meet you where you are: squarely in the digital domain where interactivity, gaming, role-playing, and file-sharing constitute our world. Frankly this world intrigues us, if for no other reason than we can design a public speaking text that will be a total sensory experience from beginning to end; and, as a result, we can stretch our ability and imaginations as public speakers in a digital age. In building this text for the twenty-first century our aim is for the organic rather than a Franken-book suffering from multiple personality disorder.

1.6 The More Things Change, the More They Stay the Same

Of course our perceptive readers might plausibly ask, how can you mention both Aristotle and digital interactivity within a few short

Know Your Greeks! Socrates [Flip Learning animation series]

paragraphs of each other? How can you invoke classical rhetoric next to neural remapping? We would emphasize from the beginning that just because an idea is old doesn't mean it's obsolete; quite the contrary. Aristotle and his ancient chums, as you'll see in what follows, still have a great deal to teach us. Of the many things we're attempting to do here, we're not trying to reinvent public speaking; many of its principles and practices are as old as civilization itself. What we are trying to do is reenergize some of the old with the myriad platforms we now have and, in so doing, re-create public speaking for our twenty-first century. Think Public Speaking 2.0. Or perhaps Athens Remixed, Rewired and Rebooted.

In creating this experience we also wanted to write against the textbook grain. In many of the other courses we teach we run as far, and as fast, away from textbooks as we can. Why? For the simple reason that not a few undergraduate textbooks treat you like third graders with limited attention spans. As literary critics have known for a long time, our prose creates its own audience; we construct our own ideal readers even as we attempt to instruct them.

Through many years of teaching, and therefore sampling the vast textbook market, it's the gifted author who treats us as an intellectual equal-or even as a partner in the exchange of knowledge.

Since we interact with you on a daily basis and we know just how sharp and ambitious you are, we think providing real examples and important concepts will suffice for you to get it. Instead of the typical text that encourages racing through bold terms and memorizing lists just before an exam (we've all been there!), our aim is to help you to understand the important stuff without forcing you a steady diet of ranked terms. And while we can provide you with as many basics as possible, knowledge, and ultimately we hope wisdom, about public speech comes in the crucible of publicly performed and embodied moments of speaking and listening.

Know Your Greeks! Isocrates [Flip Learning animation series]

A Successful Performance [Flip Learning chat]

1.7 The "Magical" Properties of Speech

Which leads us right back to communication apprehension. A course in public speaking is unlike any course you are ever likely to take. While you may take quizzes and tests in this course, the true test of public speakers is always getting up in front of your peers and delivering your message. In most other courses we test your memory, creativity, and facility of expression typically through the written word and in the silent interiority of your own head. You take an exam. You write a paper. You shoot and edit. You work through a problem set. That's the performance.

But here in your public speaking class, we've changed the rules of the game: the performance is done in real time before an audience. That's where the magic of public speech is; it's also where some frustration lies. Magic because finding your groove, snatching rhetorical edges[8], getting in the flow of speechmaking is a high that takes a while to come down from; it can even be quite addictive. But frustrating, too, because as teachers we find it very difficult to teach something as ineffable as performance; for those five, six, or seven minutes, you're up there on your own.

Gorgias and the "Sweet Sounds" of Speech

By claiming that speech has "magical" properties, we are saying nothing new. Back in the fifth century BCE, when the spoken word was first getting taught and theorized, one of the early instructors of public speaking, Gorgias of Leontini, spoke and wrote about the amazing and incomprehensible power of the inspired spoken word.[9] Through their eloquence speakers could move troops to risk death, inspire a city to change its laws, and forever memorialize a moment in time. Not coincidentally, and in a culture dominated by the spoken rather than written word, Gorgias delivered his praise of speech in a

---

8   Visit link: https://goo.gl/KVWkRZ

9   Gorgias, *Encomium to Helen*

most unforgettable manner: he rapped it.[10] That's right, before there was Jay-Z, Kanye, Nicki Minaj, Macklemore, or Biggie, Gorgias in his regal purple tunic, minus the spinner rims, was rapping unforgettable lines about the spoken word; in so doing, he was tapping into an oral consciousness and culture easily seduced by sweet sounds. These are the same sweet sounds that the Platonic Socrates wanted to interrupt with his often tedious questioning. These are the same sweet sounds that, even today, have proved so memorable.

Marble bust of Gorgias

Let's try a quick experiment. Go back a few years, or as many as you'd like, and try to remember a favorite song and a favorite artist. Perhaps it's a song that has great emotional resonance or is attached to a fond memory. Maybe it's just a good dance tune. Now try to remember the lyrics. We're guessing that you can remember some of them, perhaps all of them, once you've found the beat. This is all the more remarkable when you consider that we can hardly remember what we did or said a few hours ago. I don't even like Neil Diamond and yet when our baseball stadium at Florida State University buzzes with his "Sweet Caroline" in the seventh inning, I'm singing right along with this impromptu choir of baseball fans.

In June 2016 the Internets were buzzing over a most Gorgias-like commencement speech, delivered at Harvard University by

---

10   For the importance of speech to an oral culture, see Robert J. Connors, "Greek Rhetoric and the Transition from Orality," *Philosophy & Rhetoric* 19 (1986): 38-65.

Know Your Greeks! Gorgias [Flip Learning animation series]

Donovan Livingston.[11] Just days after delivering this address, Livingston's father was amazed that the speech had gone "virus." Note, too, how in the days after, Livingston expressed a most Aristotelian and Socratic concern: did folks really hear the message of his rhythmic address? The message, in brief, wasn't a speech delivered in poetic form in a seemingly impromptu manner, but something far more urgent.

Is it any surprise, then, that in cultures where literacy was (and is) prized by a small elite that the rhythmical spoken word dominated? Early sacred texts such as the Jewish Torah and the Greek Homeric epics were sung long before they were written down. What better way to perform them and hand them down to the next generation, many of whom couldn't read or write?

Figures of Speech

So important was sound to the ancients that they developed an enormous inventory of what we now call "figures of speech." These

---

11 Visit link: https://goo.gl/FfChGD

are spiffy/seductive/strategic/compelling ways of ordering words to achieve a certain sound effect. One of the more common modern figures that you know a good deal about is alliteration, or the practice of repeating a sound in the first syllable of a series of words. But these contrived sounds are not for merely aesthetic purposes; instead, they are intended to move you, to persuade you; above all, these sounds have designs on you. If you don't think so, have a look at and listen to Dr. Martin Luther King Jr.'s "I Have a Dream" speech.[12] The musical repetition (a most important figure of speech) of his dream still moves us more than fifty years on.

That both the Platonic Socrates and Aristotle were suspicious of orators and their sonorous sounds should give us pause.[13] Their suspicions and concerns were linked to a very specific context: the political. That is, in a direct democracy such as Athens, in which every male citizen was allowed to participate in political decision making, the stakes of public speech were enormous. Unlike American democracy and other forms of governance in which we elect politicians literally to represent us before lawmaking bodies, Athenians did it themselves in the Assembly. And they did it with public arguments in the form of speeches. And some of these citizens weren't well educated or schooled in the art of speech; as a result, they were susceptible to the appeal that sounded pleasing, the cadence that rolled easily off the tongue and performed its "magic" on the Assembly's ears. For the Platonic Socrates and Aristotle, the ethics of speech should never be divorced from its practice.

---

12   Visit link: https://goo.gl/pRWkPF

13   The Platonic Socrates—we don't think the historical Socrates ever wrote anything down—records his distrust of the spoken word in two important dialogues, *Gorgias* and *Phaedrus*. See, Plato, *Gorgias*, transl. Robin Waterfield (New York: Oxford University Press, 1994), and Plato, *Phaedrus*, transl. Robin Waterfield (New York: Oxford University Press, 2002).

1.8 The Power of Speech

You'll note that more autocratic and dictatorial forms of government don't care for a lot of open and perhaps combative speech; in fact, many governments tightly control and monitor their citizens' speech for fear that subversive ideas might take root. One of my close friends who grew up in the former Soviet Union never had the opportunity in high school or college to take a class in public speaking. Similarly a colleague born and raised in Communist China was forced into a "reeducation" camp along with her entire family for exercising speech too freely. Another colleague who traveled to a recently democratized Eastern Europe found that the first floors of most buildings had been hollowed out. Why? These were tempting (and largely hidden) places for locals to gather and talk politics. Revolutions might end with bullets and bloodshed but they begin with persuasive ideas.

"With Great Power Comes Great Responsibility"

As practitioners and listeners of public speech, we, too, have an ethical obligation. We realize you and your fellow students likely won't be fomenting plans for the next political revolution, but the consequences of our speechmaking and our listening are very important. To suggest otherwise demeans speakers and audience members. Whenever you ask another person to do something as a result of your speech, even if only to listen carefully, that act embodies an important ethical exchange. We owe it to our audiences and to ourselves to treat that exchange as a sacred one in which information is accurate and clearly sourced, appeals are logical and carefully argued, time is treated as a precious resource, and commitment is earnest and engaged but never manipulative.

If you're ever tempted to doubt the profound importance of

public speaking and that ideas, however seemingly farfetched or fantastic, have consequences, have a look at a book still banned in Germany. Of the many things Adolf Hitler's *Mein Kampf* is—autobiography, political manifesto, German history—you'll note that its author devotes an entire section to public speaking.[14] And how to make public speech "musical" to audiences big and small, ignorant and informed. What ended as the holocaust began with speech by a nobody art student with no following, fewer friends, and extreme halitosis.[15]

Talk of political revolution, public policy, and mass genocide is heavy stuff for the opening chapter in a public speaking text; this we realize. We also realize that simply giving a good wedding toast is public speaking, too–and a very important speech at that. Speaking in public, formally and informally, publicly and privately, marks our existence; as the famous rhetorical theorist Kenneth Burke claims, we are the uniquely symbol-using and misusing animal. Our aim here, then, is rather simple: to help you become better symbol users; and, in the process, we hope you discover just how exhilarating–and yes, magical–speech can be.

Chapter 1 Quiz [Flip Learning quiz]

---

14 See pages 695-716, https://goo.gl/bK7FqX
15 Visit link: https://goo.gl/UyfHcg

2 Bodies, Nerves, Delivery

2.1 Doing the Technicolor Yawn: Performance Anxiety

World-renowned violinist Joshua Bell was just twelve years old when he entered his first major competition. To put it mildly, the child prodigy was nervous. Bell had selected to play Symphonie Espagnole by Lalo, a violin concerto which features a very difficult opening sequence. With his family in the packed house, and with incredibly high expectations, Bell began. In his own words, "I began playing, and I messed it up worse than I ever could have imagined. I had never made such a terrible mistake at the beginning of a piece." Instead of bumbling through the rest of it, the gifted child made a very adult decision: he informed the audience that he'd like to begin again. And he did. And by his own account, he never played the piece better,

Episode 2: Grandpa [Flip Learning video series]
Everyone reacts to the challenges of speech day in their own way, and Laura learns to improvise.

eventually finishing third in the competition.[1]

Nervousness is the Norm

Sports fans love to debate questions such as "who's the best?"; that debate is particularly heated when it comes to the National Basketball Association (NBA). "It's LeBron!" "You're crazy, it's clearly Curry!" "No, it's Jordan and to think otherwise is just foolishness." On and on the debate runs, fueling our 24/7 sports appetite.

Occasionally the name William Felton Russell enters the debate, a center who played thirteen seasons for the Boston Celtics in the 1950s and 1960s. Remarkably Russell's Celtics won eleven championships in his career with the franchise–a record without peer in any professional team sport. But like most beginning (and even many experienced) public speakers, the great Bill Russell had his fears about performance–and they were fears he couldn't hide

---

1 Visit link: https://goo.gl/rRgLqn

LeBron James, Stephen Curry, and Michael Jordan (left to right)

from his teammates. Before nearly every game, Russell found the nearest toilet and vomited. Yes, the future first-ballot Hall of Famer and widely acknowledged "best center ever" hurled, yacked, blew chow, channeled Linda Blair, sold Buicks, did the technicolor yawn before his incredulous teammates (note: see the entire list here[2]). So ritualized was Russell's pregame routine that his coach, the famed Arnold "Red" Auerbach, made sure that his star lost his lunch before important games–just to reassure his teammates that their big man was ready to play. Note the revaluation performed by Russell, his teammates, and his coach: vomiting was actually a *desired* sign, an indication that their star was ready to perform at peak ability. The point is this: you have a choice in how you label what's going on inside you.

    We begin this chapter with the stories of Bell and Russell not to stoke your fears or make you dyspeptic but to offer our reassurance. In public speaking, as with most aspects of life, there's no such thing as perfect–and to expect perfection ensures disappointment. Even the absolute best performers commit mistakes and experience often dizzying anxiety before they go "on stage." No doubt you can come

---

2   Visit link: https://goo.gl/JFcXF9

Joshua Bell and Bill Russell (left to right)

up with others: Julia Roberts, Rihanna, Joel Osteen, Warren Buffett, Katy Perry, Adele, Samuel L. Jackson, Winston Churchill, Mahatma Gandhi, to name just a few, each suffered/suffers from severe speaking or performance anxiety. In fact, one of antiquity's greatest teachers of the verbal arts, Isocrates, was so fearful of speaking in public that he wrote his speeches rather than perform them in person before a live audience. That said, he didn't let his fear overwhelm his desire to become a great teacher.

2.2 Communication Apprehension

Speaking of antiquity, one of the more memorable episodes in the history of what experts call "public speaking anxiety" and "communication apprehension" occurs in the fourth chapter of the book of Exodus. There, a very nervous would-be speaker by the name of Moses tries to talk God out of a profoundly important leadership role. "'But, Lord,' Moses protested, 'I have never been a man of ready speech, never in my life, not even now that you have spoken to me; I am slow and hesitant.'" God counters the reluctant Moses with,

Winston Churchill, Warren Buffett, Rihanna, and Adele (left to right)

"'Go now; I shall help you to speak and show you what to say.'" An increasingly agitated Moses isn't having any of God's public speaking reassurance: "'Lord, send anyone else you like.'" Perhaps sensing that this business of speech anxiety was a more serious matter than He ever anticipated, and having lost His patience with His erstwhile leader, Yahweh finally gives in: He informs Moses that his brother Aaron will lend him rhetorical assistance: "'You [Moses] are to speak to him [Aaron] and put the words in his mouth; I shall help both of you to speak and tell you both what to do.'"[3] And thus did speech anxiety almost derail God's plans to liberate His chosen people!

Trait Apprehension

The sort of apprehension that Moses exhibits is what experts call "trait apprehension," or a generalized fear of communication that inheres in our personality and is present across many different types of speaking contexts, from one-on-one to public. Whether we're born this way or socialized into it, trait apprehension has occupied a great deal of research, leading to "therapies" such as "cognitive restructuring" and "systematic desensitization," among others. Frankly we don't want to turn you into our "patients" by prescribing therapies

---

[3]   J. Jack Suggs, Katharine Doob Sakenfeld, and James R. Mueller, eds., *The Oxford Study Bible* (New York: Oxford University Press, 1992), 65.

based on your symptoms.

State Apprehension

There's a second general type of communication anxiety called "state apprehension," or a fear induced by a unique set of speaking circumstances. For example, if you were asked to speak off the cuff before a large audience of experts in unfamiliar surroundings, we know that your state (or situational) apprehension would likely be profoundly heightened–regardless of how much trait apprehension you exhibit.[4] One of the most state apprehensive conditions has to be speaking live on national television. No do-overs, no hiding, just the glare of the camera in real time —with huge audiences. Watch what happens when General Motors' Rikk Wilde does his best to present a new truck to World Series Most Valuable Player Madison Bumgarner after the game and on live TV.[5] Sensing it had something sort of fun and unique on its hands, GM ran ads the following day that featured the tag-line "technology and stuff." We greatly admire Marjory Stoneman Douglas student, Sam Fuentes, who lost her cookies on national television—and had the best recovery imaginable![6]

We have some good news for you, though, in discussing state anxiety: in this class you're going to be speaking before relatively small, nonexpert, and friendly audiences, untrained in detecting apprehension and eager to see you succeed; you're mostly likely going to be speaking in relatively small rooms in which the acoustics are

---

4 Chris R. Sawyer and Ralph R. Behnke, "Behavioral Inhibition and the Communication of Public Speaking State Anxiety," *Western Journal of Communication* 66 (2002): 412-22.

5 Visit link: https://goo.gl/r1WCtF

6 Visit link: https://goo.gl/PQU8Hj

good; you will be choosing most if not all of your topics; your teacher wants very much for you to succeed and become an expert public speaker; you have plenty of time to prepare to achieve at the highest levels; and the novelty of speaking in public diminishes with each speech. In brief, your public speaking experience in a class like this is geared toward minimalizing state anxiety.

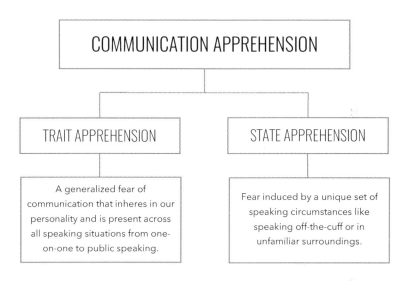

2.3 Communication Apprehension and Delivery

Of course a great deal of the anxiety-inducing part of public speaking, as Moses (and many others) knew, is in the performance; it's when we actually have to stand up, walk to the podium, and verbally perform all of our hard work that we've composed; it's a combination of trait and state apprehension. And so in this chapter, as you prepare for your first classroom speech, we've paired communication apprehension with delivery in the hopes that talking about them together will help you become a better speaker.

We've heard a good bit of nonsense about public speaking and nervousness through the years. Perhaps none is more asinine than the advice to "picture your audience naked," mocked to comic effect by Cyanide & Happiness.[7] The premise behind this counsel is to transform your listeners into less threatening people: a naked audience is somehow a less intimidating and therefore less powerful audience; simultaneously, we speakers are empowered because of its collective vulnerability. Notice that this is a very antagonist model of public speaking–a model that doesn't exist in your classroom, nor does it often exist out in the real world. Yes, we can and will encounter hostile audiences, but in most circumstances audiences want very much for speakers to be eloquent, funny, informative, persuasive, and so forth. Please, let's keep our audience members fully clothed; they'll appreciate that and you can actually spend your precious mental energies on communicating your message rather than playing the role of ventriloquist stripper.

You've heard the expression "there's power in numbers." Well, there's also power within those numbers. One of the best speakers in the world today is former president of the United States Bill Clinton, and regardless of your politics the numbers don't lie: since 2001, he's reportedly made more than $50 million giving speeches, at an average of more than $200,000 a pop. Crunching the numbers, that's about $30 per word whenever the "Big Dog" of American politics speaks. By all accounts Clinton loves to speak publicly–especially when the stakes are high and the audience is prime time. At the 2012 Democratic National Convention held in Charlotte, North Carolina, Clinton gave the nominating speech for former President Barack Obama. By commentators of all political stripes, the speech was deemed something of an "instant classic."

---

7   Visit link: https://goo.gl/CwY8L2

Physiological Responses to Speaking in Public

Take a careful look at this video[8]; more specifically, see if you can notice anything going on in the corner of Bill Clinton's mouth. The Twitter-verse erupted when it noticed the accumulating spittle as Clinton spoke. Talk about a nonverbal distraction! The technical term for this malady is Xerostomia, or what we more commonly call "cottonmouth." If you've ever spoken in public chances are you've experienced it: a drying out that really impedes the ability of the mouth and tongue to form words. It's distressing to you. No doubt it was distressing to former president Clinton. But it happens—and it can be, as he artfully demonstrates for us, managed.

How? Some speakers take a favored beverage to the podium with them—please, no booze—and this is fine with one important caveat: if you hydrate too much before going to the podium, well, nature can call at a very inopportune time. But researchers also say that gently noshing on the end of your tongue or pressing the tongue to the roof of your mouth can activate those salivary glands that have gone desert dry thanks to your autonomic nervous system launching into "fight or flight" mode. The point is, this physiological response happens to nearly everyone and we don't want you to interpret your own cottonmouth while speaking as somehow a catastrophic event. It's not. Your audience likely can't detect it, and even if they can, no worries; it happens; we can deal with it. Certainly nobody is going to tweet about it. Unless of course you're Florida senator Marco Rubio and simply didn't plan well.[9] Or you're running against Rubio in the 2016 Republican presidential primary.[10]

---

8   Visit link: https://goo.gl/B2QcmQ

9   Visit link: https://goo.gl/VtPDrw

10 Visit link: https://goo.gl/1LAC94

Of course there are other bodily signs that often decide to show up right before we make a speech. Our heart often starts racing as if we've just run a six-minute mile; our breathing becomes rapid and shallow; our palms (and even other parts of our body) start sweating; our skin can become blotchy or flushed; when we stand up our knees may start knocking or at least trembling; those movements in our stomach, the so-called butterflies, come quickly; and when blood rushes to the torso area our feet and hands might feel cold and clammy, and our blood pressure spikes. Each of these somewhat off-putting signs is simply your body's way of saying, "I'm in a stressful situation, and whether you want to or not, I'm reacting." In brief, your autonomous nervous system is engaged in its own form of public speaking. Try not to panic; it's only being "reasonable," doing its preprogrammed thing to conserve only what it considers absolutely necessary bodily functions to survive—like fending off a T-Rex, Super-croc, or the zombie apocalypse.

> Speech Anxiety Coping Strategies [Flip Learning chat]

2.4 "Practice? We're talking about practice."

Notice that we began the previous paragraph with a qualification; it's a really important one: these responses are typically happening *before* we speak. It's been our experience, reinforced by research, that many of these annoying bodily reactions diminish–and often a lot–during the course of our speech. Why? Simply because our bodies are now working on other, more important projects: namely, helping us deliver our speech in the manner that we've rehearsed and visualized it; and we're reacting to the feedback from our audience. Whether symptoms diminish or not during the speech, know that experiencing these reactions is a very normal part of public speaking, and is to be expected.

Techniques for Managing Communication Apprehension

Even so, what can we do to minimize some of these bodily reactions–called "behavioral nervousness"–before walking to the podium? Research suggests several possibilities. Perhaps most obvious, practice delivering the speech–and not just once. Even though the great Philadelphia 76er, Allen Iverson, famously disparaged practice, it is absolutely vital to reducing anxiety. Why? Because one of the greatest contributors to your speech anxiety is novelty—that fact that you haven't given a graded speech in a public speaking class before.[11] For more than twenty-years, a psychology professor has been researching how to achieve optimal performance in all kinds of contexts, from playing musical instruments to playing chess. Dr. K. Anders Ericsson's work has, in turn, influenced many, including Malcolm Gladwell and his important book, *Outliers*. What Ericsson discovered, and he and his colleagues continue to fine-tune, is what's called "Deliberate Practice." The premise is fairly simple: to achieve truly elite levels of performance, we must spend thousands of hours—many say 10,000—engaged in deliberate, carefully structured practice sessions.[12]

Yup, we know: you barely have 10 hours to practice, let alone 10,000. Us, too. But hear Ericsson out on this: carefully structured practice sessions will definitely make you a better public speaker—

---

11 Michael J. Beatty, "Situational and Predispositional Correlates of Public Speaking Anxiety," *Communication Education* 37 (1988): 28-39.

12 See for example, K. A. Ericsson, R. Th. Krampe and C. Tesch-Romer, "The Role of Deliberate Practice in the Acquisition of Expert Performance," *Psychological Review* 100 (1993): 363-406.

and immediately, not when you're in your Depends cashing Social Security checks. We know this because Helen Lie did her doctoral dissertation on Deliberate Practice; specifically, she sought to understand the practice habits of elite public speakers. If it takes musicians 10,000 hours to become the best of the best, does the same hold true for speakers? In fact that appears to be the case, but more importantly for us—for you reading this, prepping for your upcoming speech—Lie learned that great speakers prepare and practice in very specific ways. What ways? First, and perhaps most importantly, speakers have clearly defined goals for each practice session. Whether it's nailing an introduction at exactly 1:12, pausing for just the right dramatic effect, or avoiding vocal fillers, elite speakers always have clearly defined goals for each and every session. Second, repeat the session until you get it just right; you'll likely need several to get it just so. Third, try to practice in the same room in which you'll be delivering the speech for real; research shows that familiarity breeds confidence. Fourth, the best speakers like to record themselves in order to critique the practice performances, especially if they can't practice before an audience. Finally, those recorded practice sessions can then be shared with other experts or valued coaches like your teacher to help fine-tune and revise the performance.[13]

You'll hear us talk a lot about Deliberate Practice in *Public Speaking in the 21st Century*. The experts, those who study it for a living, have already cracked the code on performative excellence—and surprise: it involves a lot of hard work, but also smart work; in a word (or two), deliberate work. Growing as a speaker, just as with growing as a musician, a dancer, a cheerleader, a singer, an actor, a soft ball pitcher, or yes, even playing chess, depends on how much time, and the quality of that time, you're willing to put in.

---

13   Helen Lie, "Deliberate Practice in Professional Speaking Expertise," doctoral dissertation, University of San Francisco, 2011.

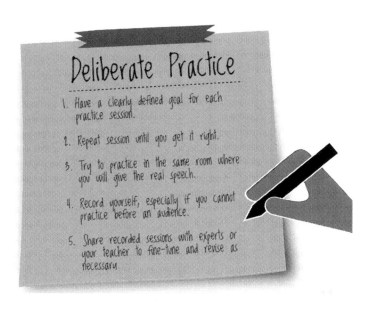

And speaking of soft ball pitchers, have a look at this clip featuring Olympic Gold Medalist, Jennie Finch.[14] One of the main reasons that Finch can make even the best hitters in Major League Baseball look absolutely foolish is because they aren't accustomed to her delivery; their visualization is all fouled up. Instead of a ball pitched at shoulder-height and sinking, Finch's pitch is delivered from the knees and it rises crossing home plate. What does this have to do with public speaking, you ask? Well, pretty much everything: proficient speakers, just like ace batters and pitchers, can lean hard on their practice sessions when the real thing occurs. You're not up at the lectern aimlessly swinging hoping to hit something, but you'll be consciously and unconsciously recalling and drawing upon your Deliberate Practice (DP) sessions. We think you're much more likely to "hit it out of the park" when you get your DP grind on. The experts

---

14   Visit link: https://goo.gl/em4Ehp

say as much, too.

So yes, practice, but practice with specific goals, seeking feedback and the expertise of others, and adjusting and editing accordingly. Even one of the greatest orators of the 20th century, Dr. Martin Luther King, Jr., took many public speaking courses when he attended graduate school; in fact, if you look closely here, you'll see that the man famous for moving mountains with his oratory was initially pretty darn ordinary at public speaking.[15]

Now that you're up to speed on Deliberative Practice, what to do about our adrenally amped up bodies? First, we can let off some steam through exercise. Whether you are a regular exerciser or not, getting a head start on the fight or flight response, because we know it's coming, is a good idea.

Having said that, we don't encourage you to go out and run a marathon or swim the English Channel; even moderate exercising on the day of your speech will lend a hand. To show up for your speech exhausted from exercise is to cut off your nose to spite your face. Walking to class, or even walking one flight of stairs shortly (not immediately) before your speech, can be enough to get the blood and breath flowing, and to help calm nerves. Along similar lines, be sure to get enough rest the night before: all-nighters and insufficient rest fueled by a burst of caffeine are only going to make your body ill-prepared for maximum performance.

And speaking of bodies in motion, in 2006, Stuart Brody, a British psychologist, made international headlines and lit up the Internet with a study involving the effects of sex on diminishing stress, operationalized as giving a public speech. His study found that sex had in fact reduced stress levels among his experimental group. The popular press quickly pounced with headlines such as

---

15 Visit link: https://goo.gl/mJkwkT

"Fear of Public Speaking? Have Sex" and "Dread Public Speaking? Have a Shag First."[16] As with most things, it just isn't quite so simple; doing the horizontal mamba is no panacea for oratorical excellence; neither James Deen nor Stormy Daniels, after all, is renowned for their eloquence.

Another scientifically proven way to reduce your stress, both as you wait to speak and while you're speaking, is simply to smile. And not in a way that barely creases your face, but rather a big ole goofy smile—what the experts call a Duchenne smile—one that causes the muscles around your eyes even to contract a bit. Experimental work conducted by psychologists Kraft and Pressman reveals that smiling helps us both relax and relieve stress. We would also add that a big, earnest smile also does wonders for your audience as it puts us in a better state of mind, too. So yes, Duchenne smiles all the way around![17]

Duchenne Smile

Practice Makes Perfect...Sometimes [Flip Learning chat]

---

16 For how the popular press interpreted Brody's results, see https://goo.gl/y4exqW. For the actual study, see Stuart Brody, "Blood pressure reactivity to stress is better for people who recently had penile-vaginal intercourse than people who had other or no sexual activity," *Biological Psychology* 71 (2006): 214-22.

17 Tara L. Kraft and Sarah D. Pressman, "Grin and Bear It: The Influence of Manipulated Facial Expression on the Stress Response," *Psychological Science* 23 (2012): 1372-1378.

2.5 Slow it Down

One of the hardest things about giving a speech is waiting. Especially if we're speaking last during a speech round, it's awfully difficult to concentrate on anything but our quaking and quivering bodies. Researchers have found, though, that deep breathing combined with tensing and releasing muscle groups (clenching and unclenching our fists, for example) alleviate some of our body's stress. We can do both activities while seated and awaiting our turn to speak.

From our years performing athletically and musically, we'd encourage an additional sensibility on speech day: very deliberately slow down. Everything. From putting on your clothes and how you get to your classroom to what you're eating for breakfast or lunch and even how you address your friends. Go slow. Really slow. Some of the best athletes, at peak performance, talk of the game slowing down. So, too, eloquent speakers often try to slow down their bodies and minds ahead of The Big Event. We already know that our adrenaline wants to speed everything up, including our rate of speaking, once our speech approaches. Very self-consciously slowing everything down on the day you speak can facilitate a very deliberative, methodical, and self-aware speech in which body and mind become one. You don't have to become the tortoise, the Slowskys of advertising fame, but we definitely don't want you to be the hare, either.[18]

Speaking of speech rate and our nerves, we can't tell you how many times a really good speech was mutilated because a racing mind translated into a racing speech rate. An average American rate of speaking is in the neighborhood of 150 words per minute, which, when you break it down, is really quite fast, nearly 2.5 words per second. The problem with fast speaking, of course, is that your audience

---

18   Visit link: https://goo.gl/QTaj9B

is going to have a very hard time comprehending what you're saying. Yes, they might actually hear you, but they're not going to be able to process the important details of your message if you're speaking like an auctioneer-on-meth or Boomhauer from *King of the Hill*; further, if you make listening difficult for an audience, guess what? They're not going to expend the energy to try and catch up with you.

As listeners to a lot of speeches, we appreciate it when speakers speak deliberately and slow down to emphasize key points. What you're doing when you slow down is signaling to your audience that this point is really important–and that you want us to concentrate hard on the specifics. We'd encourage you to make explicit to your audience that the point is very important (e.g., "this is a critical point") and to also emphasize it by slowing down your rate of speech. Build this into your speaking outline. Work on it during your practice sessions. Don't be bashful about repeating a point. Former Vice President George H. W. Bush changed his rate of speech to great effect in 1988 at the Republican National Convention when he famously intoned, "Read my lips, no new taxes." The gravity of his promise was reinforced by the deliberateness with which he spoke. On a less politically charged note, watch and listen as the Reverend Jesse Jackson delivers this wonderful eulogy to Theodore Geisel, also known as Dr. Seuss.[19] So let's remember: less is usually more–often much more–when it comes to delivering our speeches. Cramming more content into a speech under the guise of simply "speaking faster" is not the way to go.

2.6 Avoiding the Body Snatchers

One of the hardest things to do when we're simultaneously dealing

---

19   Visit link: https://goo.gl/7b2vvi

with our nerves AND delivering our speech is to actually have the presence of mind to communicate with ourselves. We've quit counting the number of times students have asked us immediately after a speech, "What just happened?" and "What did I just say?" It's almost like we've just experienced a six-minute cognitive blackout. Some sort of robotic doppelganger embodies us behind the podium and departs only once we return to our seats. Don't fret: it's happened to us, too. What is likely happening to us when this occurs is that we've given in to panic. And when we panic, as Malcolm Gladwell notes, we tend to think too little; in fact, we seem to quit thinking altogether![20] But thinking is precisely the response we need in such situations.

One of the most accomplished public speakers on the planet, Amy Schumer, didn't give in to the temptation to panic while winning an award on live national television where her heel broke; instead, she played right along.[21]

To prevent this very odd experience, we encourage you to do just a few things. First, after arriving at the podium, and having done so very deliberately (again, try to slow everything down), don't begin your speech immediately. Take a few deep breaths. Next, establish eye contact with several members of your audience (really concentrate on establishing contact with several people, not just your teacher). Hit 'em with a big ole Duchenne Smile. Then take a careful look at your outline. Silently ask yourself, "Am I ready?" Once you're ready, and only once you've explicitly answered that question, go ahead and begin your speech. What you're doing here is engaging in what we call intrapersonal communication, or communication with

---

20   Malcolm Gladwell, "Performance Studies: The Art of Failure," *The New Yorker*, August 21, 2000, 86.

21   Visit link: https://goo.gl/FJ7ARV

yourself. We engage in this sort of interior dialogue in many different contexts, and we encourage it here precisely to break the spell at the very outset of any would-be body snatchers.

The Jitters [Flip Learning animation series]
Sometimes even your body conspires against you.

Maintaining "Dialogic Self-Awareness"

Now, how can we maintain that sense of what we call dialogic self-awareness throughout the speech? How can we continue to communicate with ourselves even as we're communicating with a roomful of people? You can do this in several ways, but we'd highlight three: first, build into your speaking outline reminders, prompts, questions–"speaking cues" just for you and nobody else. They're there to slow you down and force you to be present in the moment. Understand that a two- or three-second pause isn't noticeable to an audience; furthermore, it allows the audience time to think along with you. Sports psychologists suggest using a single word to focus your cognitive energies. The great American figure skater Michelle Kwan, for example, employed the word "ooze" to great effect in winning multiple national and world skating championships. Think of

Oooooooze.

a word or phrase that concentrates the body and mind while you're giving your speech and write it right into your outline as a reminder—or use any cues that will help you effectively convey your message (slow down, make eye contact, pause, smile, etc.); we think this technique will greatly enhance that dialogic self-awareness so instrumental to performative excellence.

Involving Your Audience

Second, we'd encourage you to engage your audience by posing strategic questions throughout your speech. Such questions can take the form of "Having looked at problems, what are possible solutions?" or "How might we evaluate these answers?" They can also be much more explicit, such as "Do you know how much....?" or "Have you ever wondered why....?" Not only do questions ask audience members for answers (typically silent ones), but they ask you to slow down as your audience works through them. Remember: whenever you ask your audience a question give them a space in which to contemplate an answer. Rushing through the question tells your audience, not so subtly, that their answer isn't very important.

Third, one of our favorite tricks to break the robotic spell is to single out a specific person or a group of people in our audience when creating an example. This forces us to be present in the moment rather than racing through our speech without any awareness of what we're doing, what we're saying, how we're saying it, and the kind of feedback we're getting. It has the additional advantage of REALLY getting the attention of those you've just mentioned by name. It's easy to overlook the fact that your audience provides you with an invaluable resource for making your speech come to life. From our experience we know that the best teachers usually have the best examples. Well, some of the best examples are sitting right in front of you. Use them, always sensitively and with care, but we don't have to look far to create compelling examples.

Ideally you hope to hit that performative ideal expressed in such phrases as "feeling it," "in the groove," "locked into the zone," and "rockin' it."

Each phrase expresses something of the ineffable quality of being at the top of your game: you're aware of your performance even as you're enjoying, even relishing, every single syllable of it. Think Dr. Martin Luther King, Jr. and the 1963 March on Washington, specifically the impromptu "Dream" sequence of his address. Think Whitney Houston hitting those stunning notes in "I Will Always Love You." Think Simone Biles doing her floor exercise at the 2016 Olympics. Think Jana Kramer and Gleb Savchenko and their high-powered tango on *Dancing with the Stars*. Think Justin Verlander during a no-hitter or Kobe dropping 81 on the Toronto Raptors. Admittedly we're talking about an ideal, but there's no reason to believe that just because we're relatively new to the art of public speaking that we can't catch glimpses, even extended glimpses, of such excellence. The key, of course, is in the proper preparation.

2.7 Delivery in a virtual world

In our wired and digital world, we realize that sometimes the luxury of speaking face-to-face is just that—a luxury. Instead of the many textures of an embodied speaking performance, you will be asked to do your rhetorical work through virtual means. Don't sweat this;

	FEATURES	PROS	CONS
Google Hangouts	• Screen sharing • Real-time chat • Mobile and tablet apps	• Quick setup process • Easy to invite participants • No installation required	• 25-participant limit • Need Gmail account to host • Not as many advanced features
Skype	• Screen sharing • Real-time chat • Mobile and tablet apps • File sharing	• Familiar platform • Comprehensive chat feature	• 25-participant limit • Installation required • Adding participants is complicated
Zoom	• Screen sharing • Real-time chat • Mobile and tablet apps • Call recording	• Quick setup process • User-friendly • Browser compatible • Great video and audio quality	• 40-minute time limit and 50-participant limit • Joining can be confusing for a large group of participants
Join.me	• Screen sharing • Real-time chat • Mobile and tablet apps • File sharing	• Installation isn't required for participants • Superior screen sharing quality	• 10-participant limit • Complicated setup process • Installation required for host
GoToMeeting	• Screen sharing • Real-time chat • Mobile and tablet apps • Accessible via Chrome	• Easy to invite participants • One-click meetings	• 3-participant limit • Average video and audio quality • Difficult to find free version • Installation required for host

we've got you covered. Delivery even in our virtual age isn't terribly different from what you're doing before that real audience on campus.

By the way, you're also likely very good at it, far better than I am. Having not cut my teeth on a smart phone with video capability, I am not a digital native. There's a good chance you are, though, having ready access to that bright red record button on your phone's screen. Whether you're doing Facebook Live, Periscope over on Twitter, Skype, or sending a video Snap to your crew, you already know how to speak persuasively in this medium. But let's review.

First, if you're going to do your public speaking remotely and virtually, be aware of just what that camera is looking at. Sure, it's got you all centered and framed up and you look the part, but...what else are you sharing the frame with? Do you have some eye candy hanging on the wall? If so, remove it. The empty bottle of spirits commemorating an event? Yeah, let's hide that, too. Have you seen the video of the expert talking head speaking live from his office in his home....and his young children barge in mid-interview? We do NOT want that to happen to you, so yeah, let's set the stage very carefully so that the focus is solely on you and only you.[22]

Next, do a practice run just to see what you look like and how you sound. Part of the problem with presenting via camera is getting just the right posture—for you and your listeners. If you have a lectern and want to use it, great. Understand that if you're seated, you can look both too eager or too relaxed depending just on how you're seated. You don't want to be the virtual "close talker," all face and no body. Too, you don't want to be pitched so far back that you look like you're about to take a snooze in your recliner. So yes, let's do a test run with you and some of your favorite people to provide some feedback on what looks good.

Third, it's really hard to focus solely on that very small camera at the top of your computer or your phone of whatever recording device you happen to be using. When we give a speech before a live audience it's so much easier to scan the room, establish eye contact as we go, and engage them naturally. Let's be frank: there's nothing natural about giving a speech to a 2x2 centimeter object. This is where practice is crucial as you'll need to establish and maintain eye contact with that small object and do your best to pretend that it represents a roomful of people. Part of the juice we get from public speaking is in the immediate audience feedback, so monitoring that feedback virtually is very difficult, if not impossible.

Fourth, we'd encourage you to slow down your rate of speech even more. As we've discussed previously, our bodies are amped up to speak, and our speech rate will follow suit. Speaking virtually

---

[22] Visit link: https://goo.gl/XnEdeD

means that there is going to be a delay, however small, in what you say at your end and when it is received on the other. Sure, that delay is hopefully fractional, but it's still there, all of which means, go slowly and work hard getting the enunciation just right. Garbled speech, unintelligible speech, just really damages your ability to connect with your virtual audience. So yes, let's be a bit more deliberate with this medium.

Finally, you remember that big ole Duchenne Smile we've been talking about for several chapters, right? Now is the time to make it even more pronounced. Look, everyone involved in this exercise in virtual rhetoric understands that the set-up is not ideal; if it were, we'd be doing it face-to-face. So, let's make some lemonade out of the lemons and put on our best happy face. No, we don't want you to paste a goofy and toothy smile on your face for the duration, but we would encourage you to understand the rhetorical work done by good humor in a hard situation. Be on the lookout for the humorous moment, as it will likely present itself. Smiles do a bunch of rhetorical work.

And speaking of which, if lightning strikes and knocks out your electricity, your operating system decides to do an auto-update, or malware has just infected your computer with porn and loud sirens, know that glitches come with the virtual territory; in fact, a seamless virtual speaking event is more the exception than the rule. So don't fret, you will get reconnected and your rhetorical brilliance will shine through.

3 Language, Style, Humor

3.1 An Introduction to Language, Style, and Humor

Every year during the second week of April golf fans worldwide gather around their television sets to watch The Masters. Played since 1934 in Augusta, Georgia, and carefully timed to catch the azaleas in all their vibrant splendor, the tournament is infused with Deep South traditions–including its own preferred vocabulary. Specifically, CBS broadcasters are instructed never to use the colloquial term "fans" to describe those lining its impeccably manicured fairways; instead the more formal and distinguished term "patrons" must be used. And to say that the folks who run the tournament don't play, just ask CBS's head golf humorist, Gary McCord.

In 1994, McCord was describing on air the action taking place on the 16th hole. That day the hole was playing particularly hard because of its very fast putting surface. Rather than play it straight,

Episode 3: Invested [Flip Learning video series]
Kay learns to trust her TA's unorthodox methods...and the importance of reading closely.

per The Masters' staid tradition (e.g., saying "the greens are very fast"), McCord decided to have some metaphorical fun. He described the "body bags" piling up next to the green as the professional golfers simply couldn't negotiate the "bikini waxed" surface. Death and sex—on air, live—at a place whose tagline is "a tradition unlike any other." The green-jacketed aristocracy was *not* humored. More than twenty years later, McCord still hasn't been invited back to the tournament.

Augusta National Golf Club

Gary McCord's banishment from Augusta National tells us a lot about language, style, and humor, the subjects of the present chapter. But most important is a perception about meaning: realize that what might be funny to you and your cohort of friends—ROFLMAO funny—might be very offensive to others. The attempt to be humorous, in particular, shows us the extent to which meanings reside far more in people than in words. Samantha Bee isn't terribly funny to your grandparents' generation. Nor is Stephen Colbert. But to a much younger demographic, the two comedians deliver loud and frequent laughs on a nightly basis. Of course the obverse is also true: your grandparents' humor leaves you often scratching your head and wondering WT....

Gary McCord, Samantha Bee, and Stephen Colbert (left to right)

Humor: A Curious Omission

We should note at the outset that most public speaking textbooks don't engage the subject of humor. At all. We find this omission rather curious because humor can be an integral part of public speech, whether in informative, persuasive or commemorative settings. While we don't expect you to become stand-up comics, we do want you to think hard about the rhetorical work that humor can perform—in settings of all kinds. Back in 1984, for example, and with whispers getting louder by the day about his old age and therefore his unfitness for office, seventy-three-year-old President Ronald Reagan deflected these very serious concerns with humor. In debates with Democratic challenger Walter Mondale, Reagan joked about his opponent's youth and inexperience. And with only these minor jokes, the issue largely died. Reagan won a few weeks later by the absurd electoral vote landslide of 525 to 13. Whereas Reagan's quip came with the very high stakes of a presidential election, former President George W. Bush decided to have some fun during a Southern Methodist University commencement speech. A notoriously average student during his days at Yale University, watch as "W" addresses head-on his past exploits as a C student.[1]

Former president George W. Bush

Similarly, many other public speaking textbooks don't talk much about canon number three in the history of rhetoric: namely, style. The Romans in particular developed an enormous inventory of stylistic vehicles, or ways of saying things to achieve particular ends.[2] And while it's perhaps tempting to treat style as just more frosting on an already delicious cake, or an inconsequential side garnish next to the filet mignon, we'd beg to differ. Any and all use of language comes with a corresponding style; the Romans theo-

---

1   Visit link: https://goo.gl/YjAUPZ

2   For an online list of key figures see https://goo.gl/QnAVrL.

rized this as spanning a spectrum of plain-middle-grand, depending on the speaking occasion.[3] Some contexts call for more colloquial speech, others a far more dignified and elevated style; confusing the two can result in a Gary McCord situation. In a word, whatever we say is stylized and never just inconsequential parsley; by definition it has to be. "Dude, really?" is very far stylistically from "Excuse me sir, what did you mean?" but the two expressions convey very similar meanings. Similarly, you wouldn't likely greet your new boss with "Wassup, girl fren" or "Yo, brah" unless you wanted to start collecting unemployment checks. We need to know and be aware of how we can make all manner of language choices work for us.

3.2 Language and "Reality"

We take as our point of departure on language the theoretical work of the twentieth century's most influential rhetorical theorist, Kenneth Burke. He argued that language is always a selection of reality, not a reflection of reality. And because it is a selection of reality, and thus always partial, Burke claimed that language has to be a deflection of reality, too.[4] In other words–and Burke often needs an "in other words"–the terms we use to communicate about our world can't give us the God's-eye point of view, the all-seeing and thus always accurate perspective.

Burke argued that as the uniquely symbol-using and symbol-abusing animal, we often have other, more insidious motives. Think of how we name those we don't particularly like; history pro-

---

[3] See, for example, Cicero, *Rhetoric ad Herennium*, transl. Harry Caplan (Cambridge, MA: Harvard University Press, 1954).

[4] Kenneth Burke, *Language as Symbolic Action: Essays on Life, Literature and Method* (Berkeley, CA: University of California Press, 1968), 45.

vides a tragically full receptacle of Names for Others. It's far easier to demonize/kill/scapegoat/quarantine someone whose name connotes something dirty/evil/fearful/mysterious/ugly. Thus did he refer to language as symbolic action and language as incipient action—a program of motives can often be inferred from how we name our many "realities."

As Burke understood, names don't also just create villains; names also help us do the unspeakable: killing. In his haunting and beautiful meditation on creating soldiers and thus killers, Stanley Kubrick's *Full Metal Jacket* contains a remarkable, though brief, scene; watch the PG-13 version here. We're told on very good authority that such acts of naming still occur in the Marine Corps. Why? According to Charles Kauffman, naming a weapon functions to transfer the agency of killing from a person to a weapon.[5] In brief, humanizing a rifle with a name allows us to share the awful burden of killing with someone else. So yes, for Burke and others, naming can have very profound consequences.

Language and the "Human Barnyard"

What this means, among other things, is that communication helps us create (academics often like to use the word "construct") and negotiate our many social realities. Language doesn't simply describe; it also prescribes. Fortunately for us, and part of the great fun of language, is that it's never static; our always evolving terminology helps us navigate what Burke calls the "human barnyard."[6]

---

[5] Charles Kauffman, "Names and Weapons," *Communication Monographs* 56 (1989): 273-85.

[6] Kenneth Burke, *A Rhetoric of Motives* (Berkeley, CA: University of California Press, 1969).

We could fill a few hard drives just with new terms associated with the computer/Internet/social media revolution: tweeting, texting, sexting, friending, IM'ing, blogging, trending, and Googling populate our daily talk. Viral videos circulate in cyberspace, and Internet trolls don't live under bridges. URLs, HTML, PDFs, JPEGs, RSSs, and ISPs proliferate in our virtual worlds. Smart phones and their data plans have all but replaced land lines and long-distance phone calls–to say nothing of the increasingly obsolete busy signal. And live streaming does not refer to fly-fishing or salmon migrations. Is it any wonder that some just a bit older than us find this whole bizarre edifice rather frightening and decidedly alien?

The practice of texting has created its own acronymed vocabulary that often leaves us SMH. We live in a world where surprise is rendered as OMG, humor as LMAO, incredulity as WT..., warnings are communicated as NSFW, doubt as IDK, thanks as HT, and always, YOLO! Especially with your folks, it's TMI. This modern-day Morse code indeed functions as a rhetorical shorthand even as it alienates those who don't participate in its uniquely abbreviated lexical culture.

Technology, of course, is but one of many occupants of the human barnyard. In economics we hear of mortgages that are underwater, assets that are toxic, and the country going over the fiscal cliff; in medicine we have a bevy of new diagnoses and products from ADHD, SARS, PTSD, and Zika to statins, stents, and inhibitors; in politics, where naming is particularly freighted with rhetorical importance, birthers, the Tea Party, Obamacare, supply siders, Cheeto Jeezus, neocons, being Swift-boated, Lyin' Ted, Little Marco, and Feeling the Bern carry partisan weight; in sports, mixed martial arts has replaced boxing, moneyball is the rage among general managers in baseball, golfers putt with belly-putters and chip with lob wedges, fantasy teams are not about threesomes, porn, nor anything 50 Shades, and everybody, it seems, is (or at least was) Dabbing.

Some of our recent favorite additions to our dynamic world of language involves verbs. We've noted on our Facebook feeds the verb "adulting" frequently popping up, as in, having to put on our big boy, big girl pants and enter the hard and often stressful world of adulthood. And while we've been "Googling" and "tweeting," it seems, for a really long time, we've only be Ubering for a few years.

Similarly it's now appropriate for men to have "bromances" and for women to have "sheroes." Hollywood has great fun with names and naming: perhaps only the so-called culture industry could give us names like Gaylord Focker in *Meet the Parents* (and several sequels) or Chest Rockwell, Jack Horner, and Dirk Diggler in the adult film spoof *Boogie Nights*. And we're not even going to go down the naming-as-framing path in the James Bond and Austin Powers franchises. Ever notice that the 'Final Girls' of slasher films typically have first names appropriate to either male or female?[7] We have no idea what this brotastic surfer dude is trying to say, but we sure do love how he says it.[8]

One of my favorite places to observe what's lexically lit is over

---

7   Carol Clover, "Her Body, Himself: Gender in the Slasher Film," *Representations* 20 (1987): 187-228.

8   Visit link: https://goo.gl/tPmerb

on Twitter. For example, "gaslighting" has nothing to do with brightening a dark street; SWATting isn't about keeping pesky mosquitoes away; bots are all the rage; and doxxing is not a verb about documentary film. With its expansion to 280 characters, the Twitter-verse (aka, the crack cocaine of the social media landscape) is a place where DREAMers get debated (Development, Relief, and Education for Alien Minors), the president's spelling boners get riffed—who can forget covfefe?—and hashtags proliferate. And because Twitter still places a premium on brevity, the acronyms proliferate like kudzu.[9] Suffice it to say that even as we write this chapter we realize that by the time you're reading it we'll have new terms to help us navigate the latest in our cultural landscape. Indeed a "choice of words is a choice of worlds."[10]

3.3 Language and Gender

We humanities teachers often like to say that language constructs our realities. That's just a fancy way of saying that we can't hold up a mirror to the world and it will reflect back exactly what it sees. No, language doesn't quite work like that. But, and this is a crucial but, because language is as natural for us to use as the air we breathe, we often aren't aware of what that mirror looks like. As the metaphor a few sentences ago implies, we aren't aware of what's being constructed, or built, with our language.

Because language, to borrow a different metaphor, allows us to paint beautiful pictures, we hate it when folks tell us, "you can't say that," or "don't ever say this," or some total prohibition on what

---

9   Visit link: https://goo.gl/mXGrmc

10 James R. Andrews, *A Choice of Worlds: The Practice and Criticism of Public Discourse* (New York: Harper & Row, 1973).

we can say. We're just not down with the language police. Our use of language should always be governed by context, not cops. Period.

So, let's say in your public speaking class, you refer during your speech to your awesome instructor as Mrs. Mason. No deal, right? You're just showing respect, as your folks taught you growing up. I know when I was a child that rule was very strictly enforced! But, let's look a little closer at your construction, "Mrs. Mason." Your statement assumes that Professor Mason is married, right? Marriage has been historically a way to confer respectability and value to women who did not have equal social standing, so assuming someone goes by "Mrs" is an echo of that value system. Think about it: whether or not a man is married, he is called "Mr." Historically, only women graduated from "Miss" or "Ms" to "Mrs." In addition, until relatively recently you would be assuming she was in a different sex relationship. Even with the legalization of same sex marriage, the most common assumption is that people are married to a different sex person. You see where we're going with this. Of course you meant no harm in referring to your instructor this way; this we understand; you were just being respectful; you totally dig "Mrs. Mason." But if we're not watching and paying attention, our norms and habits of language use will often just take over and speak for us. Language can also potentially speak over others with assumptions about their lives. Language does this all the time. How about if we agree to do this: in the CONTEXT of the university classroom we refer to our instructors as Professor Mason, or perhaps Dr. Mason. Or, if she prefers some other mode of address, she'll let you know. I promise. Same for the fellas.

Here's another example I stumbled on living in the Deep South, one I never encountered growing up in Ohio. It's a form of both respect and affection to refer to men and women older than you with "Mr." and "Miss" and their first name. So I learned quickly to refer to a friend and neighbor as Miss Gladys. In the CONTEXT of our private friendship, she and her husband will always be Mr. Sam and

Miss Gladys (btw, did you once again notice that Mr. does not denote marriage the way that Mrs. does? Yup, we know, language is often gendered in very subtle ways).

Our everyday, taken-for-granted language use snuck up on the *New York Times*, one of our culture's arbiters for language use; the *Times* often devotes articles to frank discussions of our dynamic vocabulary. In a May 2016 article on Paula Broadwell and her much-publicized extra-marital affair with Marine Corps General David Petraeus, note how the author concludes: with a discussion of the word "mistress."[11] What's wrong with "mistress," you ask; after all, the term has been around for a really long time? Great question. Note the *Times*'s (and Broadwell's) answer: it has no male equivalent—as if just one person—guess who?—is to blame.

So yes, as public speakers we owe it to our audience members to be both respectful and inclusive. And we also owe it to them, and to ourselves, to become aware of how these construction materials we've inherited—our language—do their building, and what's being built. You'll also be glad to note that very recently several experts on language use (finally) gave the thumbs-up to using the singular "they" to refer to him or her.[12] So just as Penelope can now be a "they," so can Magnus. Professor Mason, too.

3.4 Style

The Romans and their preoccupation with style can be useful to us in many ways, even as beginning speakers. Specifically, their emphasis on styles that are plain, middle, and grand can usefully correlate with the types of speeches we'll often be making: informative, per-

---

11   Visit link: https://goo.gl/x6TAFj

12   Visit link: https://goo.gl/FD2Uwu

suasive, and commemorative. Let's have a closer look.

"Plain" Style

In your informative speech you'll be playing the role of teacher and aiming for the "plain" style; and, as with all good teachers, you'll want to make yourself as clear as possible: in other words, you'll want to communicate your meaning plainly and precisely. Nearly all commentaries on style over the centuries prize clarity, or the ability to see something or someone in a clear and meaningful way. Notice that we're using a metaphor–clarity, with its visual emphasis–to talk about things that aren't necessarily visual. We use the metaphor to help us understand that good teaching is clearly perceived by students; it provides a clear window on a new or unfamiliar part of the world. Note, for example and by contrast, how hard it is for us to learn when terms with which we are unfamiliar are used; specialized jargon always clouds the picture and we are usually left badly confused.

The problem is that we lapse into jargon–or the language specific to a specialized activity–when discussing something with which we're familiar. So, for example, as experts in photography and golf, it's second nature for us to speak casually of DSLRs and dogleg par fives. These terms make absolutely no sense to the uninitiated. So in playing the role of teachers in your informative speeches, never assume that the audience knows the jargon associated with your subject. Trust us: you'll see a lot of head scratching, yawning, and gimlet-eyed mouth-breathing if you use–consciously or not–a specialized vocabulary. Always assume a lay audience unless you know otherwise.

If you want to employ some of that specialized vocabulary, fine; simply know that you'll have to do some careful defining of key terms.

We'd encourage you never to introduce more than a small handful of new terms in a five- to seven-minute speech. Or, if you'd like to avoid all jargon, you first need to be able to see what's jargon and what isn't. This is where your Deliberate Practice sessions before an audience and/or recording your practice sessions can be really helpful; both can be used to very quickly identify problematic and confusing terms. We'd also encourage you to simply make a list of jargon-laden terms associated with your informative speech. Such self-awareness is vital to the clarity of your message.

Examples and Analogies

Furthermore, and as any accomplished teacher can tell you, the best teachers are the best simplifiers; as a result they have the best examples and analogies.

These can come from your own experiences–typically the most effective–or from your research. Examples and analogies also have the added rhetorical advantage of taking the form of the story; and, as rhetorical theorist Walter R. Fisher, among others, has noted, we're suckers for a good story.[13] Educators also know that we tend to learn analogically: something is like or akin to something else. So as you develop your speech be on the lookout for good examples and analogies that help your audience make sense of what's likely to be unfamiliar.

Sometimes an analogy can function to add both clarity and humor to your speech. One of my favorite writers, the late essayist and novelist David Foster Wallace, had a particular gift for the descriptive analogy. In trying to describe a professional tennis player's

---

13   Walter R. Fisher, *Human Communication as Narration: Toward a Philosophy of Reason, Value, and Action* (Columbia, SC: University of South Carolina Press, 1987).

gravity-defying hair, Wallace employed a pop culture analogy: professional tennis player Julian Knowle's hair "towers over his head at near-Beavis altitude."[14] Tall hair, stacked-up hair, piled-high hair–none works quite so vividly and humorously as "near-Beavis altitude" hair. Grandma won't likely get the analogy, but you and your Gen Z cohort will.

Julian Knowle and Beavis and Butthead (left to right)

So if you're going to employ and deploy popular culture to your rhetorical advantage, know your audience. But you don't always need popular entertainment to help you make an analogy really work. Stuck on Senator John McCain's presidential campaign bus back in 2000, Wallace found the coffee to be awful. But how to bring the full extent of awful to life? Awful, after all, is both relative and vague. By analogy, of course. Thus: the "coffee tasted like warm water with a brown crayon in it."[15] Yeah, that's bad–really bad; now we get it.

Clever and well-deployed analogies are also a staple of the advertising industry's rhetorical appeals. In trying to discern just how happy its customers are by saving money on their car insurance, Geico has moved away from British-accented geckos to witty analogies: "happier than a bodybuilder directing traffic"; "happier than Gallagher at a farmer's market"; "happier than Dracula at a blood bank";

---

14 David Foster Wallace, *A Supposedly Fun Thing I'll Never Do Again: Essays and Arguments* (Boston: Little, Brown and Co., 1997), 238.

15 David Foster Wallace, *Consider the Lobster: And Other Essays* (Boston: Little Brown and Co., 2006), 192.

and my favorite, "happier than a witch in a broom factory." Yes, good analogies sell. They also make your speeches come to life in vivid and memorable ways.

But even if you don't have a store of terrific examples or analogies for your informative speech, we'd encourage you to keep it very simple—both in terms of the organization you employ (see Chapter 7) and the language you use. Your aim here, lest we forget, isn't to impress or dazzle an audience with how smart you are; we already know that! No, the point is to teach and thus inform your audience with as much clarity and concision as the subject allows. Trust us: having listened to far too many speeches in which speakers spoke over the audience's heads, opting for the plain style will boost your credibility and, more important, help you achieve your speaking aims.

On Analogies [Flip Learning animation series]
Colorful language always spices up a speech. Just use your discretion.

"Middle" Style: Repetition

While we heartily recommend the "plain" style for informative speeches, you can also use it for your persuasive speeches; while

Language, Style, Humor   61

Aristotle's Golden Mean

Plain   Middle   Grand

you're playing the role of advocate, you'll also likely be doing some teaching as well. But because we're advocating for a course of action or a change of some sort when we speak to persuade, the middle style might also be usefully employed. Such a style is what Aristotle called a golden mean, a style midway between the plain and the grand. In terms of clothing, think of a middle style as business casual. Persuasive speeches offer you the opportunity, depending on the subject and the occasion, to aim for eloquence. That eloquence can take many forms and figures of speech, but we would highlight just two here. First, notice that some of the greats in speechmaking use plenty of repetition: Dr. Martin Luther King, Jr. repeated "I Have a Dream" to great rhetorical effect at the March on Washington; former President Barack Obama employs repetition frequently and powerfully; and British Prime Minister Winston Churchill used repetition to stunning effect in rallying his nation during World War II. Watch and listen, too, as a remarkably poised young Pakistani woman, Malala Yousafzai, addresses the 2015 Oslo Education Summit.[16] Malala had been targeted for assassination in 2012 by the Taliban for

---

16   Visit link: https://goo.gl/o5QbmA

Malala Yousafzai speaks on the systemic nature of gender inequality and bringing about change.

her efforts to bring education to young girls in the Northwest region of Pakistan. Watch and listen as her powerful use of repetition–"I am here"–functions rhetorically to underscore her role on behalf of millions of young girls seeking to attend school.

Let's be clear about using repetition: the grandeur and idealism of King's dream just isn't going to work in your small speech class; this is akin to wearing a tux with tails or a formal gown on a first date. But strategically repeating key phrases, those of particular persuasive importance, is certainly appropriate for a persuasive address as it adds a layer of formality and emphasis to what you're attempting to do. Never overlook the fact that when you attempt to persuade someone you're actively seeking access to their world–and that's a really big deal, certainly a bigger deal than your intentions in the informative speech.

Synecdoche

The second figure of speech that we find particularly useful in persuasive speeches is synecdoche (sa-nek-doh-key), or the use of a part to stand in for the whole. For example, in baseball commentators speak of "arms" (for pitchers) and "bats" (for hitters); we know that a pitcher is more than an arm and a hitter is more than a bat, but you see the point. But we'd like to expand synecdoche to include bigger parts standing for bigger wholes. Television news, for example, uses synecdoche all the time, though they would never call it that. But

when they attempt to communicate a very complex issue like Medicaid waivers in just a two-minute time bloc, they almost always reduce the complexity by having a part stand in for the whole; in this case only one family will likely be used to stand in for how Medicaid waivers are affecting a nation of families. In reducing this complex policy issue to one family, televised news is not only greatly simplifying things but also dramatizing at the same time. What about those smiling faces on your university's web site? Sure, those students represent the entire student body. High draft picks in professional sports often talk about becoming "the face of the franchise." That face, their face, stands in for the entire team, so that stakes are really high. In politics, heads of state stand in for the entire country, especially when that person represents the country abroad.

We like stories with memorable characters and easy plots. We don't like abstract numbers and plots riddled with complexity and contingency. You only have six to eight minutes to persuade a skeptical audience; as such, we need all the help we can get to dramatize our subjects. Synecdoche, or the use of a single to represent the many, is a powerful figure of speech that can greatly enhance your persuasiveness.

Understand, though, that when you use a part for a whole you have an ethical obligation to represent just as accurately as you can; selecting the anomaly rather than the typical will get you in hot water with audiences–just ask many pundits who loudly and confidently proclaimed that Secretary of State Hillary Clinton would handily defeat Donald Trump in the 2016 presidential election. Rather than looking globally at many polls, they selected one or two polls/parts that favored Mrs. Clinton. Needless to say many commentators were confronted by a lot of angry and confused viewers/readers on The Day After. How could they have been so wrong? Easily, especially when you employ synecdoche for very partial, and thus deceptive, ends.

"Grand" Style

As for the third type of style, which the Romans called elevated or grand, the most appropriate speech for this style is the commemorative. When we speak to praise, memorialize, or celebrate, we're elevating a person/event/idea, and what better way to elevate than in dignifying our speech–dressing it up, so to speak. Just as you wouldn't wear jeans and a T-shirt to a good friend's catered wedding reception at the local country club, so too you wouldn't want to use slang or ordinary speech when you want to praise something or someone important; instead, you'd like to dignify the occasion by taking a little extra effort, ironing out any wrinkles, and making sure everything matches just so. Is it any wonder that the ancients often referred to style as adornment?

Alliteration

But how can we achieve elevation, dignity, and grandeur in our speech? The possibilities are endless, and you can and should consult the long list of figures of speech, but it's hard to beat alliteration and metaphor, two of our favorites. Because we often compose commemorative speeches to be delivered from a manuscript rather than a speaking outline, we have the opportunity to compose with a bit more attention to detail. Even so, we're still very concerned with the sound of our words, and alliteration, in particular, functions to link sounds together; specifically, it repeats the same sounds, either at the beginning of words or in the syllables stressed.

The street hustler turned black nationalist Malcolm X spoke of "the ballot or the bullet"; the remarkable woman suffrage advocate Elizabeth Cady Stanton spoke memorably of "the solitude of self"; former Vice President Spiro Agnew derided the nation's press corps with the unforgettable epithet "nattering nabobs of negativity"; former President George W. Bush campaigned in 2000 on the slogan "compassionate conservatism"; and Malala Yousafzai's call for "books not bullets" continues to resonate with audiences across the world. In each case the speaker appeals to our penchant for melodious and pleasing sounds, a weakness of ours since at least the days of

Malcolm X and Elizabeth Cady Stanton (left to right)

Gorgias of Leontini, who employed such cadences to great sonic effect in fifth century BCE Athens.

Metaphor

If alliteration emphasizes the beauty of sound, metaphor can create the beautiful image. Technically a metaphor is a comparison of two different things that share something important in common. Some metaphors become so useful to us, so culturally ingrained, that we forget they're metaphors at all; we call these "dead" metaphors even as they're very much alive. Take the common expression "a politician's stance on the issues." Last time we checked, politicians don't stand on anything save for their feet. Similarly, we talk of a candidate's run for office. Frankly, we haven't seen too many political candidates, local or national, mimicking Usain Bolt or Zola Budd. The point is that to "stand" and to "run" are two very common dead metaphors.

    George Lakoff and Mark Johnson write about "metaphors we live by" and it's true: metaphors help us make sense of our often confusing world.[17] When former President Obama's approval rating was the lowest of his two terms he talked about "losing that new car smell." Late in his term as president, Ronald Reagan's advisors talked about how the "landing gear was down." At a recent wedding reception a groom was informed that "he'd outkicked the punt coverage" in marrying his wife. Television pundits talk frequently about politicians "doubling down" on a controversial policy, "kicking the can down the road" in delaying a decision, and "dog whistling" to highly informed true believers. Someone, it seems, is forever being "thrown under the bus." And when asked about his longevity, a cynic

---

17   George Lakoff and Mark Johnson, *Metaphors We Live By* (Chicago: University of Chicago Press, 2003).

responded that "he was still circling the drain." Driving metaphors seems particularly in vogue just now. We've been hearing about "pumping the brakes" to slow something down, and "staying in your line" to keep someone from trespassing on another's expertise.

Metaphors that resonate deeply across time and cultures, are called archetypal metaphors. Communication scholar Michael Osborne has identified several of these, including light and dark, the seasons, and the sea.[18] Americans are particularly infatuated with metaphors that feature journeys and hoped-for destinations: we speak of a "rendezvous with destiny," a "shining city upon a hill," and "towards a more perfect union." Roads and paths–crooked, straight, and forked–are common as we seek to reach our future. "The road less traveled" and "a fork in the road" are powerful metaphors suggestive of change and struggle.

Metaphors are limited only by your imagination and creativity. In seeking to embrace the diversity of the nation, presidential candidate Jesse Jackson spoke of the nation as a patchwork quilt and later as a rainbow coalition. Both metaphors are powerfully visual and convey the beautiful diversity and pragmatism symbolic of the American character. Novelist J.K. Rowling, author of the incredibly popular *Harry Potter* series, employs the power of metaphor to convey the depths of her own failures before the 2008 graduating class at Harvard University. From 8:17 to 9:30, watch and listen as Rowling employs two very common metaphors to great rhetorical effect.[19] You don't need to look to great literature or great speeches to find compelling metaphors; they're all around you: that rosebush in your

---

18   Michael M. Osborn, "Archetypal Metaphor in Rhetoric: The Light-Dark Family," *Quarterly Journal of Speech* 53 (1967): 115-26; Michael M. Osborn, "The Evolution of the Archetypal Sea in Rhetoric and Poetic," *Quarterly Journal of Speech* 63 (1977): 347-63.

19   Visit link: https://goo.gl/6CdhNM

front yard, that lamp on your desk, that sturdy support wall behind you, the yarn on your sweater, the circle formed by your ring, and the window in your study—each has enormous metaphorical potential. We encourage you to take the time and engage in a bit of what Kenneth Burke calls "verbal atom cracking," or the rhetorical collision of two unlike things.[20] The results can indeed be powerful and spectacular.

Jesse Jackson and J.K. Rowling (left to right)

The Power of Synechdoche [Flip Learning chat]

---

20 Kenneth Burke, *Attitudes Toward History*, 3rd ed. (Berkeley: University of California Press, 1984), 308.

3.5 Humor

Even as words form, re-form, and reflect our cultural landscape, we can't help but notice how important humor has become to our everyday existence. Whether it's yet another new comedy series or the most recent iteration of *Jackass*, the latest viral video or advertising campaign featuring talking animals (Geico) or supposedly undersexed women (pick any male "grooming" product), our culture puts an enormous emphasis on the comedic. So much so that recent trends in dating and courtship reveal that if you're not very funny, you might want to find the nearest nunnery, monastery, or desert island. Poll after poll reveals that a sense of humor is a top five requisite in the dating game.

One recent poll conducted by *Men's Health Magazine* caught our attention. When asked to specify the most desirable personality trait in men, 77 percent of the women surveyed selected "sense of humor." Ranked a very distant second, at 55 percent, was "intelligence." Long gone are the days when "being a good provider" topped these same polls year in and year out. No, in our present age of relative gender equity and women outnumbering men on college campuses, home appliances are out and punch lines and irony are in. Coupling isn't the only area in which humor is key; research finds repeatedly that professors who are perceived as funny are far better teachers, according to their students, than their unfunny peers.[21]

Research in the communication field hasn't yet caught up with the contemporary comedic moment, however. In fact, back in the early days of communication research, scholars claimed with a very straight and perhaps long face that humor had little, if any, effect

---

21   Sarah E. Torok, Robert F. McMorris, and Wen-Chi Lin, "Is Humor an Appreciated Teaching Tool? Perceptions of Professors' Teaching Styles and Use of Humor," *College Teaching* 52 (2004): 14-20.

at all on persuasive speeches. Professor Lull (no, we're not making this name up) and his colleagues, though, shouldn't be faulted for their findings; clearly early 1940's America did not place much of a premium on being funny.[22] In an age of economic depression–and the name "depression" is its own important selection of reality–and world war, survival was far more important than laughter, however much needed.

Using Humor in the Public Speech: Pros and Cons

What, then, do we know about humor in the context of public speaking? Even though it is vastly understudied and undertheorized, here's what the research indicates about humor: (1) it is effective when it's a means to an end rather than an end in itself; in other words, it has to be relevant to the speech's objectives; (2) it can increase the audience's attention to the speech; (3) it tends to enhance the speaker's credibility and the audience's mood, especially when witty self-deprecating humor is skillfully employed; (4) it can increase interest in a speech; (5) it can help an audience remember a speech's contents; and (6) it must be employed judiciously to achieve maximum effect.[23] We'd call particular attention to number 5. In one of the most unforgettable student speeches we've ever heard, watch how Georgia Tech engineering student, Nick Selby, blends humor, music and the theatrical to stunning rhetorical effect.[24]

You can see even by these fairly tentative findings that the use

---

22 P. E. Lull, "The Effectiveness of Humor in Persuasive Speech," *Speech Monographs* 7 (1940): 26-40.

23 Charles R. Gruner, "Advice to the Beginning Speaker on Humor—What the Research Tells Us," *Communication Education* 34 (1985): 140-44.

24 Visit link: https://goo.gl/FE3LWd

of humor has a negative flip side: employing humor out of context, too frequently, and without purpose can do more harm than good. We would also emphasize that humor can be very idiosyncratic: what's funny to you and your cohort might be very un-funny to your grandmother and her posse. Frankly, Dave Chappelle, Amy Schumer, Ellen DeGeneres, and Sarah Silverman don't translate well to many senior citizens. In fairness, Jack Benny and the Three Stooges might not work well in the twenty-first century, either. All of which is to say that humor is a wonderful rhetorical tool that needs very careful calibrating.

Here's a bit of advice when it comes to that calibration. As you know, humor can offend–deeply. If you have any question at all about the appropriateness of your humor, run it by your teacher first. The last thing you want to do is be perceived as bigoted or dismissed as inappropriate, however laudable your intentions.

Humor in the Subject

Back in your grandfather's day, it used to be a staple of nearly all speechmaking to begin with a joke, something to lighten the mood and gain rapport with one's audience. Oftentimes that joke had very little to do with the subject matter in question–a joke for joke's sake, in other words. Ideally humor should spring organically from the subject, the occasion, and its interaction with the cultural moment. And humor can take place at any point in your speech. For example, even an ostensibly un-funny subject such as blood (take your pick: blood types, blood tests, blood diseases, blood properties, blood donation) is dripping with possibilities: vampires, zombies, leeches, mosquitoes, and a host of other allusions, comparisons, and popular culture possibilities.

And speaking of grandfathers and attempts at speech humor, I was recently at a commencement ceremony in which 10,000 plus people packed a convention center to celebrate student achievement. I can't remember much about the speaker that day other than the fact that he was older—and his attempt at humor was painfully awkward. Whereas jokes about Dolly Parton might have gotten a chuckle in the last millennium, these days, uhm, no, just don't go there. Fetishizing women's body parts (or men's) just isn't funny anymore. Trust me: you don't want to hear 10,000 people audibly groan.

Furthermore, campus-specific topics—and we're partial to selecting topics that are quite local to our immediate audience—involving everything from tuition, financial aid, required courses, student-teacher ratios, campus history, career development and placement, campus hot spots (wired and otherwise), philanthropy, parking (always parking), student governance, study abroad, food, career development, town and gown, housing, commencement, majors and minors, to invited speakers all have their own humorous possibilities. And if you don't find those possibilities, that's fine; not every speaker has to be witty, clever, funny, or hilarious. We simply encourage you to take a good, hard, creative look at what's possible—what the ancient Greeks called invention, the creative energy that makes a speech really hum and offer unique and memorable insights.

Humor in the Occasion

Next, and in keeping with our local theme, try to find humorous possibilities with what's happening in your own speech class and speaking occasion. As communication theorist Owen Lynch has noted, one of humor's principal functions is to reduce tension—and in your speech class you're likely going to have a LOT of tension; it comes with the territory of nerves and bodies that we discussed in Chapter

2.[25] Keep an eye out for the funny stuff going on right in front of you. Many times we've been lecturing and something very unplanned happens: a construction worker fires up a concussive jackhammer right outside the room; a car alarm that can be heard from three states away is tripped–and nobody deactivates it; somebody pulls the fire alarm; the lights go off, back on, then off again; a student laughs loudly, by herself, at an inopportune time; students in the class next door start singing–loudly; a student walks into the wrong classroom–and begins talking; a student's cell phone is ringing and he can't shut it off, or better yet, the teacher's phone unexpectedly goes off; you enter the URL whitehouse.com with the classroom LED projector on and expect to share a presidential press conference and instead you see a very different kind of presentation; while sharing pictures of a campus event posted to your Facebook page with students, a friend instant messages you a rather ribald greeting; and always, it seems, something is crashing to the floor.

Each of these occurrences has happened to me, and each is loaded with comic opportunity. One of my students a few years back brought an enormous caffeinated beverage to class and proceeded to sit down in the front row. She promptly forgot about the drink as she pondered her speaking outline and then knocked it off her desk, splattering pumpkin latte all over her professor's shoes and pants. Though not terribly funny at the time, it became hilarious by the end of the term, in part because the class was willing to play along and because giant beverages exploding proximate to professors is kind of funny.

---

25   Owen H. Lynch, "Humorous Communication: Finding a Place for Humor in Communication Research," *Communication Theory* 12 (2002): 423-445.

Humor in the Moment

But if 64-ounce drinks aren't spilling in your classroom, no worries, we bet you can have some fun contextualizing your speech in the context of other people's speeches. What if, G/god forbid, the student speaking immediately before you speaks on the exact same subject? Our advice is, to borrow a cliché, take the lemon and make some lemonade. Write a quick note on your speaking outline acknowledging your predicament. Or what if the student again speaking right before you can't complete her speech and flees the room in panic? You have to follow this rather uncomfortable predicament. Perhaps you might mention your impeccable timing or some other self-deprecating comment. Such situations aren't that unusual; in fact, we've recently invented a catch-all cultural buzzword for such uncomfortable moments: "awkward." It doesn't even need a verb as we repeat it–usually in a sing-song voice. Audiences appreciate it when you can improvise in a humorous way; it gains our sympathy since we know it just as well could've happened to us. And getting your audience to laugh along with you early in your address lightens the entire room and it shifts the attention back to you and your message.

One of the all-time best public speakers is (semi-) retired late-night comedian, David Letterman. Watch as this Ball State communication major does his best to deal with a very bizarre guest, Joaquin Phoenix.[26]

One of our favorite comedians is the late/great George Carlin. While Carlin gained no small fame and notoriety from his "Seven Words You Can't Say on Television," he was also a brilliant commentator on language. As you've no doubt observed, the English language is full of comic possibilities. Watch Carlin's brilliant and inci-

---

26 Visit link: https://goo.gl/KS2q7Y

sive commentary on the difference between baseball and football.[27]

As you can no doubt see, language, style, and humor are intimately related; we've simply separated them out here in Chapter 3 to call attention to each one. We encourage you to see the building blocks of our collective humanity– otherwise known as language– less as sort of a boring mirror reflected onto the world and far more as a unique inheritance teeming with rhetorical potential. Lest we forget, language reflects our world just as it also selects it. Just ask Gary McCord.

Favorite Skit [Flip Learning chat]

Chapter 3 Quiz [Flip Learning quiz]

---

27   Visit link: https://goo.gl/z6rfuA

4 Selecting a Topic

4.1 We All Have Expertise

If we had a dollar for every time a student has approached us with some variant of "I just can't find a decent topic for my speech," we'd be Bill Gates-wealthy. Even more than the perennial issue of nerves and fear, topic selection seems to induce all manner of panic and/or brain freeze. Students often respond to our advice to "explore your interests" with "But I don't really have any interests that someone's gonna want to listen to." Oh, but you do. Your Facebook page, among other places, likely contains a lengthy list of just how interesting you are—and the many things you like or are attracted to. Whether it's *The Catcher in the Rye*, *Eternal Sunshine of the Spotless Mind*, *Breaking Bad*, Drake, the Miami Heat, going vegan, spelunking, or Sentence Diagramming for Dummies, you have interesting interests. So let's clear this ground first: you do have interests that can help you select

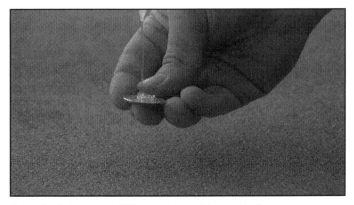

Episode 4: Quarters [Flip Learning video series]
In Episode 4 of our video series, Laura struggles to find a satisfying speech topic, but Calvin knows just what to do.

a topic suitable for a public speech.

    These interests, by the way, also suggest a certain level of expertise that is vital to speechmaking of all types— informative, persuasive, and commemorative. Aristotle called ethos—the root term for ethics—the "controlling factor" in compelling speechmaking.[1] Think of your ethos in terms of your expertise but also your character. Audiences respond best to speakers who not only have authority on a given subject but communicate that authority with goodwill, trustworthiness—and lots of dynamism. Because your ethos is potentially so persuasive, Plato, Aristotle, and their Greek and Roman colleagues understood rhetoric as a moral art with profound consequences. We don't need to invoke the League of twentieth century Villains—Hitler, Stalin, Idi Amin, and Pol Pot—to make the point about ethos and character: the salesperson who sold you the defective (fill in the blank) because of his or her perceived ethos makes the same point on a much more personal and local scale.

---

1   Aristotle, *On Rhetoric*, transl. George A. Kennedy (New York: Oxford University Press, 1991), 38.

And speaking of sketchy salesmen, have you ever noticed in low-budget and poorly produced local television advertisements how ethos gets tied somehow to excitement? In other words, because the person selling the furniture/used cars/pest control products/monster truck shows has pretty much zero initial expertise/ethos (since we don't know them), listen to their voices. You'd think by their rate of speech and tone of voice that The Flesh Eating End Times were immediately upon us—or a Bieber concert had just broken out at the local middle school. You absolutely don't have to stretch your vocal chords like this guy hawking used cars,[2] this guy selling furniture,[3] or this guy advertising the monster trucks coming to town.[4] Yes, the voice conveys excitement and passion, but let's stick with indoor voices; your ethos will shine through, even among the zombies and Beliebers.

Out in the world, away from your speech class but likely in your near future, you will be asked to speak on matters that involve your expertise: at work you'll be asked to summarize to a board of directors your unit's new advertising campaign; the local garden circle will ask you to instruct them on the basics of rose pruning; and the state Kiwanis convention wants your counsel on which nonprofits need financial assistance in your area. And if we stretch the concept of expertise just a bit further, you might also be invited to give a wedding toast as a best man or maid of honor. Even as these invitations might arouse our anxiety, they also provide a certain measure of reassurance: after all, these are things about which we know a great deal; people are seeking us out for our expert counsel.

Not so in our speech class; our speaking is mandated and not

---

2   Visit link: https://goo.gl/TPxfhs

3   Visit link: https://goo.gl/X7okn1

4   Visit link: https://goo.gl/41Cq5N

invited. Thus our collective unease and uncertainty and timidity. Back to the first sentence of this chapter and Mr. Gates. So, where does all this talk about expertise, (non)invitations, and character leave us? Actually, in a very important place.

> TED Talks [Flip Learning chat]

4.2 Integrating Personal and Audience Interests

Our best advice when it comes to selecting a topic for your speech class is to explore your passions—but with one qualifier: how do your passions intersect with an audience of your peers. In nearly every public speaking book that's ever been published you'll note that "Topic Selection" and "Audience Analysis" each have their own separate chapters—as if they were different areas of inquiry. Authors do this out of convenience and tradition rather than understanding the two areas as unrelated to each other. Let's be clear: topic selection should always be intimately connected with audience analysis. Frankly, if you don't care much about the needs of your audience, that feeling will be reciprocated—and then multiplied by the number of listeners in the room.

Sample Topic: The Mountain Pine Beetle

Let's say, for example, that you have a fascination with the genetic make-up of the Mountain Pine Beetle. Your interest is both personal and academic: your family farms pine trees in the Northwest and your college major is biology. Bottom line: you find the MPB exceptionally compelling. But your audience of fellow undergraduates won't. Not yet anyway (stay tuned). You would be speaking over their

Mountain Pine Beetle

heads since your audience won't likely have a clue about carapace genetics or about pine trees and pulp wood farming. The speech would be one massive snooze or an interlude for coy email/text checking and perhaps even a Snap or three. That glazed look and gimlet-eyed mouth breathing...yeah, those are never good signs.

So yes, absolutely: the first place to explore potential speech topics is in the mirror. But remember: your own beguiling reflection should never distract you from your immediate listeners. Recall that the mythic Narcissus died from staring at himself; however, you're not going to "kill it" with an audience if you think only about your own interests. So be very practical: if you can't make this particular interest of yours interesting for a group of peers, that's fine; move on to the next subject. The best public speakers are always audience centered, which means every component of their speeches, including the topic, takes into consideration the unique dynamics of an audience.

Caravaggio's *Narcissus*

Another way to think about the relationship between yourself and an audience in the context of public speaking is in this Venn diagram, where your own interests are represented in green and your audience's interests are represented in dark blue.

Our "go" spot is the area of overlap, or where green and dark blue turn to light blue. This little football-shaped area represents something of a match.com moment of potential bliss. Now just because there's overlap doesn't mean your speech will be a smashing success; it simply indicates that conditions are auspicious. We would add that this relatively small light blue shape will increase with your skill and creativity as a public speaker. That is, with experience, hard work, and imagination, you will be able to shade your audience's particular interests closer to yours. But you can only do this by being exceptionally audience centered; getting an audience to care about what you care about is part of the magic of invention. We'll have much more to say about this magic in the chapters to follow.

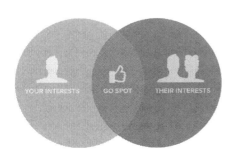

At this point we hear your plaintive plea: "But how do I know what topics will interest my audience?" In answering this really important question, let's have a closer look at that ugly Mountain Pine Beetle. With just a bit of Internet searching (and more on Internet searching later), we'll quickly discover that this tiny five-millimeter beast has wreaked havoc on the mountainous western regions of North America, deforesting millions of acres of pine trees. Now notice: whereas a classroom of your peers might not be terribly interested in your family's tree farm or the beetle's DNA sequencing, put in the much bigger context of deforestation, we might generate a bit more interest. Going further, why has this bug become a problem only in recent years? Interesting question. Furthermore, what are the short-term economic and climate impacts of this devastation?

A mountain pine beetle-infested forest in British Columbia

Very interesting question. You see in what direction we're moving with this: the closer you can bring this handlebar-mustachioed critter in need of a good leg waxing to your audience's concerns about climate change, ecology and economics, the better. Generally speaking, the bigger and more inclusive the context, the better. So what might have begun as a personal/family matter is now of much more global concern—a concern to those sitting in front of you.

4.3 Brainstorming Geography to Identify Speech Topics

Beyond our own passions, where else might we find compelling speech topics? They're all around us; we just need to pause long enough and give them a careful look. Try, for example, to generate your own Speech Table, in the same manner as we do below.

	PLACES	EVENTS	GROUPS/PEOPLE	CURIOSITY
GLOBAL	VATICAN CITY	RAMADAN	VIKINGS	STONEHENGE
NATIONAL	NATIONAL PARKS	VALENTINE'S DAY	ABOLITIONISTS	MT. RUSHMORE
REGIONAL	STONE MOUNTAIN	MARDI GRAS	HONEY BEES	NORTHERN LIGHTS
STATE	ROSEWOOD, FL	GASPARILLA	SEMINOLES	RED TIDE
UNIVERSITY	THE SWAMP	FREEDOM SUMMER	MARY MCLEOD BETHUNE	SOD CEMETERY

Selecting a Topic

Here are twenty topics that could easily make for compelling informative speeches. If you're more globally inclined, and perhaps you've traveled there, you'd like to speak about the creation of Vatican City. Or maybe you're a practicing Muslim and you'd like to inform your audience about the month of Ramadan. At a national level, perhaps you're interested in the group of activists known as abolitionists, whose mission it was to abolish slavery. Turning more regional, maybe you grew up in the upper Midwest and were treated to the dazzling astronomical displays known as the Northern Lights (Aurora Borealis) or you're concerned about what's been happening to the region's key workers, otherwise known as honeybees. More locally, and having grown up along the coast of Florida, perhaps you're dismayed by the frequent red tides and accompanying fish kills. At the most local level, or what's in your backyard as a college student, perhaps on your way to class during freshman year you passed some sculpture that eventually piqued your interest, and you learned that it commemorated the university's involvement with an important chapter in the civil rights movement.

Each of these topics has the potential to be the focus of a terrific informative speech. Over many years as speech instructors, we've noted a tendency for some of the best speeches to be more local in character; that is, audience members tend to be attracted to things close to home. Here at Florida State University, for example, one of the topics covered frequently by speech students are the murders committed at the Chi Omega sorority house by the infamous serial killer Ted Bundy back in 1978. As sad and awful as that story is, what happened at the Chi Omega house serves as an important bond among our students and the history we collectively share. On a much lighter note, we're also rather (in)famous for being at ground zero of the student streaking "movement" back in the early 1970s.

Your campus, too, has many interesting and important stories waiting to be told. Go and find them. A great place to start is in your university library where units of "archives" and "special collections" are often housed.

Of course check your library out virtually first. Who was your university's first president? Who helped form the first Black Student Union? Who was the first female faculty member? Who are some famous alumni? Was the mascot always the same? What important event happened at a location on campus? How did the student newspaper editorialize about an important subject? You see where we're going with this advice: what we can see and touch daily can offer an added importance and urgency to our speechmaking; moreover, in sharing an identity as a Seminole, a Buckeye, or even a Banana Slug (go U.C. Santa Cruz!), you share something very important. So go ahead: add a new layer to that identity.

4.4 Brainstorming Academic Interests

Another great place to find potential topics for informative, persuasive, and commemorative speeches is your academic major. Think about it: your major (or prospective major) represents an area of academic interest unique to you—and presumably you're passionate about and engaged by the topics it covers. In addition, because of your burgeoning expertise in the area—you're the major after all—audiences, per Aristotle and ethos, will likely find you more credible, believable, and even engaging. Don't be coy about advertising this small but really important fact; if you have academic expertise your audience wants to know about it—and so does your instructor!

Sample Topics: French Impressionism

Let's have a closer look. Say that you're an art history major and you've found the work of the French Impressionists particularly fascinating. While your audience might not have any expertise at all in

Claude Monet, *The Water Lily Pond*, c. 1917-19

this area, they have likely seen or heard about impressionistic styles of painting. Great. Go ahead and inform your listeners about why this style of painting emerged when it did or to what the style was responding. Or, show us a prominent example of impressionism (perhaps Monet and his water lilies) and walk us through what an artist is attempting to convey. Even better: let's say you're an aspiring impressionist painter. Go ahead and demonstrate for us (by literally drawing during part of your speech) some of the layering techniques at the heart of the style. There's a reason that a posthumous Bob Ross is still incredibly popular on Saturday morning public television: watching him create art from a blank canvas is absolutely mesmerizing. And his gentle narrative style featuring "happy accidents" makes him a most compelling public speaker/painter. And that hair!

Repairing Torn Knee Ligaments

Or let's say that you're a sports medicine major, with plans to go on to pursue either physical therapy or medical school. One of the major injuries suffered by athletes and non-athletes alike is tearing a knee ligament. With a suitably detailed visual aid, you might give a speech on how knee ligaments (interior, anterior, or posterior) get repaired. Or, given the proliferation of artificial replace-

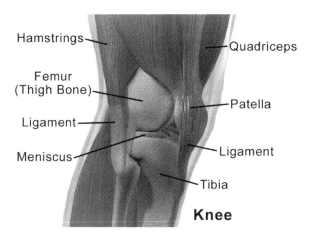

Anatomy of the knee

ments, perhaps a speech on how hip replacement works would be fascinating. Of course we'll need to be mindful about the specialized vocabulary that comes with such topics, but surely we can give a compelling speech on important medical technologies that many of us are already dealing with because of aging parents and grandparents. Or perhaps your interest in the medical field stems from something far more personal: you suffer from migraine headaches and you want to work on a cure. Your audience will likely be not only sympathetic to your suffering, but also have some degree of interest in the subject by virtue of a friend or family member who suffers from the same affliction. Tell us what a migraine is, as opposed to a "regular" headache. What are treatment options—Eastern and Western? What is acupuncture and how is it being used to treat these debilitating headaches? What is literally happening inside of our heads when we get a migraine?

Perhaps you're a history major and attending a college in the Great Plains. You've recently taken a fascinating course on Native American history and read extensively on the battle of Wounded Knee. Great. Go ahead and give a speech on what happened there and why it's so important to our collective history. Or maybe you

Crazy Horse Memorial

recently visited the remarkable rock carving just south of the iconic Mount Rushmore, the monument to Crazy Horse; this experience, along with your interests in history, suggest a potentially compelling speech on this Lakota leader emerging out of the South Dakota Badlands.

And speaking of Badlands, you geology majors have a literal landscape of treasures to work with—from how Kimberlite rocks form diamonds to how a new technology called "fracking" is revolutionizing the natural gas industry. Most of your audience members will be interested to know more about diamonds, to say nothing about how oil and gas is being mined here in the United States to fuel our cars and heat our homes—and with what consequences.

We could go on, but you see the point we're driving at: your major(s) serves as a very rich source of potential speech topics. Sure, we should always be mindful about translating the technical areas of our majors into common language since we're speaking to non-experts, but your passion for the subject and your credibility as an expert are unique and very important rhetorical resources upon which you can and should draw.

> Generate Topics from Academic Interests [Flip Learning chat]

> Generate Topics from Current Events [Flip Learning chat]

4.5 Brainstorming Professional Interests

Another important place for speech topics is notable for how often people overlook it: where you work. Students often think that because they have a relatively low-paying job in the service sector of our economy that they should look elsewhere for speech topics; nothing interesting happens where I work. Well, not so fast; you might have something really important to share with your audience. Let's say you work part-time as a receptionist at a blood bank. Furthermore, just a bit of brainstorming will reveal an enormous number of really important topics centering around that place you call work: blood products, blood donation, blood screening, blood shortages, blood properties, blood tests, and so forth. More to the point of your audience, blood is one of those universals: we've all got it, we all need it, and it tells us some remarkable things if we look carefully for its secrets.

Or perhaps more commonly, you work as a waiter/waitress/host/hostess at a local restaurant. You're not wild about the job, but it helps pay the bills and the hours are flexible for a student. But go ahead and look carefully around you; see that restaurant anew—as a source for speech materials. For example, you might want to talk about issues related to the minimum wage and its effect on tipping behavior; an entertaining speech on common customer mishaps (with accompanying stories) might be a lot of fun; how does the county or state regulate restaurants for cleanliness; what happens behind the scenes back in the kitchen area might be very informative; how is technology changing the restaurant experience; the logistics of running a restaurant are complex and potentially very interesting, from food prep and inventory to scheduling and seating. Or perhaps as a budding chef you want to show your audience how to create a delectable dessert—with ease and on the cheap. The key here is to let your imagination run amok: see that place of work in a new light; see it as a place where the magic of invention can happen with just a bit of creativity.

Generating Topics from Current Events

A final source of topic inspiration comes from current events. One of the reasons that news outlets of all kinds publish 24/7 is to keep us updated on what they deem important and newsworthy. In other words, news outlets always have topics that appeal to audiences of all kinds—if they don't, they won't be in business much longer. So, if you just take a stroll around the Internet you'll be inundated with interesting new(s) topics. That stroll might include such stops as: major newspapers such as *USA Today*, *The Guardian*, the *New York Times* or the *Wall Street Journal*; magazines such as *The Economist*, *Time*, *Newsweek*, the *New Yorker*, *National Review*, the *New Republic*, and of course *The Onion*; always local and campus newspapers; major news organizations such as the Associated Press, Reuters, National Public Radio, and the British Broadcasting Corporation; and basically any Internet browser homepage. On any given hour of any given day you'll find topics from the bizarre—porn elbow—to the extremely useful—top apps for college students—and always those Buzzfeed or Letterman-inspired top ten lists for any and all matters. Of course if you're really desperate you can always type in "topics for speeches" at Google and immediately get back six figures' worth of relevant hits. And if you want to see those topics performed, YouTube provides an extensive archive of germane possibilities.

4.6 Taboo Topics

We should also say a word or two about taboo topics—topics from which you should probably steer clear. As much as you'd like to push the edge of the envelope, we'd encourage you to think hard about whether a speech topic might offend. We have a very long list of prominent public speakers who perhaps meant well but whose remarks ended up short-circuiting their careers. So, what are those topics? In general, any topic that generalizes negatively about a group of people, or a prominent person, yeah, you'll want to avoid that. On our Facebook feeds we'll occasionally see postings about "Walmart people," "Republican wing-nuts," or "White Girl Problems," or fraternity this or sorority that. In brief, we're really advanced when it comes to insulting others based on a certain pattern of behavior or system of beliefs. If you're a Democrat and think that Donald Trump or Ted Cruz is Lucifer with a red tail and pitchfork, and eats kittens that's fine—but you'll want to realize that several (many?) in your speech class have a different political affiliation than you. Don't assume otherwise. Or if you believe that former President Barack Obama read Karl Marx to his cabinet and continues to pray five times a day to Allah, that's fine, too. But many in your speech class won't and would be insulted to hear as much. So we'd counsel you to steer clear of generalizing about groups of people and prominent public people who function as lightning rods of (usually) political controversy. By all means, don't be afraid to examine important political topics, especially policies and the debates they inspire, but gross generalizations are usually just that: gross.

A second category of taboo pertains to that ubiquitous three-letter signifier, S-E-X. Now we don't mean to come across as prudish or old-people-repressed; in fact topics related to sexualities and policy are potentially really interesting and worth exploring in a speech class (topics such as transgender advocacy, gay and lesbian adoption laws, contraception, family planning, medicalizing sexual conditions, criminalizing deviancies, etc.). No, we're talking about the *Cosmo-* and *Maxim*-inspired detritus like, "how to pick up hot guys at the next Panhellenic shindig," "best pick-up lines to use at Club 21," "measuring hotness on campus," or "how to Facebook stalk your future boyfriend." The list could go on. And on. Social media, pop culture, and the Internet in general traffic heavily in our sexual needs and insecurities. Tell you what: let's let Dr. Ruth, Dr. Drew, and the "experts" at *Cosmo* and *Maxim* deal with this stuff. In general, privileging pop culture's views about such a sensitive area runs a much higher risk of offending rather than informing, persuading, or entertaining. But, as always, if you have any doubts or questions about propriety, consult your speech teacher.

As we're discussing topic ideas with students, we occasionally get asked about language taboos—generally something like this: "Is it okay if I cuss?" or more specifically, "Can I drop the term D'bag?" And our answer usually goes something like, "Yes....but." Taboo words have their own fascinating histories, especially with marginalized groups, but understand that swearing gratuitously runs a very big risk of alienating members of your audience, not to mention diminishing your credibility. And the older that audience is, probably the more of a risk you run. Most of our grandfathers never swore. Ever. For their generation and their specific socioeconomic class and religious affiliation, to swear was to lower oneself, to be uncouth, to be profane, uneducated. We won't even talk about our grandmothers, who lived with their own gendered speech taboos. So our advice about swearing redounds to a simple but important question: is it fulfilling some important rhetorical function in your speech? If so, what is it? If not, don't do it; the risks outweigh the rewards. Maybe "uncouth" is rhetorically more advantageous than "D'bag."

When in doubt, ask your teacher.

4.7 Narrowing a Topic to a Specific Purpose

Once you've selected a topic, the fun is just getting started; the work, too, is just beginning. But after a careful consideration of your interests, your work, and your passions, you're now ready to begin "building" your speech. We use this construction metaphor very purposefully. Think of topic selection this way: selecting a neighborhood in which you'd like to live. Now we need to start putting together that blueprint—or what your house will look like. Let's call this part of your work determining the Specific Purpose.[5] That is, "specific" refers to something very definite while "purpose" refers to what you plan to accomplish. In sum, the Specific Purpose refers to the aim of your speech. You don't want to build just any old house but one with very purposeful features. And on a very solid foundation.

In talking about your Specific Purpose, perhaps we should put some *bells and whistles* around this part of our text. Why? Because our experience is that if students don't have a compelling and very clearly stated Specific Purpose, the architecture of the speech just collapses and you're left with just an empty shell. So let's talk about the phrasing for specific purposes.

Phrasing the Specific Purpose

Specific purposes should begin with, "To inform my audience that/about/how to..." or "To persuade my audience to..." or "To commemorate..."

You'll want to avoid phrasing that is very vague, asks a ques-

---

[5] The terms *Specific Purpose* and *Central Idea* come from Stephen E. Lucas and his fine speech textbook, *The Art of Public Speaking*.

tion, employs a sentence fragment or features figurative language. The word "and" should be avoided as it conveys at least two thoughts.

Here's a lousy specific purpose:

> "Donating blood."

Here's another stinker:

> "To persuade my audience that donating blood doesn't suck as much as you think."

And another:

> "To persuade my audience to donate blood and get your cholesterol screened."

And one more:

> "Praising Robert Moses."

Now, here's a good specific purpose:

> "To persuade my audience to donate blood."

But, we think there's one better; watch:

> "To persuade my audience to donate blood at the next campus blood drive."

This last Specific Purpose adds the very important detail of when and how so pivotal to calls to action with persuasive speeches (more in Chapter 9). Especially when it comes to persuasion, audience members often need to be able to act upon your speech—especially when you're asking them to take very specific steps. If your community is like ours, there are a number of different organizations involved with blood donation. But if your audience is college students, let's make it real easy for them: "the local bloodmobile is coming on Friday, February 13, from 8 a.m. to 6 p.m. in front of the student union." Let's take it a step further: have them take out their smart phones and enter it into their calendars. Now they have no excuses for not knowing the when, where, and how of your speech.

And just who is Robert Moses? Well, he's a terribly important civil rights figure who repeatedly risked life and limb to bring the state of Mississippi into the twentieth century. In many ways he was the antithesis of Dr. Martin Luther King, Jr., who led with his soaring oratory. No, Moses led a movement on the ideal of it being largely leaderless—or if it had to be led, let the locals lead; as a result we don't know a lot about this remarkable man. But in terms of phrasing a specific purpose, we can do a lot better than:

> "Praising Robert Moses."

How about:

> "To commemorate for my audience the civil rights work of Robert Moses."

Such a statement allows you to focus on a handful of important events from Moses's long and consequential life—events that should be near and dear to your audience as well.

But let's go back to our furry friend, the Mountain Pine Beetle, and a speech to inform. Here are some poorly worded Specific Purpose statements:

Selecting a Topic

> "To inform my audience about the Mountain Pine Beetle."

Note that this is much too vague; you could spend the rest of your adult life talking about this insidious insect.

> "To inform my audience that the federal government needs to better fund research to kill the Mountain Pine Beetle."

Notice that you're now giving a persuasive speech rather than a speech that tries to inform. A common mistake that students often make when it comes to the informative round of speaking is they end up acting as advocates rather than educators.

Here's another poorly worded Specific Purpose:

> "What is the Mountain Pine Beetle?"

Again, don't phrase your Specific Purpose as a question. Instead be very clear and specific about your intentions. Moreover, we find it very useful for students to state the specific purpose somewhere in their introduction. Why? Because leaving your audience guessing about your aims will only lead to confusion—which usually leads to texting/mouth-breathing/daydreaming/sleeping or annoyed audience members. Perhaps all of the above. So in general, audiences like for you to be very explicit with them; speechmaking is just not the time for being vague.

A really good question at this point is: where do good Specific Purposes come from? How would I find or create them? Invariably the answers will come from doing research on the subject. Unless you're already an expert on the subject, you simply won't "happen upon" a compelling Specific Purpose. No, you'll need to do some careful research in multiple venues (see Chapter 8) before settling on a Specific Purpose. One newspaper article won't do it. Neither

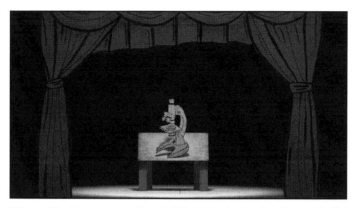
Where Do Ideas Come From? [Flip Learning animation series]
That age-old question, answered by science.

will two magazine articles. You'll want to consult and read as much research as you can in order to develop the expertise that will carry the day with an audience. Don't you owe it to your listeners to be as informed as possible? Sure, you can't read everything ever written or said about the Mountain Pine Beetle, but if you treat audiences with the great respect they deserve, you'll want to give them expert counsel.

Let's say after consulting a number of credible sources that you've decided on this as your Specific Purpose:

> "To inform my audience about the environmental impacts of the Mountain Pine Beetle."

Note that this statement is very specific—environmental impacts—and we're playing the role of educator, not advocate. Great. At this point we have a very good blueprint for what the exterior of our house will look like.

We've settled on the theme of environmental impacts because our research has revealed that this is a very important consequence of the beetle's infestation; that is, a number of writers and researchers are talking about this subject since it's so important to so many people. These same writers and researchers are also talking about the economic impacts of the Mountain Pine Beetle, but this is another "house" altogether. An important one, but a different one.

> Develop a Specific Purpose [Flip Learning chat]

4.8 Developing a Central Idea

We're now ready to talk about our next important step in the speech-building process: specifying in more detail the Specific Purpose. Let's call this specification the Central Idea, or what key points you will develop in the speech. Let's repeat the point for emphasis as it, too, is vital to your future public speaking success: the Central Idea develops in more detail—typically three main points—your Specific Purpose. Those three main points—along with an introduction and conclusion (see Chapter 6)—function as the rooms in your house. Again, the Central Idea is developed from the expertise you develop in researching the topic.

Phrasing the Central Idea

So back to our friend the Mountain Pine Beetle:

▷ Specific Purpose:
To inform my audience about the environmental impacts of the Mountain Pine Beetle.

▷ Central Idea:
Rising temperatures have allowed the Mountain Pine

Beetle to survive winters leading to massive deforestation and several additional environmental consequences: increased water runoff leading to increased soil erosion, a rise in microorganisms such as E. coli, and a potential decrease in air quality.

Your speech is now taking on that all-important characteristic of form (see Chapter 7 for organization). Rather than a random bunch of unrelated facts, we now have a clear, cogent, and well-articulated set of points, each related back to the Specific Purpose—in this case the environmental impacts of the Mountain Pine Beetle. Furthermore, each of the three main points mentioned in the Central Idea can be directly related to your audience. After all, a depopulated forest can lead to water runoff, which causes dirty rivers leading to a dirty water supply, which leads to more sources of contamination—each of which directly and indirectly affects us. In brief, the infestation of the Mountain Pine Beetle has consequences well beyond deforested areas of the Rocky Mountains. The ecological chain reaction of cause and effect also provides an excellent organizational structure to your speech. Moving from a dead tree to later arrive at the air we breathe and the water we drink can provide a powerful explanation of the destruction wrought by our five-millimeter pest and a slightly warmer climate.

Let's pause to take careful inventory of the all-important Central Idea:

- ▷ It's an elaboration of what's been stated in the Specific Purpose.
- ▷ It's generated only after careful research and a consideration of possible alternatives.
- ▷ It's phrased in such a way that a speaker's main points are easily identifiable.

- ▷ It should always speak to a specific audience's need or needs.
- ▷ It should be calibrated very carefully to fit within the time parameters of the assignment.
- ▷ It should be stated in terms that a non-expert audience of your peers can understand.
- ▷ Oh, and did we say it's an elaboration of the Specific Purpose?

The same principles also hold true if our speech aims to persuade or commemorate. Let's go back to our Specific Purpose regarding persuading our listeners to donate blood at the next campus blood drive. Here's our aim:

> To persuade my audience to donate blood at the next campus blood drive.

Now, after you've done a bit of research, what might your Central Idea look like? Let's do the same with Robert Moses. Recall our Specific Purpose:

> To commemorate for my audience the civil rights work of Robert Moses.

A bit of "Googling" should turn up several interesting and important sources. That said, be sure that you're not researching the famous urban planner from New York City.

As we close this chapter, let's not forget our master metaphor: building a well-designed house with clearly differentiated rooms will be vital to our public speaking success. Sure, having a vivid, even inspired delivery will certainly matter in terms of how our speech is received. But to speak with passion and flair without the bedrock of a carefully researched and definite Specific Purpose and a clearly refined Central Idea is to construct a house on beguiling but precarious sands. Instead, let's build a solid and deep foundation with a carefully detailed floor plan. We would also remind you that you are a font of potentially fascinating topics; to think otherwise is to demean your many experiences, passions, experiences, and ambitions.

> Constructing a Speech Table [Flip Learning chat]

> Chapter 4 Quiz [Flip Learning quiz]

5 Audience Analysis

5.1 Epic Fail: Know Your Audience

In the summer of 1998, my grandmother Eila Lee Coffeen passed away at the age of eighty-two. Over the preceding ten years she and I had gotten to be pretty good friends. She was funny in ways that I never expected a grandmother to be: she was quick with a retort, could role play in telling her own stories, and just had a fun and mischievous way about her. So when she died, I wanted to offer something of a eulogy (literally eu [good] logos [words]), a brief speech commemorating her long and interesting life, and our shared past.

Let's just say the speech did not go over very well with the gathered mourners at First United Methodist.

In the years since, I've often reflected on that speech—so enjoyable for me to give, yet so poorly received by my immediate audience. So what went wrong? In hindsight, there were two problems,

Episode 5: Elementary [Flip Learning video series]
A first date, a job interview, and student government... What could possibly go wrong?

one of a demographic nature and the other more situational, perhaps even architectural. Regarding that first problem, I was speaking primarily to a group of eighty-year-olds who'd attended more than one eulogy in recent years. And by sharing several funny stories about my grandmother, I was violating the "code of conduct" of public speaking behavior at funerals. In brief, I was messing with their expectations—and older folks don't tend to cotton to messing with long-established speech traditions. They wanted piety and sadness and eternal life—none of which I offered. The second problem, not unrelated to the first, was the setting: we were in a church—and churches for most octogenarians are not places for humor or mirthful storytelling, certainly not during a eulogy. And so I'm guessing not a few folks from my grandmother's funeral returned home muttering about the smart-assed and disrespectful grandson who'd screwed up a perfectly morose funeral service.

Most of us can easily see where age matters to all manner of public speeches and settings. Race and culture matter, too. A few years back I was involved with planning a fall festival for a Boys and Girls Club in a small rural Deep South community that was still largely segregated along racial lines. As part of the planning committee,

I had helped develop a fun day of activities, events, music and food for the mostly black boys and girls and their families served by the organization. At a committee meeting an elderly white woman from the community brought up the subject of law enforcement: Shouldn't we have an on-site police presence given the size of the expected crowd, she asked. It was a well-meaning and important question. The black men and women at the table looked at each other with a bit of discomfort. Nobody was very quick to respond. Awkward looks.... awkward silence. Not wanting to be "that" white guy at the table, that guy who condescendingly speaks "for" black people, I tried to hide a bit behind my education as well as my work in the community. I said something to the effect that while having law enforcement in the general area was a good idea, having them walking the grounds during the festival might not be the best thing to do.

Confused white looks. So I went a bit further. Perhaps we should keep in mind that many black members of the community see the police as less a keeper of the peace, I offered, and more of a perceived threat. And because of this some people might stay home rather than attend the festival.

Some black nods, but a lot of confused white looks now starting to look a bit more hostile; my little local history lesson wasn't going terribly well. And so I backpedaled: Can we agree that if we want to have a police presence that they simply have some personnel in the general area? Sensing the awkwardness of this interracial moment, we agreed and quickly moved on to other less vexing matters like bounce houses and extension cords. I'm guessing that a few left that meeting wondering, "What kind of problem does Houck have with the police...jeeeesh, get over it." Or something to that effect.

We're guessing that you have your own stories about how audiences affect messages. We recently learned, for example, that an unemployed British woman, Joanne Rowling, was coaxed into changing her writing name. She wondered, what's wrong with my name?

Her publishing company thought that since her book was addressed to young boys, the pen name J.K. Rowling was much more appropriate since it concealed her biological sex. That choice seems to have worked out pretty well for Joanne Kathleen—the first author to have reportedly made over a billion dollars on their writings. And speaking of audiences and the Boy Wizard, when things are going badly in lecture, I only have to drop the name Harry Potter and the classroom dynamic changes in the instant. No lie.

While I didn't grow up with *Harry Potter*, I did grow up in a family that liked cars; my grandfather was something of a connoisseur of fine European motorcars. On a recent trip to California and the Bay Area, I noted to a good friend who lived there, wow, lots of Teslas on the road here. She did NOT seem terribly impressed by Elon Musk's revolutionary and very pricey electric car; in fact, she seemed sort of hostile to all the men driving the car along the 280. I asked why. Karen replied, "I just have a hard time liking a car whose logo looks exactly like an IUD. Tesla clearly didn't consult with women on its design." Since I knew as much about an IUD (Intra Uterine Device) as an IED (Improvised Explosive Device), I did some quick Internet research. Uhmmm, Karen was on to something. In fact, more than 80% of recent Tesla owners turn out to be men.[1]

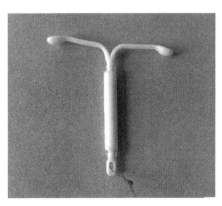

Mirena IUD & Tesla Motors logo (left to right)

---

1   Visit link: https://goo.gl/9eKnk8

> #LifeOfWomen Promotional Video [Flip Learning chat]

5.2 The Ancient Greeks on Audience Analysis

We're guessing that you have your stories, too, stories that feature awkward or embarrassing moments based on the rather obvious fact that different situations and demographics often lead to different meanings. From the very beginnings of rhetoric's long history, theorists have been concerned about audiences—who they are and how that all-important questions of "who," "where," and "when" influences the speaker and the message. Part of our aim in this chapter is to sort through some of these complex questions as we think about our topics and how best to present them.

As a general rule, audience members are nothing if not selfish—not in a crazy hoarding way that shows up on late-night cable television but in a way that says, "hey, what's in this for me." We should always remember the costs of public speaking: you're asking listeners to tune in to you rather than do something else. To be audience-centered is to acknowledge those costs and in so doing, to transform them into benefits. Crafting listenable messages means seeking to communicate in ways that resonate with our audience rather than pander (catering to the whims of the audience by abandoning our own convictions) or condescend (by being ethnocentric—assuming our cultural norms or perspectives are superior).

A Hierarchy of "Souls"

One of the earliest attempts to explore how audiences influence speeches is Plato's immortal dialogue, *Phaedrus*. In this sublime and sometimes embarrassingly sensual dialogue on the oddly paired topic of love and rhetoric, the Platonic Socrates informs his admiring and flirtatious interlocutor, "In both cases [rhetoric and medicine] you have to determine the nature of something— the body in medicine and the soul in rhetoric—if you're going to be an expert practitioner, rather than relying merely on experiential knack."[2] That same expert practitioner, moreover, will expertly lead souls to achieve his desired end.

Earlier, in his rapturous second speech, Socrates has outlined a hierarchy of souls, beginning with the best (philosophers, of course) down to the worst (tyrants).[3] Furthermore, each soul will have a corresponding type of speech that best moves it; in this manner Plato is attempting to create a "science" of rhetoric in which the fitting speech will have predictable results in moving certain types of audiences. Once the expert rhetorician has a knowledge of souls

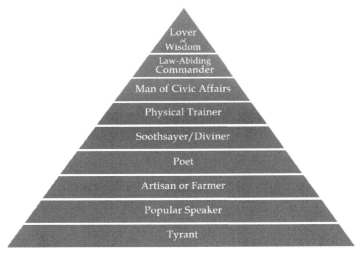

Socrates's Hierarchy of Souls

---

2   Plato, *Phaedrus*, transl. by Robin Waterfield (New York: Oxford University Press, 2002), 61.

3   Plato, *Phaedrus*, 31-32.

and speech types, leading souls will be a fairly simple business. Of course Plato leaves out one important detail: What happens if you have many different souls present for the same speech? Yeah, that's gonna be a problem, even for the sagely Socrates.

Plato's student, Aristotle, also takes up the matter of audiences in his magisterial book, *On Rhetoric*. But rather than rank-order and spiritualize audience members with the term "souls"—Plato's world revolves around the afterlife, we mustn't forget—Aristotle looks instead at the dirty ways of the Mediterranean world to observe (literally) what influences audiences. And while Aristotle doesn't go into great detail when it comes to demographic ("demos," meaning the people) audience analysis, he has some interesting things to say about the young, the old, and the middle-aged, as well as how political constitutions affect speechmaking.

Hierarchy of Souls [Flip Learning animation series]
Socrates urges you to understand your audience in order to perfect your speech.

Aristotle on the Young, Old, and Middle-Aged

The young, for example, he claims are: prone to desires of the body, especially sex, quick-tempered, filled with good hopes (are optimists), easily deceived, courageous, trusting, impulsive, keen to achieve victory, sensitive to shame, eager for companions and fond of friends. Aristotle also claims that the young always err on the side of excess, they think they know it all, and "they are fond of laughter and, as a result, [are] witty; for wit is cultured insolence."[4] We especially like this last one —and tend to agree with it. But what of the others? Have things changed in the past 2,400 years, give or take? Or has Aristotle put his finger on something "universal" here?

As for his take on "the old," and Aristotle doesn't specify numbers here, they are: skeptical, cynical, suspicious, small-minded, stingy, cowardly, chilled (not chill, but literally cold), fond of themselves, nostalgic, not concerned about their reputations, self-controlled, querulous, and "not witty nor fond of laughter."[5] It's clear from this list that Aristotle was not looking forward to old age; it also explains something of my troubles at First United Methodist circa 1998 and Eila Lee Coffeen. But is Aristotle painting with too broad of a brush? Or is he accurately describing how life's myriad ups and downs affect those fortunate enough to experience "old age"?

Now if you know anything about Aristotle, you know he also put great faith in the Golden Mean—literally the arithmetic place midway between two extremes. His classic manifesto on ethics, the *Nicomachean Ethics*, offers a detailed exploration into the "virtue" of the middle way. Here in *On Rhetoric*, Aristotle not surprisingly offers his views on those midway between young and old, people in the "prime of life," (the body between the ages of thirty and thirty-five; the mind at forty-nine??). They are: neither fearful nor confident, neither trusting nor distrusting, neither impulsive nor de-

---

[4] Aristotle, *On Rhetoric*, transl. by George A. Kennedy (New York: Oxford University Press, 1991), 165-66.

[5] Aristotle, *On Rhetoric*, 167-68.

sirous, combine prudence with courage, and in general, "whatever advantages youth and old age have separately, those in their prime combine, and whatever the former have to excess or in deficiency, the latter have in due measure and in a fitting way."[6] In other words, Aristotle takes great stock in the middle-aged navigating a middle, and presumably wise, way.

For Aristotle, Politics Matter

Kim Jong-un and Miley Cyrus (left to right)

But beyond the arithmetic mean, Aristotle also understood something important about the human condition and age: politics matter, too. That is, Aristotle understood that merely knowing an audience's age wasn't good enough; the smart speaker also needed to know the country and its form of constitution to really know what an audience really values. An eighteen-year-old North Korean, for example, is not going to have the same sensibilities as her American counter-

---

6   Aristotle, *On Rhetoric*, 168-69.

part. Kim Jong-un is not Miley Cyrus.

Aristotle identified four different types of politics in *On Rhetoric*: Democracy, which values freedom; Oligarchy, which values wealth; Aristocracy, which values education and law; and Monarchy/Tyranny, which values self-preservation. Sure, not all democratic audience members value freedom in the same way or to the same extent; remember that Aristotle is painting with a very broad brush here. But his point is still an important one: political culture matters to what audience members value. We often see these political values clash in a classroom context where our native Chinese students tend to avoid eye contact with us and rarely raise a hand to ask a content-oriented question. In stark contrast, American college students are taught to value eye contact and critical examination of course content—and yes, even disagreement with their professors.

5.3 The Perils of Generalization

While Aristotle had politics on the brain for most of *On Rhetoric*, economics is just as important in our present age. Many of you will enter careers in which audience analysis will be first, second, and third on your list of important job duties and skills. Given that we live in a service and information economy and that economy depends to a significant degree on consumption, knowing how to reach those consumers and persuade them will be absolutely vital. Marketing and advertising, just to name two of the most obvious careers, are primarily audience-based activities; persuasive messages simply can't be created without a nuanced sense of who your audience is. Those messages, moreover, can tell us a lot about audiences.

Take a careful look, for example, at national network news, and the commercials that mark the thirty-minute broadcast. What you'll notice is a great majority of the advertising is geared toward Aristotle's "old people," that cold and cynical and supposedly un-funny cohort. Why is that? Companies have done their homework and discovered that a lot of elderly people tune in to watch the national news. A twenty-something watching the national news might be nonplussed by all the stool softeners, hemorrhoid creams, bone strengtheners, and financial services being advertised. Similarly, though, the elderly might be flummoxed by the conspicuously bosomed cheerleaders diving on nerdy ectomorphs, rum-swilling pirates, and orgasm-inducing shampoo—all broadcast during a Beavis and Butt-head rerun.

Generalizing from Demographic Categories

Most public speaking books contain something of a laundry list of demographic categories that students can then supposedly leverage to strategically design their messages. These categories typically include age, sex, sexual orientation, religion, race and ethnicity, and group membership. The problem, of course, with such lists is that they essentialize or homogenize entire groups of people, as if there were no diversity within each separate category. We've all probably known sixty-year-olds who have the spirit of a twenty-year-old, and vice versa. We've known gay, lesbian, and transgender Christians who regularly attend church—and the synagogue. We've certainly met very conservative black men and women who don't identify with the "black community." And we've also known more than one woman into arm wrestling and motorcycle maintenance. You might also note a very conspicuous absence in such lists: hetero white guys. That's because hetero white guys (thus Plato and Aristotle) usually create the list and the center begins from their position from smack in the middle of it. Moreover, the faulty assumption is that we don't need to do audience analysis for this group since they're the default center that everything deviates from; why analyze the already known?

Researchers at the Pew Research Center, just like our friend Aristotle, have attempted to do both two and three dimensional analyses based on four huge audiences: Millennials (24-38), Generation X'ers (39-53), Baby Boomers (54-74), and Silent Generation'ers (75+). Millennials, not surprisingly, are quite different from their older cohorts. Using broad data trends, here's what researchers think they know about their age group: they're suspicious of institutions (political, religious and legal); they're slow to marry; they're politically progressive even as they tend to distrust traditional parties; they're digital natives comfortable with forming and maintaining relationships digitally; racially they are very diverse; they lack economic security; they're exceptionally well-educated; they're not very trustful of others; but, they remain quite optimistic, especially when it comes to their economic future.[7] Interesting trends to be sure—especially when compared with older generations of Americans. But, and as the good folks at the Pew Center readily admit, these are enormous generalizations about millions of people using small samples of self-report surveys. Where am I, you ask? Great question. Generation Z (ages 3-23) is still being studied by the good folks at Pew.[8] But remember the point: big data makes big generalizations about big age groups; the researchers at Pew aren't interested just in the twenty students comprising your speech class.

In thinking about the problems of generalizing from demographic data we would also add: since we aren't a large multinational corporation seeking the lowest common denominator for a marketing/advertising campaign, can't we paint with a much finer brush? Can't we do pointillism instead of wall painting with a roller? Shouldn't we? Your public speaking class might very well be popu-

---

7   Visit link: https://goo.gl/tZK5rj

8   Visit link: https://goo.gl/MbkfCX

lated by second-generation Hispanics, European and Asian exchange students, gay and lesbian students, members of fraternities and sororities, atheists and Catholics, "Gingers," returning students, members of the military, and members of the Black Student Union. White hetero guys, too. In brief, our very multicultural world has rendered a lot of traditional audience analysis categorizing and generalizing as quaint and out-of-date, perhaps even dangerously misleading. In our world of instant access and real-time person-to-person contact, we think we can do much more granular (and accurate) audience analysis in our speech classes, analysis that doesn't rely on broad two-dimensional categories but rather nuanced three-dimensional questions and answers.

> #UnplugYourDay PSA [Flip Learning chat]

5.4 Situational Audience Analysis

We'll return to the "how" question of doing such audience analysis in a moment. For now, though, we would highlight some very consequential audience concerns that have little to do with demographics and everything to do with the myriad situations in which you might physically speak. As you might have guessed, this sort of work is called situational audience analysis and being attuned to its variables will make you a much better speaker.

Adapting to Your Physical Surroundings

Many times we simply don't control the environment or the time of day on which we speak. As such, being smart about when you'll be speaking, in what physical space, and to what size audience can have a direct bearing on how your speech is received. Or isn't. You've likely been an audience member in a space, for example, where it was very difficult to hear the speaker—through no fault of that person; the venue was just too big and there was no amplification. Or perhaps you've listened to a speech in which the noise outside the room drowned out the speaker's words. The key here is to be very flexible as a speaker, to be prepared to deal with the unexpected even as you've prepared under more ideal circumstances.

Similarly, there are better and worse times to give a speech on a college campus. While I love to teach bright and early, my students are less than enamored of listening to speeches at 8 or 9 a.m. So, how do you deal with such constraints; after all, the early slot was the only time open for you to take the course. First, and perhaps most importantly, acknowledge that fact: yes, it's boot camp early; yes, it's hard to focus; yes, we'd all rather be deep asleep, but here we are. You might find there develops a group solidarity around being The Early Crew. Or, The Rock Stars of Campus Parking. Perhaps like me, you bring your travel coffee mug with you to the lectern; that's fine, it can also combat cotton-mouth in addition to giving us a caffeine jolt. We've also been known to, when things were particularly quiet and low energy, to do group jumping jacks or run in place—something to get the heart pounding just a bit harder.

Let's say that your public speaking classroom is rather cavernous, with a lot of desks and students scattered all over the place and in various stages of slouched mouth breathing. What to do? Here's what I do: we ask (always politely, but firmly) that students fill in all the seats in the first few rows —every one of them. Of course there's a lot of moaning and groaning but this changes the entire classroom dynamic—immediately and to our rhetorical advantage. What was once a bunch of separated individuals is now a more unified community in much greater physical proximity to you, the speaker. You'll also note that it's a whole lot easier to get audience feedback, and adjust accordingly, from a closer proximity. From audience members' points of view, they can now be seen and they are much closer, engendering a more intimate and engaged environment. They likely also have neighbors on either side of them now; good, let's have more shared space where we interact verbally and nonverbally with each other. As the speaker you also have the added bonus of not having to yell to the back of the room.

Making Meaning in/through Public Spaces: The "Town Hall" Format

If you think space in a public speaking setting doesn't much matter, have a look at the video clip from the 1992 presidential campaign in the flipped activity at the end of this paragraph. Note the format, which back in 1992 was a radical departure from previous campaign debates. We have three well-dressed men at what appear to be bar stools and small tables. You can't hide behind a bar stool the way you can a lectern. But read what a very young governor from Arkansas does in addressing a question which with then president George H. W. Bush was struggling mightily.[9]

There's a reason that Bill Clinton soon became known as the "I-feel-your-pain" president. By walking to the very edge of the venue and addressing the questioner directly, Clinton conveys a powerful connection that translates: I get it; I empathize; I'm not afraid to be vulnerably close to you (something that would later get him in a bit of hot water). Because Clinton so decidedly "won" the debate based on his nonverbal behavior, this moment has literally changed the way presidential candidates (and a host of other public offices, too) debate. We now do town hall style debates regularly—and if you

---

9   Visit link: https://goo.gl/QiueVz

can't empathize you might as well go home.

You're not running for president, we get that. We also get that you're not interested in running for the county commission either. You are interested in doing your best in a speech class and Bill Clinton provides us with some important lessons regarding space and proximity, or the nonverbal cue of proxemics–the way in which we use space and distance to communicate. When he speaks, there's very little mouth breathing; he commands our attention even as he's willing to get out of his comfort zone and connect with an audience.

Your classroom or speaking venue may also be much too hot (Florida), much too cold (Minnesota, pretty much year 'round), or much too small (transformed broom closets). Unfortunately you're kind of stuck when it comes to room temperature unless there happens to be a functioning thermostat. So, too, with room size. Again, part of the key here is in acknowledging that you and your audience might be uncomfortable. Empathy, again. And when that jackhammer starts in the middle of your speech or when the fire alarm goes off, we need your sense of humor and willingness to adjust to shine through—even though such things can be incredibly irritating.

Often when we lecture the entire class will hear an odd and random noise from who knows where: loud thumping, students yelling, toilets flushing, people singing, and always the unmodulated cell phone talker having a meltdown with his girlfriend, to say nothing of the very late arriving student who has no clue about door-shutting etiquette. And invariably in the South: booming thunderstorms and loud rain. You're going to have to roll with it, to adjust—and even better if you can do it with a smile on your face and a timely quip; best yet, if you can fold the moment into your speech. You're right, you can't script these moments, but what we'd encourage you to do is first acknowledge that your speaking environment likely won't be perfect...and plan accordingly. Then run a few mental experiments about what you can do if x, y, or z happens during your speech. Your speech teacher empathizes with you here since s/he has to deal with the same sorts of situational uncertainties.

As we mentioned in a previous chapter, if possible, definitely plan on practicing your speech in the very place you'll be delivering it for "real," or in a place that simulates it. If you cannot practice in the space in which you'll be speaking, at least make mental notes while in the classroom. Perhaps you can begin to get a better sense of what situational variables might affect your speech. Is the room big or small? Does it sit very close to a noisy road or construction site? Is it hot or cold? Is there noisy ducting in the room? From where will a late arriving student enter and exit? What about a lectern: do you have a heavy wooden one you can perhaps lean on a bit, a flimsy skeletal one more fit for a trombone player than a public speaker? Or is there one at all? Can you move it? Do you have to hold your outline or can you rest it on a level surface? Will the students be in long narrow rows or a semicircle? Which do you prefer? How are the acoustics in the room? Does sound tend to bounce or is your voice muffled? When we speak in a large lecture hall with lots of carpet and sound panels, we really have to speak louder because our voice gets absorbed in several different places. If sound in the room tends to bounce, go slower and enunciate with precision; you might even be able to speak more softly. If there are windows, will the sun be pouring in or will students be walking by? Are there shades on those windows? We love to lecture in bright and airy rooms; others like very dark movie-theater-like venues.

> Jury Consultant [Flip Learning chat]

5.5 Speaking Style and Audience

Most of you will be speaking before relatively small audiences during your public speaking class. Whether it's 15, 18, or 22, this is a small, intimate group to communicate with. Furthermore, as college students they expect you to address them with a carefully prepared speech, and to do so in a manner fitting the speaking occasion. Let's go back to where we opened this chapter: a large and older church audience awaiting a eulogy expects formality; the language should be elevated and dignified. Think suit and tie or blazers, skirts, and blouses. Not quite a state dinner or the senior prom but certainly not a night out clubbing either. If you're giving the keynote address before 2,000 people at a state Chamber of Commerce meeting, you're going to want to elevate your game; this is not the time for the sort of language you'd use to address a group of five good friends in your living room. Let's reverse the situation: Dr. King's elevated discourse at the March on Washington in 1963 is decidedly not appropriate in your speech class; he's addressing the nation, not a small group of millennials gathered to deliver their commemorative speeches.

The Romans might help us here: Cicero and his fellow rhetoricians liked to talk about a low, middle, and grand style—styles attuned to the speaking situation; in a word they were doing situational audience analysis, too. How we say things is intimately related to the occasion in which we're speaking.[10] In hindsight, my style was much too low for the assembled crowd at First United Methodist; I was violating the all-important variable of propriety—and notice how such a violation immediately goes right to judgments of character. That is, if you can't gauge the dynamics, if you can't calibrate

---

10   Cicero, *On The Orator*, Books I-II, transl. by E. W. Sutton (Cambridge, MA: Harvard University Press, 1942); Cicero, *On The Orator*, Book 3, transl. by H. Rackham (Cambridge, MA: Harvard University Press, 1942).

your language to the occasion, well, there must be something wrong with you—so much so that I just can't trust you. Not unlike the young man who shows up for the Proctor and Gamble job interview with a nose ring, propriety speaks directly to character. This isn't quite as bad as Kanye stealing Taylor Swift's microphone—for which he was deemed a "jackass" by our very proprietary former president—but you see the point: getting the language and the occasion to match is important rhetorical work.[11]

Former president Barack Obama, Kanye West, and Taylor Swift (left to right)

Let's return for a moment to your speech class and propriety. Your audience expects a well-prepared and well-rehearsed speech; your teacher does, too. They don't expect to hear slang throughout the speech and they don't expect to hear a lot of verbal fillers ("know what I'm saying?"; "you feelin' me?"; "ya know"; "I know, right"; "she was all, like, you know"; "I was like..."; "come at me, bro," and always, "uhmmmm," "aaaahhh," or some variation on these overused and often very unconscious expressions). No, your audience expects a certain level of formality that communicates you've prepared, you care, and your audience's expectations matter. Most students aim rightly at the middle way—a style that isn't too formal or too infor-

---

11   Visit link: https://goo.gl/Dsr5Rs

mal but communicates that you understand the situation and your role in it. A really good speaker, by the way, can riff from both the low and the high to arrive at that same middle way—and, as audience members, we can appreciate that performance of stylistic artistry.

5.6 Constraints in the Speech Classroom

Let's go back to the physical space in which you'll be speaking. Let's say the room is ideal: the temperature is 72, the acoustics are pitch perfect, the seating dynamics are just right, the lectern is steady and well positioned; in other words, the setup is all working in your favor. But there are going to be six speeches on this particular day, and you're the lucky sixth speaker. Most public speaking textbooks are unfortunately silent on this very important matter of speech order and how it affects the room and the people in it.

Time of Day

First off, let's be very frank: the energy in the room is not the same for speaker #1 compared to speaker #6; it just isn't. Time is dynamic and careful listening is hard work, and by the end of that fifth speech, audience members are often hungry, tired, eager to leave for their next class, very preoccupied by that vibrating device in their pocket, stuffed full of rhetoric for the day, and in general wishing that only five people were speaking. And you're the sixth speaker. How can we make this difficult situation work for us?

As you've no doubt noticed by now, we're advocates of candor, and in this case, let's make some lemonade out of the lemons we've been forced to accept. So here are some possibilities. First, acknowledge the situation; help the audience understand that speaking sixth is hard—even on the best of days. Empathize with them by understanding how tired they are (even God had to rest after the Sixth Day,

we're told). Furthermore, perhaps you can artfully make some connections among those who spoke before you and your speech topic. But the point is to try and acknowledge the moment; your audience will very much appreciate it. Being last can also work to your advantage; knowing this is The End can certainly bring your audience's attention to the fore, a point to which we'll return in discussing the all-important conclusion to your speech in Chapter 6. Just like a coach trying to get that last something extra from her team before calling it quits for the day, you, too, can get that last bit of rhetorical juice from your listeners. But it will likely take some prodding. Let's never forget: listening is very hard work and the easier, the more interesting, and the more pleasurable we can make it, the better.

Speaking Order

Speaking last is hard. What about the situation where you're not only speaking last, but just two speakers prior, a speech on the same topic was given!? Should you flee the room in panic, convinced that you're doomed by the Rhetoric gods? Of course not. As we like to remind our students, no two speeches are the same—even speeches on the same subject. So don't panic and certainly don't flee; you can make this admittedly awkward situation work to your advantage. The first step, of course, is admitting the obvious: another speaker has just presented something similar. Perhaps more importantly, a simple statement about how your speech will be different or build on what a previous speaker offered will generate lots of empathy.

Dealing with Time Limits

Let's move to that all-important situational variable called time, or in nonverbal nomenclature chronemics—the meanings we attach to use of time. You will absolutely ruin a speech—however eloquent, clever, and audience-centered—if you trample on the time limits. Now in your speech class time limits are prescribed and rather strictly enforced. Trust us on this one: when your instructor says six minutes for an informative speech, s/he means six minutes, give or take a bit on either side. If you're in the eight- or nine-minute range, you will not be receiving smiles from the back of the room. More likely you will see someone pointing at a watch—which is awfully disconcerting when you're behind the lectern. A strange phenomenon happens, by the way, when you're speaking: time simply morphs into a series of truncated blips; we experience it in ways we've never imagined. And what seems to us like thirty seconds, has, in actuality, been seven minutes—or more. Again, this is why we urge you to practice with great care and to stick very carefully to that outline. Freestylin' might be great with your crew at a club, but it can be absolutely deadly in front of a public speaking audience.

The same advice goes for public speaking outside of the classroom context: speeches that run too long are just poorly received and can end up reflecting badly on your character, that all-important Aristotelian proof called ethos. No doubt you've experienced a speaker/speech that has simply run on and on and on: people start shuffling uncomfortably in their seats, whisper to the person seated next to them, look at their watches and phones—and completely tune out the speaker. Since you don't have a teacher in the back of the room keeping a keen eye on the clock, you'd be wise to either bring a watch/timer to the podium or perhaps have a friend or colleague seated nearby give you hand signals at agreed-upon time intervals.

But before you've even begun to prepare to speak you'll want to ask the organizer(s) of the event about speech expectations. Moreover, coming in under the time limit can have its own positive effects. Don't forget that brevity, rhetorical power, and eloquence can and do go together. What took Edward Everett two hours to say at Gettysburg back in 1863 took Abraham Lincoln less than five minutes. As a general rule if it's going to take longer than fifteen to twenty minutes, you'd better be a really captivating orator, or be giving a victory speech before partisans. In any case, brevity is a much-appreciated virtue.

Abraham Lincoln and Edward Everett (left to right)

5.7 Audience Surveys

Let's close this important discussion on audiences by going back to the question of just how we can get critical information from our immediate listeners. Recall that even the best-intentioned efforts at demographic audience analysis force us to make some pretty sweeping generalizations about certain "types" of people: not every twenty-five-year old white male thinks the next bottle of Dos Equis is going to turn him into The Most Interesting Man in the World. Or Brad Pitt covered in catnip, etc. No, if you're genuinely interested in understanding your audience, do what the pros do: send out a brief survey. With websites such as surveymonkey.com and many others, combined with the interactivity here in *Public Speaking in the 21st Century*, you can easily design a survey to get important information about your audience members.

Three Types of Survey Questions

There are three general types of survey questions: the fixed-alternative question, which offers a limited choice among two or more options; the scaled question, which offers a range of possible answers; and the open-ended question, which allows respondents great freedom to express answers. Let's take a closer look at each of the three. Let's say you're interested in giving a persuasive speech on the not uncontroversial subject of adoption by gay and lesbian couples; furthermore, you're curious to know whether your audience has an informed opinion on the subject, and if they do, what it is. So here's a fixed-alternative question you might ask:

> ▷ Is adoption for gay and lesbian couples legal in every state?
> Yes ___
> No ___
> Not sure ___

Or you might ask a more specific question:

> ▷ Is adoption for gay and lesbian couples legal in Florida?

Yes ___
No ___
Not sure ___

Since this is a persuasive speech and you're trying to induce your audience to accept the claim that it should be legal, you'll want to know where your audience stands on the issue. So we might elicit a scaled response by stating:

▷ Gay and lesbian couples should be able to adopt children in the state of Florida:
Strongly disagree ___
Disagree ___
Don't know ___
Agree ___
Strongly agree ___

Or if you're interested in a more unstructured set of answers, you can simply ask:

▷ What is your opinion about legalizing adoption for gay and lesbian couples in the state of Florida? Why do you hold this opinion?

While each type of question has its advantages, we're fond of the open-ended question since we can use the responses to our question to refine our main points and supporting evidence—and also to inform our objectives. But we can learn important things from each of the three types of questions.

Let's say, for example, that 4 out of 18 respondents to your scaled question said that they "strongly disagree" with the claim that gay and lesbian couples should be able to adopt children in the state of Florida. Furthermore, when asked to specify why they held such a belief they noted that their beliefs were informed by what the Bible says. Let's also say that four respondents "strongly agreed" and justified their beliefs on the legal grounds of the Fourteenth Amendment, and its emphasis on equal protection under the law.

Now, should you at this point pick another topic? Not necessarily. Just because you have some polarized opinion among your listeners doesn't mean you should search for some ersatz subject that won't be controversial. According to our admittedly limited math, you have at least 10 "persuade-ables" in the room. These students comprise what we call a "target audience," or that group of listeners who are most likely to be persuaded by your message. Sure, you're not likely to persuade all 10 of them, but this group is likely to give you the fairest hearing since their commitments are not so entrenched that they've made up their mind for all time. No, their scaled responses indicate that they can move on that scale; they just need a bit of persuading.

What might persuade them? Well, we'd be advised to go back and look at how informed they are and why they believe the way they do. Perhaps you can persuade some by showing them that an opinion might be held in factual error. Perhaps you can persuade others by detailing the often tragic effects of the foster system or the number of special-needs children looking to be adopted. Still others you might reach by summarizing studies that show the long-term positive effects of having a two-parent household—gay or straight. And who knows, your speech might be so compelling that even a few on the extreme end of the scale might be moved to reconsider their opinions.

The point is: before committing to any subject, but especially controversial ones, it's important to know what your audience believes—and why. No demographic data point is going to tell you that; we've got to go and unearth that ourselves.

To close this chapter, we must remember that audiences are at the very heart of public speaking; if we didn't have them, we'd be engaging in something but it wouldn't be called public speech. And from the very beginning, rhetorical theorists have been trying to figure out ways to unlock the mystery of audiences—by age, by politics, by economic class, by sex, by religion, by region, by nationality, by ethnicity, by group membership—even by souls. Each of these categories once promised to unlock the mystery of how to effectively influence such groups. And while these categories offer would-be speakers important information, we would do well to always remember that demographics never tell the whole story; we're far more complex than the sum total of our demography. Back in the day, these categories had a lot more stability and predictability, but in our present postmodern era, these same categories are far from stable. In fact we perform multiple identities during the course of any given day—and none of these identities necessarily defines us.

Think of it this way: Does your status as a 21-year old white female Republican from Minnesota, majoring in fashion merchandising and who attends a Lutheran church regularly determine which messages you'll find persuasive or interesting? We didn't think so. These details merely provide the good public speaker points of reference, places to begin thinking hard and strategically about speech topics, audience members, and their interaction.

While good speakers are always audience-centered, they are also very attuned to the situational dynamics that always influence speechmaking. From the overcrowded and hot room, to the noises outside of it and the order in which we speak, we need to be aware of how the physical and mental environment can add or detract from our message—and always to be aware that situations, like identities, can also be very fluid.

If only a younger (and much skinnier) Davis Houck had thought these things through circa 1998 at First United Methodist Church.

But then again, I like to think that even in spite of her age, sex, and political preferences, somewhere, Eila Lee Coffeen was getting a good laugh at/with her grandson.

Audience Analysis Survey [Flip Learning chat]

Public Speaking and the Physical Environment [Flip Learning chat]

Nelson Mandela Survey [Flip Learning survey]

Chapter 5 Quiz [Flip Learning quiz]

6 Beginnings and Endings

6.1 Memorable Bookends

Then again, we should've known Ted was a bit "disturbed." It wasn't so much in his pale and unaffected countenance, or his untethered curly hair, but just the blank way he stared at us. His mind seemed to be preoccupied by something far more involved and grim than his first graded speech at the University of California, Davis. Just what that was remained to be seen.

I wasn't really thinking much about Ted on this particular Monday morning. No, I was thinking far more about what could go wrong in this first round of graded speeches. Did I prep the students well enough? Had the students taken my advice to heart? Were they ready? Was *I* ready? After all, this was my very first time grading real, live speeches; I'd be assigning grades in ways that influenced lives. This wasn't the driving range anymore, but the real golf course. All

Episode 6: Stumped [Flip Learning video series]
Laura and Mal face off in student elections, much to everyone else's chagrin.

this was a bit heavy for a Monday morning.

I called out the speech order; Ted was first. I watched from the back of the room as Ted made his way slowly to the front of the class—with his book bag. How odd that Ted would bring his entire Jansport to the lectern, I thought. He began methodically emptying its contents on a shelf built into the lectern—a shelf I couldn't see, nor could anyone else in the room. Then a wry smile from Ted. With his left hand he began rolling up the sleeve on his right arm. He next reached for an object, and then opened it. A straight-edged razor, the kind barbers used for shaving in 1930s-era gangster movies. With his left hand Ted began slowly cutting at his right wrist, a line of blood following the incision. Students in the front rows shrieked. The back of my scalp grew hot and damp almost immediately. Ted's wry smile grew wider. More shrieks. What to do? How can this be happening? A student committing very public suicide on our first day ever of graded speeches! Do I stop everything and call 911? This can't be happening....

Then Ted laughed, closed the razor blade and rolled down his sleeve. "Well, that's my attention getter. I'm going to be a visual effects designer in film one day." Never did Ted look so pleased. The room exhaled noticeably. Tragedy had been avoided. A student was not dying in my midst. I think I could've killed Ted. Then again, nearly twenty-five years later and I haven't forgotten Ted or his "magical" opening. I suspect Ted might be working on the *Saw* franchise by now, or some sordid remake of *The Texas Chainsaw Massacre*.

Ted's story reminds me of another remarkable beginning that also began without a single word being uttered. Several hundred people had assembled at McGaw Chapel on the campus at The College of Wooster. It was part of the college's fall 1988 speaker series, as I recall. A student body leader introduced a middle-aged woman to assembled faculty and staff. She approached the lectern with careful deliberation. She very methodically put her speaking materials in their proper order, and then she started the scan: to her right she slowly looked out at her audience. By the time she reached my section in the middle it had been a full thirty seconds. But she still kept right on with her slow scan of the audience. Once she had completed her scan, she stopped and looked placidly out at the large auditorium and then down at her notes. By this time things were getting uncomfortable. Some fidgeting. Some murmurs. Was this woman having a medical emergency? Did she need some help? The seconds at this point felt like minutes. And still she kept staring. Finally, after about 2 minutes she said, "Now that I have your attention I should begin." It was an amazing performance of silence.

And she absolutely had everyone's full and undivided attention as she began her address. I may not remember her name, but I've never forgotten her beginning.

A Great Catharsis

You've likely heard the expression "ending with a bang." Easier said than done. I was seventeen years old, listening to June commencement exercises in a very hot gym in Mansfield, Ohio. The speeches promised to be an epic snooze. We weren't there to hear speeches but to see some older friends graduate. A speaker was introduced, a nondescript dark-complexioned, dark-haired middle-aged man. He began speaking. As much as we wanted to tune him out and think about the parties later in the day, his words captured our attention. He spoke simply but eloquently of growing up poor, addicted, and disabled on an Indian reservation. Midway through his speech he had every member of that sweat-soaked gymnasium on the edge of the bleachers. Nobody was inflating beach balls or whispering to the mortar-boarded and polyestered senior seated left or right. Something was building, you could just feel it; his story was moving in a direction that had all of us participating moment by moment in the suspense of his speech. He played the hushed concentration beautifully, drawing out a word here, pausing dramatically there. And still the speech kept building. Finally the moment of dramatic release—Aristotle called it catharsis—came when after describing the devastation of a wound in his throat, he came to a close not by talking—but by belting out acapella several lines from a song. We don't remember what song it was; we could have cared less. It was a moving and unexpected ending to a stunning story. As the last notes rang off of the gym's walls, the audience erupted with loud and sustained applause. We could hardly believe what we'd just witnessed.

That commencement address in that sweaty Ohio gym, especially the speaker's closing, reminds us of what public address scholars rate as the best American speech delivered in the twentieth century. That speech, perhaps not surprisingly, is Dr. Martin Luther King, Jr.'s 1963 speech at the March on Washington; you likely know it as the "I have a dream" speech. Now a civil rights anthem that captures a uniquely American moment, what many don't realize about this address is that a good bit of it was improvised—including the climactic closing. While the speech has its own musical cadence and rhythm, the last five minutes in particular sing with the rhythmic power of repetition.[1] Moreover, everyone in the massive audience knew the split second the speech was over—such was King's oratorical power and mastery of timing. Dr. King's speech closing less than five years later in Memphis, Tennessee rivals his Dream speech for sheer rhetorical brilliance; it, too, sings with the soaring power of a prophetic voice—a voice that would be silenced the following evening on April 4, 1968, thus marking it as King's final rhetorical act in a life filled with oratorical brilliance.[2]

Martin Luther King, Jr. at the 1963 Civil Rights March in Washington, D.C.

Number nine on that same list of "great speeches" is Ronald Reagan's eulogy to the astronauts killed aboard the space shuttle in January 1986. Watch and listen as Reagan closes the address, a beautiful meditation lasting less than three minutes, in a masterful and moving allusion.[3] It was most fitting that the former president and his speechwriters chose to close the eulogy to the seven astronauts by quoting from a poem, "Flying High," written by a young American aviator, John Gillespie Magee, who died tragically in an airplane crash during training exercises over England in 1941. To "slip the surly bonds of earth" to "touch the face of God" renders this

---

1   Visit link: https://goo.gl/ie7kdx

2   Visit link: https://goo.gl/bDbg4U

3   Visit link: https://goo.gl/EQZFGM

Beginnings and Endings

The crew of the Challenger Space Shuttle

awful national tragedy into poetic and transcendent terms—terms that pilots, astronauts, and everyday Americans could understand.

> Media Scavenger Hunt [Flip Learning chat]

6.2 Why Great Beginnings and Endings Matter

We hear what you're thinking at this point: I'm not Martin Luther King, Jr., Ronald Reagan, and I can't even carry a tune—publicly or in the shower. Got it. But you certainly can be Ted among many other possibilities. No, you do not have to cut yourself to get our attention, but with just a few prompts and creative brainstorming, we think you can indeed invent very memorable beginnings and endings.

Building Anticipation

One of the things we shouldn't forget as we begin planning our speeches is that beginnings and endings provide unique moments for speakers and for listeners. That is, from an audience's perspective, we are just plain curious to know what's coming: what will this speaker offer and how will she do it? There is tension and curiosity and anticipation all mingling in that one moment. As speakers we absolutely have to seize it and use it as a springboard into our speeches; we will never get another moment quite like it, so we have to prepare carefully for it. Think of the first few minutes of a favorite film, the first few notes of a treasured song (has there ever been a more inspired set of opening notes than the Rolling Stones' anthem "Satisfaction"? And I don't even like the Rolling Stones), the opening to a memorable novel, play, or poem, even the first few explosive minutes to Monday Night Football: each beginning compels us to want more and to know more as these carefully designed openings create expectations about what is to come. Speeches can do the same sort of rhetorical work. Sure, we don't necessarily have visual pyrotechnics and a heavily amplified guitar lead, but we have our voices. And we have silence. Our bodies, too. Each of which mingles in important ways with expectations.

Achieving Closure

While it's hard to argue against introductions being the most important part of a speech, conclusions shouldn't be slighted just because they are the caboose to the louder locomotive. Plato uses the analogy of the head (introduction) and the feet (conclusion), and indeed, bringing the speech to an inspired close serves a number of very important rhetorical purposes—not the least of which involves your audience's memory and its ability to retrieve some of what you've said; because you are one of many speakers, the audience's ability to retrieve is very important. In fact, "primacy-recency", a psychological theory that suggests we are more likely to remember the first and last items conveyed orally in a series than what comes between, reinforces the importance of the head and feet.

When it comes to said feet, our experience has been that nothing triggers an audience's willingness to listen like the words "to close" or "in conclusion" or "let me end by saying…" Such small and seemingly insignificant signposts function to get everyone in the room paying careful attention to what you're about to say. There are also not many things worse in a speech than to experience one that has no conclusion, no fitting end. Like the bad noir film or the too postmodern novel, or a game that ends in a tie, so, too, a speech without an ending is deeply unsatisfying for an audience—and also not the least little bit awkward for a speaker trying to navigate a way back to his seat. Let's look at beginnings and endings in more detail and figure out ways to make them work to our rhetorical advantage.

> Policy Issues [Flip Learning chat]

6.3 How to Begin Your Speech

Do you recall those popular and big-haired television commercials for a certain anti-dandruff shampoo, the tagline of which is "you don't get a second chance to make a first impression"?[4] The same, for better and worse, also applies to public speaking: audiences make judgments, some of which are unconscious, just seconds into your speech; as such, it's imperative that we shape those judgments to our advantage, lest our "flakes" be visible. Okay, so that first thirty seconds: we encourage our students to script this critical time very carefully, perhaps even writing it out on your outline.

---

4   Visit link: https://goo.gl/mQK1y5

Involving the Audience

There are several possibilities for what might be in that script. We like, for example, a dialogical approach to beginnings: starting with a question or a series of questions asks your audience to be immediately involved in your speech, to catalyze its curiosity, and while you don't necessarily want them to answer out loud, you do want them to form an answer. One bit of advice when it comes to asking your audience questions, though: be sure to give them enough time to in fact form that answer. Too often really good questions get obscured by a speaker moving through them much too quickly. If you want your audience to answer a question, be sure to give them plenty of time to form an answer. If you're asking for a show of hands, take careful note of them.

What might that question be? Well, the possibilities are many, but here are a few suggestions. Did you find a remarkable statistic or finding during your research, one that really surprised you? Great, use it. Thus, "If I asked you to guess how many...?" Or "Did you know that...?" You can also ask your audience members to take on a role related to your topic: "Have you ever imagined what it would be like to...?" Jokes often function as questions, per the (in)famous knock-knock jokes, though a joke just for the sake of eliciting laughs is not the best way to spend your precious class time. But because there is tension in the room at the beginning of speeches, defusing it with laughter can be a great way to begin; audiences are usually eager to share a laugh, if only to feel more comfortable themselves. So we often love to hear, "Hey, have you heard the one about..." Even the form of the question usually elicits a smile: we know a joke is coming and we appreciate the form you've invoked to clue us in. In his now-famous 2005 commencement address at Kenyon College, listen as the late David Foster Wallace nails his opening with a joke about

Walter White and Tyrion Lannister street art (left to right)

fish and water.[5]

We once had a student who began his persuasive speech not with a joke but with a memorable question: "Have you ever seen the bumper sticker, 'If it's hootin' I'm shootin'?" Thus began his memorable speech on the Northern Spotted Owl controversy. While each of these possibilities invites dialogue, and therefore audience participation, asking students to raise their hands in response to a question has the added benefit of getting your audience both mentally and physically involved in your speech.

When National Basketball Referee Dick Bavetta delivered his Hall of Fame Acceptance speech in 2015, he feigned a lack of energy to begin his address. Watch how he skillfully (and humorously) uses the large and enthusiastic audience to get his juices flowing.[6]

---

5   Visit link: https://goo.gl/8cg1m5

6   Visit link: https://goo.gl/AvWphf

The Art of Storytelling

Another great way to begin a speech is with a story. The story can be one that you discovered during the course of your research, one that relates directly to you or someone you know, or perhaps it's a story that you've created. The point is we love a good story. Rhetorical theorist Walter R. Fisher has gone so far as to claim that what makes us unique as human beings is that we are hardwired to tell stories: we are homo sapiens and also homo narrans.[7] Fisher is definitely on to something here. From the Homeric epics, Aesop's Fables, and the parables of Jesus to our seemingly insatiable desire for *Harry Potter*, *Breaking Bad*, *The Bachelorette*, *Flavor of Love*, *Game of Thrones*, and of course *The Handmaid's Tale*, we crave stories—high and low. We homo narrans so desire the narrative form that we get hooked on comic books, Manga, and even scrapbooking. So hooked are we that we're even willing to watch the same season of *Downton Abbey* several times. And if you think your Facebook page doesn't offer its own story, you're kidding yourself.

Speaking of the popularity of stories and storytelling, a graduate of public speaking recently informed us of a new and entertaining outlet for this rhetorical form: check out *The Moth*.[8] The organization sponsors storytelling competitions and features some of the best examples on its website. Many of the featured stories are just straight-up hilarious. Others are more poignant and feature a moral. All are carefully choreographed to develop characters, create a plot, build to a climax and close at just the right moment. How

---

7   Walter R. Fisher, *Human Communication as Narration: Toward a Philosophy of Reason, Value, and Action* (Columbia, SC: University of South Carolina Press, 1989).

8   Visit link: https://goo.gl/qp16rR

curious that in our hyper-mediated, hyper-fast and get-it-done-now world that this ancient face-to-face rhetorical form is also finding a sizable digital audience.

You probably also know some really good storytellers, aunts and uncles, friends and neighbors, who just seem to have a gift for telling compelling stories. Most likely that gift has been carefully cultivated over the years. The award-winning sportswriter Rick Reilly, whose knack for inspired storytelling has led to his winning the National Sportswriter of the Year award an incredible 11 times, informs us that his abusive and alcoholic father was directly responsible for his gift. How so? Because Reilly's dramatic and funny stories functioned to distract his father when he was in yet another drunken rage. In oral cultures storytellers such as the West African griot hold very esteemed places as they are the keepers of history, tradition, rituals, and memory. In our age of secondary orality, watch what happens on the nightly national news broadcast: reporters almost universally dramatize difficult policy-oriented stories (think healthcare, civil rights, unemployment) by situating that complexity in a person, a couple, or a family. The Jordan family from Jonesboro, Arkansas is interesting and engaging and very real; far less so are numbers, graphs, pie charts and talking-head "experts" that don't connect to a larger story.

We're guessing that you, too, are something of a raconteur, someone who can transform the quotidian details of daily life into something far more dramatic and compelling. Just on your way to class, for example, that skinny-jeaned skateboarder that got a bit close to you on the sidewalk, the texter in the VW Cabriolet who took "your" parking spot, and the email at 3 a.m. from an ex—this is almost enough material for you to write your own reality TV episode. Stories and storytelling, per Fisher, are in your DNA at this point. Great. They're also in your audience's DNA, too.

So yes, a story is a great way to begin a speech, one that skillfully told, will have your audience quickly immersed in what you have to say. So conversant are we with stories that your audience doesn't need to hear a preamble to the effect of, "I'd like to begin with a story," or "I'd like to tell the story of...," or if you're riffing a commonplace, "Once upon a time..." or even "A long time ago, in a galaxy far, far away..." We'd advise you just to dive right in: "Cathy Adams couldn't believe her good fortune..." or "It was a day like any other day, but when I...," or even, "Then again, we should've known that Ted was a bit disturbed..."

The Element of Surprise?

There are, of course, other ways to begin a speech. Many textbooks encourage you to "shock" your audience—no, not with a cattle prod but with the unexpected. Thus Ted and his straight-edged razor. Watch and listen as Pamela Meyer nails the opening to her TED talk on liars and deception with a bit of "shock and awe."[9] There are as many ways to shock an audience as you have creative ideas, and we certainly like the idea of violating an expectation or norm to our rhetorical advantage. But we'd also encourage you to think carefully about this word, *shock*; if you've ever received one, you know they can hurt and surprise in a very unpleasant way. And the last thing we want to do as speakers is hurt or wound. Bringing in a live animal? Probably not. Weapons such as switchblades and guns? Uhm, no. Taking off your clothes to reveal a "hidden" tattoo? That's going to get uncomfortable. Fireworks and other inflammables? Bad idea. Alcohol and illegal substances? Take it somewhere else. While perhaps very well intentioned, these props are going to hurt far more than they help (and most are illegal on the majority of college cam-

---

9   Visit link: https://goo.gl/gHPjy7

puses). As teachers, we want to post your good grades, not your bail. So when it comes to shocking your audience, just know that there is a delicate line between rhetorical brilliance and really bad judgment. And as always, if you have questions about where that line is, consult your instructor.

Sharing a Memorable Quotation

A fourth way to open a speech is with a quotation—famous, obscure, or one you've created. We have a thing for memorable phrases. Think of John F. Kennedy's "Ask not what your country can do for you, ask what you can do for your country"; Franklin D. Roosevelt's "The only thing we have to fear is fear itself"; Fannie Lou Hamer's "I'm sick and tired of being sick and tired." Of course you don't have to use a quotation from a famous political figure to get the attention of your listeners; Forrest Gump is eminently quotable as is Bart Simpson. This one has been riffed a lot, too.[10] Given the myriad anthologies and websites that traffic in our fondness for aphorisms, you won't have any trouble finding one that fits your subject matter. Per our earlier comments about beginning your speech with a question, make sure that your audience can hear and absorb the quote. Sometimes quotes bear repeating just so that these important little gems have a better chance of staying with your listeners.

Building Suspense

A fifth way to open your speech to great rhetorical effect is to build suspense. Typically what speakers are "suspending" is the revelation of the topic; in other words, you might begin your speech by repeat-

---

10   Visit link: https://goo.gl/3mqomx

edly referencing an "it" or a "they" or a "him" or a "her." Done well, such rhetorical flirtation functions to heighten the curiosity on the part of the audience as it is left guessing as to what in fact the topic will be—and when it will finally be disclosed. Just like a good suspense film might show you a dramatic moment in the very first scene and not reveal the perpetrator, so a suspenseful opening to a speech engages our need to know. Unlike the film, though, you will want to disclose your topic sooner rather than later; to continue to defer that disclosure will only frustrate your listeners.

> The Moth [Flip Learning chat]

6.4 How to Organize Your Introduction

Disclose the Specific Purpose

This leads us to our next important point about what content to include in an introduction. Effective introductions get our audience's attention, clearly reveal our topic/purpose, establish listener relevance, establish our own credibility, and preview our main points. Once we've got our audience's attention, and though it seems like a no-brainer, you might be surprised how many times public speakers forget to disclose their Specific Purpose (see Chapter 4) somewhere in that opening minute or two. Don't make this mistake. Early in your speech we need to know what you're up to— if for no other reason than to help structure our listening. We can't make judgments about your intentions without knowing exactly what those intentions are; furthermore, if you withhold or greatly delay them, your audience will likely have long ago tuned you out.

Preview Main Points

Once we've captured our audience's attention and clearly revealed our purpose, we need to provide listener relevance—that's to say we need to let our audience members know why what we have to say is, or at least should be, important to them. How will they benefit from paying attention to us? Will they learn something new, something helpful, something that will make them more well rounded, something that will make them more interesting at parties? Don't leave it up to your audience to figure it out; let us know exactly why we should want to listen. If you are going to talk about honeybees, letting us know that honeybees are important to life on the planet—to *our* life on the planet, and ultimately to our survival—is going to compel us to listen. The point is: make what's important to you important to your listeners.

Establish Credibility

Now that we know why we should listen, tell us why we should listen to you: advertise your credibility.

Now out in the world things may be different for you as a public speaker: when you're asked to make a public speech, most likely you'll be speaking precisely because you have some unique expertise on the subject; as such, you'll have no compelling need to discuss your credentials; in fact, when you're introduced, those credentials will likely be carefully rehearsed and presented by the person doing the introducing. But as students of public speaking, the persons seated next to you have no idea what you may or may not be expert in. Think of it this way: part of the dialogue you're having with an audience in creating your speech should address these interrelated questions: So, why should I listen to you? What authority do you have on the subject? We don't mean to pose them as hostile questions but as questions any skeptical listener might bring to a classroom setting. Especially when it comes to persuasive speeches, good listeners, careful listeners, critical listeners, want to know about your expertise before they commit to expending a lot of precious energy listening to your speech.

So how can we go about meeting such expectations? We like the direct method: tell your audience how you've acquired this expertise. Is it part of your course of study in a particular major? Is it because you have a great deal of personal experience with the subject? Is your expertise linked to a hobby or part of your work experience? Have you spent considerable time researching the subject because of a particular interest? We have a close friend, for example, who has a rare condition called Mitochondrial Disease; she sends us research material about the disease and what new clinical trials are underway. Perhaps you, too, have a friend or family member with a debilitating disease or condition. Similarly, former First Lady Nancy Reagan became a very influential advocate for stem cell research because of its promise in preventing Alzheimer's Disease, which afflicted her husband. Like us, you're not a medical doctor, but your personal involvement with the subject and the homework you've done can make for a compelling informative or persuasive speech. Remember, you're not giving a speech to a group of medical experts but to a small group of classmates who might not know much, if anything, about the subject in question.

So beginning a speech with a story about our close friend with the disease, revealing our topic, and then transitioning to our involvement and expertise with it could make for a very effective opening. It's easy to overlook, too, that your classmates are eager to know more about you. Over several decades of research, Charles Berger and his colleagues have studied the phenomenon called "Uncertainty Reduction," typically in the context of interpersonal relationships.[11] But the need to reduce uncertainty about people we don't know also holds true in group contexts like public speaking. We're eager to know more about our classmates, and the sort of disclosure necessary to advertise your expertise satisfies some of our mutual curiosity. For those of you more modest and shy about your credentials, we would remind you of a favored aphorism: "it ain't bragging if you can do it." We don't think you need to be BIG and LOUD in a Muhammad Ali sort of way,[12] but as Aristotle noted many moons ago, ethos is often the "controlling factor" when it comes to influencing audiences. Yes, we need to know about your bona fides, so don't be coy; artfully disclosing your expertise will go a long way in creating a more receptive audience.[13]

Along similar lines, and finally, you'll also want to reveal your Central Idea by way of previewing your main points. You don't have to reveal your purpose and central idea all in one long sentence (at this point you should have clearly revealed your topic), but both need to be in your introduction. Your instructor will be listening for them. Your audience will be, too. Media experts take advantage of the important concept of signposting all the time. Whether it's your local newspaper previewing what's coming in a special section on Sunday or David Muir of ABC News telling us what's next after the commercial break, as consumers of information we are keen to know what's next; not only does it build anticipation but it also satisfies that anticipation, closing a very important rhetorical circle.

---

11   Charles R. Berger and R. J. Calabrese, "Some Explorations in Initial Interaction and Beyond: Toward a Developmental Theory of Interpersonal Communication," *Human Communication Research* 1 (1975): 99-112.

12   Visit link: https://goo.gl/P1qZgF

13   Aristotle, *On Rhetoric*, transl. by George A. Kennedy (New York: Oxford University Press, 1991), 38.

One of my favorite programs is ESPN's "Pardon the Interruption," where hosts Tony Kornheiser and Michael Wilbon spend 30 minutes arguing over the day's sports news. At the beginning of each episode a list of topics is included on the right side of the screen, effectively previewing for viewers what is to come. Watch the first 50 seconds of an episode.[14]

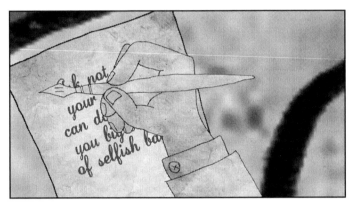

Rough Drafts of History [Flip Learning animation series]
Four score and seven drafts ago...

> Speed Dating for Introductions! [Flip Learning chat]

6.5 How to Achieve Closure

Let's move now to talking about closing your speech. And about how to achieve closure. We think there's an important difference between closing and achieving closure. We want you to aim for the latter as closure provides formal satisfaction; in more colloquial terms, done

---

14 Visit link: https://goo.gl/8vMojG

well, an ending brings us "full circle" and lets an audience know that you've completed your address.

Using Signposts

But the first thing we need to do in our quest for closure is to let our audience know that we are in fact going to be finishing shortly.

As we noted earlier, those magic words "To close," "In conclusion," and "I'd like to close by...," function in a Pavlovian way to ring the bell that dinner is coming. As teachers the only other thing we can compare these magical phrases with is when we're lecturing and say something along the lines of, "This list features four important items" or "A likely test question..." We can almost guarantee that every pen, pencil, or laptop in the room just got busy, so ingrained have the importance of lists and tests become for undergraduates. Don't ever overestimate the amazing rhetorical work that can be done with simple signposts; you will want to let your listeners know that you're about to finish. This will bring any straying eyes and ears back to your speech, and while you have their attention, let's make sure we communicate one more time our specific purpose and central idea.

Aiding Memory

We love it when speakers not only briefly repeat their topic and key points, but also go the extra mile to give listeners something to help us remember—most often referred to in speech as a "clincher." Some speakers offer something of a mnemonic aid to remember these important points. In a speech about diamonds, for example, a student left us with the four Cs: color, carat, cut, and clarity. Alternatively, we've often heard key arguments and points distilled to a memorable acronym such as MAIDS when discussing the history of rhetoric: Memory, Arrangement, Invention, Delivery, and Style. A perceptive student did us one better: I'M SAD for the same holy rhetorical fivesome. Such summative acronyms not only summarize, but they provide a terrific cue for our very crowded memories. I'M SAD is a whole lot easier to retrieve than trying to remember the five canons of rhetoric; one memorable phrase always trumps five separate parts.

Let's pause for a moment and note that endings differ just a bit in the persuasive speech. That is, there's one additional element that we'd highlight: repeating your call for what you'd like us to do as a result of your speech.

Since you have your audience's attention, let's make explicit just one more time what it is that you'd have us do—especially if it involves a specific course of action (e.g., registering to vote, going to the blood drive, attending a student government meeting, downloading an app, signing a petition, etc.). This appeal doesn't have to be longer than a sentence or two–in fact it might only require a few words–but repeating a call to your listeners is a good idea. No, we don't recommend shouting that 1-800 number six different times, per so many bad furniture advertisements or late-night infomercials, but repeating a call to action by directly asking your audience to fulfill your specific purpose is an essential part of concluding a persuasive speech.

Closure vs. Closing

So we've signaled that we're ending and we've done some important summary work, now what?

Should we take our seat now that we are finished? Technically yes, we're done, but again, let's aim for closure, not just closing. Before we talk in more detail about that, though, just a cautionary word about an error we occasionally see students make when it comes to conclusions. Sometimes students add an extra main point or a key piece of evidence in their conclusions. We'd urge you to keep them where they belong, which is in the body of the speech (see Chapter 7). Remember that the rhetorical function of a conclusion is to summarize and to achieve closure—not introduce new material. Including new material at the close of your speech will only serve to confuse your audience.

Complete the Circle

Let's get back to talking about closure and how best to achieve it. In public speaking terms, we call this the clincher—to formally wrap up our speech in a memorable way. If we conceptualize the speech as a circle, a really fine conclusion simply closes the circle. To be more specific, if you began your speech with a story, great, go ahead and finish that story at the close. We see this strategy executed all the time, often with great impact, in the world of film and television. Good storytellers know that if they give only a glimpse of the story at the outset, they'd best finish it by the close. Again, this rhetorical device literally "rounds things out" and provides a formal and satisfying close to the narrative.

Similarly, if you began with a question or a series of questions, go back to them and perhaps provide answers. If you began with a quotation, sure, refer to it in a manner that brings closure. Let's say, for example, that you're giving a speech on Medicaid, a federal government program that subsidizes health care for the poor. You started your speech with that memorable quote from Mrs. Hamer, a poor and often very sick Mississippi sharecropper who didn't have Medicaid until much later in life: "I'm sick and tired of being sick and tired." Returning to that same quote in the conclusion, perhaps we could glimpse a future of better health care in which that aphorism no longer holds. You see where we're going with this: to return to our beginning shows your audience where we've been and it satisfies a formal urge for unity—an urge that our speech has created magically in the first place. Regardless of how you begin your speech, the best cue you have for how to finish is in that first minute or two. You don't need to wrack your brain grinding over a fitting end; it's there right in front of you.

One of the more epic conclusions in the history of student speechmaking went down in Atlanta, Georgia in August 2013. Sophomore engineering student, Nick Selby, delivered this remarkable welcoming speech to the incoming class at Georgia Tech. If you're interested in the conclusion, it starts at 5:25, but the entire speech is well worth your time. Watch and listen as Selby enacts the very principles that make Georgia Tech great—all while achieving a unique closure that nobody in that auditorium will ever likely forget.[15]

Twenty-five years on we don't remember Ted's ending on a Monday morning at U.C. Davis. But you can bet we would recall it if he had rolled up his right sleeve. Again. A convention in novels, a staple in films, never forget that endings and beginnings function best when they speak to each other.

Chapter 6 Quiz [Flip Learning quiz]

---

15 Visit link: https://goo.gl/UW74gZ

7 Organizing the Body

7.1 Getting Out of Order

Getting Out of Order—Advantages

Have you ever watched Quentin Tarantino's masterpiece, *Pulp Fiction*? Among its many memorable moments—comfortable silences, getting Medieval, Parisian quarter pounders, accidental gun shots—the plot's non-linearity stays with you long after the credits roll. Recall from Chapter 6 that a great way to achieve closure is to circle back to where you began. Tarantino does this masterfully in *Pulp Fiction*, where the holdup of a restaurant serves as both the opening and the closing scenes. In between, though, Tarantino is having just a bit of fun messing with our expectations about how time functions in a film.

That is, film conventions have it that we are told a story—in

Episode 7: Grrr Argh [Flip Learning video series]
An epic game of Humans Versus Zombies throws the timeline out of order.

sequence. A beginning, middle and end occur in just that chronology. Many filmmakers use flashbacks (see *Titanic* where Old Rose narrates about young Rose), but Tarantino isn't interested in this slick convention. No, in *Pulp Fiction* the chronology is disrupted (spoiler alert) just when we think we're dealing with a standard story. While Vincent Vega (John Travolta) leaves the restaurant with sidekick Jules Winnfield at the film's close (Samuel L. Jackson), we know that his hours are numbered; after all, we've already witnessed Vincent's death at the hands of Butch (Bruce Willis) during a poorly planned bathroom break at his apartment. This little secret that Tarantino lets his viewers in on comments rather artfully on the always vexing issues of chance versus choice, volition versus "stuff happens."

Quentin Tarantino at the 2015 San Diego Comic Con International

But notice what Tarantino accomplishes here: by violating our expectations about organization, he makes a memorable point about it.

Now we should be very clear here: we don't expect you to make artful and sophisticated meta-points about the process of speech-making in your speech. Neither does your instructor. Let's leave that work to the existential philosophers, filmmakers, and the folks who wear a lot of black. Or at least we'll leave it until the Advanced Public Speaking class. Tarantino, after all, had 2.5 hours with a visual medium to achieve his memorable results; we get 5-7 minutes, no popcorn or Hot Tamales, no Thurman/Jackson/Travolta/Willis, and primarily just our voices. So our aim in the present chapter is to get you thinking about very pragmatic ways to structure your speeches in order to accomplish your specific purpose.

Getting Out of Order—Disadvantages

Growing up, we had a good friend whose little brother was a pesky nuisance in ways typical of little brothers. One of his favorite things to do was to inject a statement or ask a question that had absolutely nothing to do with what we were talking about. In technical terms, he was engaged in what the Romans called a non-sequitur, literally translated as "does not follow" (think of the Latin term as "not sequenced"). Perhaps you know some folks artful in the use of the non-sequitur? In any case, one evening our buddy's dad put a memorable but temporary end to his youngest son's "not following." After interjecting yet another non sequitur, an exasperated father exclaimed, "Jeff, honey, slice your own pineapple." Dad's non-sequitur was a perfectly-timed retort—one we later employed frequently when Jeff again got "out of sequence."

It's not hard to get out of sequence when we're organizing our speeches; what seems eminently logical and "follow-able" to us might not sound the same way to our listeners. Moreover, because listening demands so much concentrated energy, it's easy for our audience to get a bit out of sequence, too. But if we pay careful attention to how we construct our speeches, we can greatly aid our listeners' ability to sequence what we're saying.

Isocrates & the Pineapple [Flip Learning animation series]
The master of pragmatism teaches us a useful skill.

'Out of Sequence' Films [Flip Learning chat]

7.2 Creating Logical "Flow"

One important way to think about organization is to consider what it fundamentally is: namely, to be logical. We don't mean this in a formal sense such as if a = b, and b = c, then a = c. We'll have much more to say about logic in a later chapter. No, what we mean is that something necessarily follows from something else. A compelling speech is one in which, yes, the delivery might be dynamic and the audience analysis spot on, but it's also going to proceed in a manner that helps the audience comprehend the subject in question. Have you ever noticed that the best teachers also tend to be the best organized with the best examples? Their lectures seem to flow seamlessly as they skillfully move you through the subject. You "get it" in no small measure because you've been guided to see what's important or how a relationship functions. Often when we don't "get it" it's because we've not been expertly guided and relationships haven't been made clear; the flow has been interrupted.

Let's revisit our construction metaphor from Chapter 4 for a moment here. Recall the house that you're designing. The rooms in that house are your main points and the hallways linking those rooms are called connectives. Without a hallway or portico you're going to be trapped in that room for a while; moreover, we don't want you leaping out of any windows. Our experience is that students build three or four discernible rooms, but they often overlook the fact that those rooms function best when they're connected, each to the other. Architects as well as proponents of Feng Shui often talk about flow, or the dynamic and artful movement among and between places. Yeah, that's something of what we're aiming for when we organize our speeches: an artful and also logical flow. Not random pineapple slices. We'll be talking more about how to employ these connectives in what follows.

The Feng Shui compass (or "luopan") can be used to determine the precise orientation of a structure or building.

Aristotle's Arrangement

So important was organization to the Greeks and the Romans that they gave it its own special place in rhetoric's history, better known as arrangement. While Aristotle, that great organizer himself thought arrangement could be reduced to just two things, proposition and proof (or, argument and evidence), the Romans offered a much more detailed schema for how speakers might organize their main points, beginning with a statement of the facts (*narratio*) and division (*partitio*) and moving then to proof (*confirmatio*) and refutation (*refutatio*). Notice that this four-part organizational pattern might be great for a persuasive speech in which a case is being advanced, but not so relevant for an informative or commemorative address.

Let's take a look, then, at other patterns for organizing, ones useful to different types of speeches.

7.3 Chronological Order

One of the most common patterns for organizing both informative and commemorative speeches is what is called a chronological order. As the term suggests, the logic of this type of pattern is premised on time—usually a movement from early to late, or beginning to ending. But that sense of time can also relate to things involving a process. Let's say, for example, that you want to give an informative speech on how to make a nutritious and inexpensive smoothie. It is logical that you would proceed through the body of your speech by walking your listeners through a temporal sequence: we start with this, we next do that, and we finish by doing this. "How to" speeches, especially when they include visual aids to help us see exactly what you're doing, are very compelling but they also need to be sequenced very carefully. If you've ever built a model, programmed a computer, assembled anything from Ikea, or made an elaborate French pastry, you know all about careful sequencing!

Example: Commemorating Oprah Winfrey

A chronological order can also be very useful when it comes to certain types of commemorative speeches. Let's say, for example, that you want to do a speech of praise on über woman Oprah Winfrey. You not only loved her in *The Color Purple*, and *Beloved*, but you also admire her rise from poverty in Jim Crow Mississippi and her philanthropic work in South Africa. Notice that you've got three main points here, but they need sequencing. How about putting them in chronological order, beginning at the beginning in Mississippi, working through her work as an actress and concluding with her school in South Africa? Notice that the chronological approach is a natural fit with telling a story, whether it's a partial story of Oprah's remarkable life, or the "story" of making that healthy and tasty smoothie.

Example: Persuasive Speech on the Dangers of Drinking and Driving

This is not to suggest that the chronological form can't be put to good use in a speech to persuade; indeed it can, as we've suggested in an earlier chapter. One way to persuade an audience about the dangers of drinking and driving and not to engage in it is to cite statistics, punishments, and costs. Another entirely different and more compelling way is to tell the story of your friend/colleague/family member who was involved in a DUI accident. Again, as homo narrans, we have a seemingly hard-wired affinity for this form—an affinity that many producers of messages are only too eager to employ. Do you recall your senior year in high school when you showed up at school one morning to find a badly mangled car in the middle of campus? We do, too. That car was there for only one reason: the story it contained. Like us, you wanted to know what happened.

Example: Fannie Lou Hamer's 1964 DNC Speech

One of our favorite speakers is the Mississippi sharecropper-turned-civil-rights-activist, Fannie Lou Hamer. In perhaps her most famous speech, captured live on national television, and which occurred in 1964 at the Democratic National Convention, she was given only 8 minutes to try to explain to the country and the Democratic Party how and why blacks were being disenfranchised in her home state. Now of course Mrs. Hamer could have recited county-by-county statistics that revealed rather blatant discrepancies in white vs. black voting; she could have talked about literacy tests and constitutional interpretations used by white registrars; and she could've talked about how federal voting laws were being violated. But she didn't. Instead she tells two relatively short personal stories. In telling them she mesmerized the entire country; she also entered American history that afternoon in Atlantic City. Have a listen.[1] Each of Mrs. Hamer's stories proceed chronologically, the first story taking place in August 1962 and the second occurring in June 1963; each story is carefully narrated for profound rhetorical effect.

Fannie Lou Hamer at the Democratic National Convention in August 1964

So yes, a chronological pattern is often well-suited to your

---

1 Visit link: https://goo.gl/bDWmtZ

speaking objectives in the informative and commemorative speeches, but it can also be employed effectively in your persuasive speeches. As you look carefully at designing that specific purpose and central idea, see if you can in fact impose a chronological pattern on the subject matter. If not, no worries, but understand that employing a narrative structure in your speech can yield remarkable results. Telling the "story" of that fruit smoothie (informative), Oprah Winfrey (commemorative) or voting in Mississippi (persuasive) resonates—often deeply—with our rhetorical instincts as homo narrans.

> Fannie Lou Hamer's 1964 Speech [Flip Learning chat]

7.4 Spatial Sequence

A second type of organizational pattern that you might find useful is a spatial sequence. As suggested by its name, this method encourages us to find a directional logic in our speeches. That logic can be north to south, east to west, clockwise or counterclockwise, top to bottom, bottom to top, out to in, in to out, front to back, and back to front. Not to give you vertigo, but think of it this way: if your speech topic involves movement, especially one that can be visualized by your listeners, spatial ordering might be just the ticket.

Illustrating Geographic Places

Let's say that you're giving an informative speech on historically important locations on your campus. Great, this should be an engaging topic, but how best to organize it? We would encourage you to get out that campus map, or pull it up online, and see what makes the most sense directionally. Granted, in our world of GPS technologies where sophisticated and suave-sounding-voices-who-are-never-lost instruct us what to do and where to go, you need to be that voice for your listeners. Here's one idea: if you can pull up the campus map for your classmates using projection technology, you can begin your journey to these locations from the classroom in which you are speaking, moving from closest to farthest away. Similarly, you could work in a number of different directions—just so long as those directions offer a logical and consistent movement. The last thing you want to do, though, is move randomly, jumping from one spot to the next. The important point to remember is that if you're working on a speech that involves geographic places, spatial ordering should work well.

Describing the Relationship Between Parts and the Whole

Spatial ordering is also very useful when it comes to showing parts and their relationships. Let's say, for example, that you're a biology major and want to share some of the basics of cellular structure and function with your classmates. Again, you're probably going to want a really detailed visual aid to do this (and some great analogies to reduce the complexity), but in thinking about how best to organize the speech, it seems logical to move from the outer cell wall (the cellular membrane) inward to the cytoplasm and then to the nuclear membrane and finally to the nucleolus. Sure, the cell functions as a unified organism, but for the sake of your speech, you need to divide the cell into its key components. But that division allows us to learn about the important parts

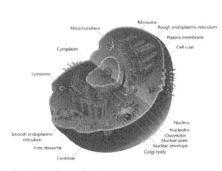
Eukaryotic cell structure

and how each part, in turn, functions within the larger whole.

Let's revisit that Oprah Winfrey commemorative speech for a moment. We'd earlier decided that the chronological pattern was best suited for our specific purpose. Note, too, that you can also combine a chronological pattern with a spatial one. How so? Well, we can begin with her early years in Mississippi, work west to Hollywood and her mid-career films, and then keep heading west, to halfway around the globe and South Africa to see her more recently created school for girls. So, just because you've isolated one organizational pattern, don't assume that there aren't others that you might combine to form an even more compelling pattern.

Oprah Winfrey's Leadership Academy for Girls

Lawyers do this all the time as they make their cases to juries. That is, they combine a detailed and very careful chronology (what happened and when) with where an alleged crime happened. Especially with our advanced technologies, times and places are much easier to determine. Whether it's surveillance footage from a local 7-11 store, to a time stamp on a smartphone picture, issues of where and when have gotten infinitely more sophisticated. Lawyers for Duke Lacrosse player and accused rapist, Reade Seligmann, for instance, had a time stamp from a Durham, North Carolina ATM machine to prove that he couldn't have been a perpetrator of the alleged assault. And even though the case never went to court, the defendants' lawyers were prepared to make a case based on both chronological and spatial patterns of logic and organization.

Organizing the Body   165

7.5 Topical Approach

Now that we understand chronological and spatial organizing, let's take a look at a third helpful sequence, known as the topical approach. Think of the topical pattern of organization as a movement within rather than a movement across. That is, instead of moving across time and place in the manner that chronological and spatial patterns do, we employ a topical approach to help us subdivide a single subject into its more discrete parts. We're guessing that when you talk to a friend or family member about your smartphone, you talk about a specific brand with certain features. You don't have a smartphone; you have an iPhone X or a Galaxy J7 or any number of other alternatives. Drilling down further, you note certain features of your specific phone. Similarly, you don't drive a car; you drive a Dodge Charger or a Bugatti Veyron (one day!). You see the logic here: we're moving from something fairly broad (smartphone, car) to something rather specific (brand, features).

If we wanted to have a bit of self-reflexing fun here we might say that organizing your informative speech is best understood topically: it features three approaches: chronological, spatial and topical.

Example: Informative Speech on Eight-Legged Arachnids

The topical approach is best suited for informative and commemorative speeches insofar as each type of speech aims to teach us something we might not know a lot about. And by breaking a given topic down into its smaller parts, we're showing relationships and learning in greater depth. Let's say, for example, that like us you have a shark-week-like fascination with those eight-legged arachnids that seem to flock to your house and garage. Moreover, you'd like to give an informative speech on spiders, but in researching a specific pur-

A non-poisonous Palm Spider in Moyenne Island

pose statement you quickly realize that a speech on types of spiders or habitats of spiders is simply too broad. Proceeding in the other direction, you realize that a specific purpose on the mating habits of the tarantula is probably much too narrow for your particular audience. But your research also turns up important information on venomous spiders, particularly those native to your area of the country. A specific purpose informing your listeners on how they can identify the three most common venomous spiders in your area might prove to be very useful information. Per our earlier counsel, please leave the live "pets" at home; Ted, and others, will thank you.

Example: A Topical Approach to Skin Cancer

Here's another idea for a topical approach to a subject: let's say that skin cancer runs in your family and you want to do a speech on it. Good topic, but notice that the subject of "skin cancer" is an enormous area of medical research; moreover, there's myriad different approaches to the subject, including things like genetic predisposition, prevention, self-examination, and risk factors, among many others. During your research, though, you come across different types of skin cancer and what they look like. Reading further, you decide on a specific purpose that informs your audience about the three or four most common types of skin cancer and how to identify them. Such a topical approach to the subject allows you to take a very

Organizing the Body   167

broad subject and begin narrowing the possibilities. Again, if you need to err on one side or the other, we'd encourage you to aim for the more narrow topic rather than the less manageable larger one.

Topical Approaches to Commemorative Speaking

Topical approaches to commemorative occasions function in a similar manner. Perhaps in your role as either the maid of honor or the best man at an upcoming wedding, you know you're going to be making a toast, which functions much like a speech of praise. Toast rhymes with roast, so we also know we are expected to have a bit of fun at the bride or groom's expense. We were at a recent wedding reception where the best man did an artful (and hilarious) job of dealing with a bit of a touchy subject: the groom was a full ten years older than his very young bride. So in taking a topical approach to his subject—embarrassing stories about groom Matt—his best man regaled us with the story of being Matt's roommate in college, and how as roommates they often talked about meeting The One. He shared some of the details of their shared fantasy, artfully building the story to its unanticipated climax: "...and little did Matt know it, but his dream girl Elizabeth was then eight years old."

But regardless of whether the subject is funny stories about the groom or bride, a topical approach to commemorating functions to take a category like achievement, honors, heroism, generosity, sacrifice or bravery, among others, and break it down into specific instances. Let's go back to Oprah one more time. Recall that we could organize our commemorative speech about her using a chronological and/or spatial approach. We might also do it topically. Let's look again at our three main points. Her upbringing in Mississippi speaks to her ferocious determination; her achievements as an actress speak to her creative talents; and her school in South Africa speaks to her generosity. To be determined, talented, and generous—each functions as a type of character that we admire.

Topical Approach to Persuasive Speaking: The Case of Monster Trucks

Recall, too, that we claimed that a topical arrangement functioned best with informative and commemorative topics; this is true. But it can also be used effectively in persuasive speeches as well. How so? Perhaps think of it not as a speech but colloquially first: you're trying to persuade a close friend to attend the monster truck show with you on Saturday night. In anticipation, your head is throbbing pleasantly with loud Auto-tuned reverbs of "THUNDER, THUNDER, THUNDER!!" But you need to offer your friend some good reasons for going to this rather curious cultural event. You settle on three: people watching; loud, jacked-up trucks pulsating dangerously to country music; and the coliseum has great wings, which you'll spring for. You see what's going on here, yes? Each of your reasons functions as a sub-topic for why your (former?) friend should attend the monster truck show with you.

In general, whenever you're offering a list of reasons as to why a certain course of action should be undertaken or a belief held, you're in the realm of topical arrangement. Whether it's giving blood, buckling your seatbelt—and we've heard a lot about giving blood and buckling up through the years —volunteering at a local animal shelter, or becoming a vegan, each reason functions as a sub-topic for something larger. When taken together, though, those combined reasons can exert a compelling and persuasive force on audiences.

In sum, then, when we think about topical arrangements, we're moving progressively deeper into a subject, and in so doing making relatively abstract ideas, subjects and appeals much more specific. Teaching, commemorating and persuading each makes use of the topical approach.

7.6 Causal Organization

Let's look at a fourth approach to organizing, one very useful in both informative and persuasive speeches. Causal organizing encourages us to see our topic as two interrelated parts: this outcome was caused by these factors, or these factors caused this outcome. Generally speaking, we're attracted to causal organization and causal arguments because they offer a certain and very precise explanation for why things happen. It is very reassuring to know, for example, that the cause for your phone "being dead" this morning is because you forgot to charge it, not because your operating system has been corrupted. Or the unusual behavior you're witnessing by your roommate is caused by public speaking anxiety and not by something far more serious.

We have many important public policy debates that hinge upon issues of causality. For example, are outbreaks of severe weather such as hurricanes, tornadoes and flooding being caused by global warming? Is a reduction in serious crime being caused by "stop and frisk" policies? Are higher rates of childhood obesity being caused by easy access to sugary snacks and beverages? Does online bullying cause young adults to commit suicide? Do early childhood inoculations cause autism?

A Word of Caution

We have to be careful whenever we organize or argue by cause and effect that in fact we're doing so logically, that event x comes about only because of y. Did eating too much sugar really cause Dan White to kill San Francisco Mayor George Mosconi and his colleague Harvey Milk? His attorneys put forward the infamous "Twinkie" defense to make such a causal argument. Did injections of Propofol cause Michael Jackson to die of cardiac arrest? Did listening to Marilyn

Manson's music cause the Columbine, Colorado school shooting massacre? Closer to home, did that black cat you saw as you walked under a ladder on your way to school cause your girlfriend to break up with you and to get fired from your job? Did an encounter with the number 13 cause you to fail your math test? Yeah, we have to be careful when it comes to attributing causes to certain effects. Often, upon closer inspection, two events have nothing in common but coincidence.

Example: Informative Speech on the Causes of Honeybee Population Decline

But let's get back to that informative speech; more specifically, as an agricultural economics major you've become fascinated with the economic power of....bees! That is, a huge reduction in the honeybee population has had important economic consequences. But you're curious to know why: why has the honeybee population declined so dramatically? After your research you settle on this specific purpose: to inform my audience about the causes of the honeybee population's decline. The body of your speech will begin with an effect (the decimation of the population), followed by causes why (such as increases in certain pesticides).

Instead of being an agricultural economics major, let's just say you're an economics major—and you've noticed that college textbook prices are, in your estimation, ridiculously high. Determined to find out why, you learn through your research that the used textbook market is causing publishers to issue new editions of their textbooks more frequently and at a higher cost to recoup revenue lost from used bookstores, who pay no royalties and often have a monopoly on a local college market. Thus, your specific purpose: to inform my audience about the causes for high textbook prices.

Again, you begin your speech by showing an effect (high prices) and then move to explaining the causes for those prices (used textbooks and a lack of competition).

Example: Persuasive Speech on the Causes of Sever Weather Outbreaks

Let's move from causal organizing in the informative speech to the persuasive speech. As you'll see, the logic of causality undergirds both types of addresses. Let's say that you're an atmospheric sciences major and you're very interested in the phenomenon of global warming, or the earth's rising temperatures caused, claim many, by our consumption of fossil fuels such as coal. Furthermore, you'd like to persuade your listeners that, in fact, global warming is causing outbreaks of more severe weather—colder winters, hotter summers, more severe hurricanes and longer droughts. You decide on a specific purpose: to persuade my audience that global warming is causing more severe weather. As such, the body of your speech will begin with a cause, global warming, and then move to documenting its effects. You won't have an easy case to make, especially in 6-7 minutes and given your audience's existing beliefs, but as a budding scientist you are persuaded by one side of the research.

Example: Persuasive Speech on the Effects of TWD Laws

Speaking of controversial attributions of causality, here's a very interesting public health issue that's not going away anytime soon; furthermore, many reading this sentence engage in it to some extent: TWD—texting while driving. If you've done it, you know it's not good for you (or others). Experts claim it's three or four times more toxic than DUI—driving under the influence. But as a political science major (and inveterate texter), you're intrigued by a recent story making the rounds on a lot of news programs: banning it is actually making the problem worse, not better. Huh? But wait, I thought TWD causes more accidents, injuries and fatalities. Indeed, you're right; it does. But our question is this: have laws to ban it caused the problem to become worse? After more research you determine a specific purpose: to persuade my audience that laws to ban texting while driving are actually making the problem worse. The body of your speech begins with a cause (state laws that ban TWD) to its surprising effects (what researchers are finding is that texters, to avoid detection by law enforcement, are holding their phones well below the steering wheel, thus diminishing lines of vision and causing more accidents; in other words, the law is not a deterrent to texting, per lawmakers' assumptions).

Our experience suggests that audiences have a real affinity for causal organization patterns; they provide the cover of a scientific logic in the realm of contested public policies. In employing them though, we have to be cautious, maybe even skeptical, about concluding too easily that x always causes y. Most of the time we just don't have definitive proof in the way that dropping a book will cause it to hit the ground. Complex weather patterns, honeybee behavior, high textbook prices, and texting behaviors can elude even the scientists.

7.7 Problem-Solution Order

A fifth approach to organizing your speech, one most common to persuasive speaking, is the problem-solution order. This approach stresses the relationship between two points: the first one specifies a problem and the second one attempts to solve it. Cognitive psychologists have argued that we are susceptible to persuasive appeals that help us to resolve an "imbalance" or perceived problem. As you might have guessed, the problem-solution approach is most useful in a persuasive speech, where you're trying to induce us to believe that your solution should be adopted. The key here is two-fold: first, demonstrating that there is a compelling problem that needs to be solved; and, second, that your solution actually would solve that problem as you've defined it.

So first we need to concentrate on determining if, in fact, there's a problem. Are federal income tax rates for those making more than $250,000 too low?; is the out-of-state tuition rate at your college too high, or tuition in general?; are college students graduating with too much loan debt?; are mandatory minimum sentences for certain types of drug convictions too punitive?; do your state's employment laws discriminate against same-sex couples?; does your county's animal shelter put down too many stray dogs and cats?; is protection of the endangered white sturgeon creating more problems than it's solving? You see what we're doing here: establishing that there is a problem is absolutely essential to the success of your speech.

Aligning Solutions with Problems

Now, about those solutions. First, does your proposed solution solve the problem? Be careful here: you need to demonstrate persuasively that your solution directly addresses the problem. We've noticed over many years of evaluating speeches that occasionally a proposed solution just doesn't line up with a problem. So, if you've identified three critical aspects to the problem, have your solution address those same three aspects; in this manner your audience can see exactly how that problem is getting solved. Second, you might also need to show that your solution won't create another round of problems; this is the perennial concern with any solution to a major problem—what some call the law of unintended consequences. So, for example, over the past several years we've heard an outpouring of public discourse that the Affordable Health Care Act (aka "Obamacare", a solution to out-of-control costs) will only make our health care crisis worse. So, too, critics of new voter identification laws (a solution to fraudulent voting) claim that they will disenfranchise young and minority voters. Or the legalization of medical marijuana (a solution to the side effects of chemotherapy) will create a climate of acceptance for non-medical marijuana use.

Addressing Unintended Consequences

One important thing you can do when it comes to addressing the issue of unintended consequences is look around for precedents. Proposed solutions are often most persuasive when you can show that other campuses, other counties, other states, other countries even, have implemented similar solutions—with positive outcomes. We'll have more to say about arguing by precedent and by analogy, but know that the best lawyers and the best policymakers almost always argue by precedent and analogy. So, let's see if we can find them; chances are, other creative minds have been working on similar problems. Digging deep, the subject of our next chapter, perhaps we can persuade our listeners that our careful research has turned up logical and achievable solutions.

Before moving on, allow us to introduce you to a slightly more elaborate version of the problem-solution pattern: Monroe's Motivated Sequence, or MMS. Created in the 1930s by Communication scholar Dr. Alan Monroe, MMS is sequential pattern that follows the human process of thinking, helps to emphasize what our audience members can do, and includes five steps: gaining our audience's attention, demonstrating a need, providing satisfaction, visualizing results, and calling our audience to action. Don't let the terminology scare you: need = problem and satisfaction = solution. MMS invites our listeners to invest—to want to take action to solve the problem rather than feeling helpless. This organizational pattern is one we see in policy debates, advertising, public service announcements, and—to be sure—infomercials!

> Monroe's Motivated Sequence [Flip Learning chast]

7.8 Refutative Design

Our sixth and final form of organization is one that you see on a lot of *Law & Order* type of programs, but it's also one favored by the ancients—namely, the refutative design. As the name suggests, a refutative organizational design takes the major points advanced by our opposition and refutes them point by point. One of the reasons we seem drawn to courtroom dramas of all sorts is the intense verbal dueling, and a critical part of that dueling involves refuting an opponent. While it's not quite the physical dueling of college football, Mixed Martial Arts or professional wrestling, such rhetorical contests play into our tendencies as homo narrans to want to see a competitive drama resolved with good arguments and compelling evidence. Think of the losing "bad guy" lawyer of crime dramas as the "heel" in professional wrestling.

Refuting your opposition's arguments, though, isn't limited to the courtroom; such an organizational strategy is at home in the corporate boardroom as well. Public relations professionals and communication theorists call it "stealing thunder," which involves directly engaging with the opposition's arguments in order to refute them. Such a strategy functions rhetorically to give the appearance that your side isn't hiding; no, your side is willing to directly and forcefully challenge what the opposition is arguing. And you and I seem to have a thing for standing up to perceived bullies. Such a strategy also functions rhetorically to reduce the power (the "thunder, thunder, thunder") of your opponents' arguments. How? Because an audience isn't hearing those arguments for the first time. That is, if you can beat your opponents to the starting line, you're several steps down the track before they're even in the starting blocks. For some listeners, the argument has already been refuted before the opposition has even made its case. Good lawyers, good public relations practitioners, and yes, savvy politicians, are keenly aware of the power of refutation.

Example: Persuasive Speech on State Legalization of Medical Marijuana

But let's leave the boardroom and the courtroom and the legislative chamber for a moment and return to your public speaking class. How might we employ a refutative design in our persuasive speeches? Let's say that you want to give a speech arguing in favor of the legalization of medical marijuana in your home state. In your research, though, you continually find the same three or four arguments advanced by those opposed to its legalization; moreover, you think those arguments can be refuted by evidence you've discovered based on its legalization in other states (arguing, again, by precedent). Here's one way, then, to state your specific purpose: to persuade my audience that the arguments against the legalization of medical marijuana aren't true. Or, here's a more positively stated specific purpose: to persuade my audience that medical marijuana should be legalized. Both specific purpose statements could be supported by a central idea that features three or four arguments, and their refutation, by the opposing side. Additionally, each refutation functions simultaneously as a point for your position: by proving that something isn't so, you can also advance a positive argument. How so?

Let's say that your first point addresses the opposition's claim that legalizing marijuana for medical purposes will lead to increased non-medical use across all demographic groups, but especially among 16-22 year olds. Your research, though, indicates that rates of non-medical marijuana use did not increase significantly in several (all?) states where medical marijuana is legal. Notice that refutation does two things: yes, it refutes the opposition's claim, but it also advances a more positive point: that rates of use have remained the same.

Strive for Accuracy and Fairness

The refutative design can be a very powerful strategy in persuasive speaking. But we'd also caution you to be very careful in its use. In our very heated public sphere, it's not hard to find opponents trying to score very loud rhetorical points by caricaturing their opponents' positions. In other words, that desire to win often trumps accuracy, nuance and careful argument, and when this happens nobody wins; in fact, we'd argue that everybody loses. When characterizing an opposing side our aim as ethical speakers should always give pride of place to accuracy and fairness. Look back at the preceding paragraph. Did you note something important about how we characterized our evidence? What if two out of ten states revealed higher rates of non-medical marijuana use after legalization among 16-22 year olds? What should you do with that piece of evidence that doesn't work to your rhetorical advantage? Do you remain silent? We would encourage you to make your refutation as transparent as possible; after all, eight states still saw no increases in usage.

Refutations done well are always transparent, even if there's some conflicting data. As critical evaluators of a persuasive message, and not partisans at a WWE event, your listeners will appreciate and value your candor, which, of course, goes right back to that all-important Aristotelian category of character.

In summary, then, we have numerous organizational patterns: chronological, spatial, topical, cause-effect, problem-solution and refutative. But when it comes to organizing speeches, our advice has less to do with using just one of these six patterns and more to do with your specific purpose statement. You can't go wrong organizationally if you can find a good answer to one question: what is the most logical way to organize my purpose for this topic? As we mentioned at the outset, organizing is nothing if not a logic—a logic of what should follow what. And so as you sit down to assemble the parts of your address, don't make the mistake of beginning with one of these six patterns and forcing your ideas to fit it; our commemorative speech on Oprah after all fit three different categories rather coincidentally. We didn't set out to create a commemorative speech about Oprah that used just spatial logic. No, answer the question, what is the most logical way to proceed to fulfill my specific purpose? Chances are good that whatever you decide will fit with one of the six patterns of organization, or perhaps a combination of them. Remember that the "magic of invention" doesn't require six predetermined organizational boxes, nor two or three, to work its magic. Perhaps your creative genius will invent an entirely new way for how to organize a speech.

7.9 Using Connectives

Let's close this chapter by connecting driving down a few roads or connecting several "rooms." When you deliver your speech in class you'll likely notice your instructor somewhere near the back of the room scribbling/typing like The Great Cornholio on Meth.[2] Don't sweat this: your instructor is merely trying to get all the details of your speech so that they can have it for later recall, and so that s/he can provide you helpful feedback. One of the things sure to bring

---

2   Visit link: https://goo.gl/7ESnr5

a smile to your instructor's harried face, though, is your compelling use of connectives, those seemingly trifling little words and phrases that link together the different parts of your speech. Stated differently, in order to achieve that flow between rooms that we described earlier, the careful and deliberate use of several types of connectives is vital. It's sometimes easy to forget as speakers that our audience simply doesn't have access to any visual information of where we are in our speech. Our aim, then, should always be to let our listeners know where we are, what we've done and where we're headed. You simply can't go wrong with big and bright hallways that lead from one room to the next or a good navigational system that helps you get to where you're going.

Transitions

As you look at your outline you'll note that you have many points and subpoints. One of the best ways to connect them verbally for your audience is with transitions—phrases that show movement from one point to another. Phrases such as, "Let's begin with the environmental role of the honeybee," or "now that you understand the effects, let's look at the causes," or "Oprah not only is a talented actress, but she's also a generous philanthropist," each tell your listeners what you've done and where you're next headed. Structuring your listener's ability to process your message in a clear manner is vitally important. Please don't assume that your talents as a dynamic speaker are good enough. Frankly, dynamism and personal charisma are going to take you only so far. We also need points and sub-points that are clear and clearly differentiated from each other.

Signposts

Signposts, as the name suggests, are another type of connective that give a sort of verbal GPS "I am right here" notification to your listeners. Phrases such as, "my first point," "my second reason for . . ." and "to conclude," each functions to allow listeners to "see" where in fact you are even as they structure our listening. If you're like us you hate to be lost and have no clue where you're going. Out in the swamps of south Georgia this can induce great anxiety; in a classroom during a speech it can induce deep sleep, extended mouth breathing or surreptitious texting. Never forget, listening is hard.

Internal Previews

A third type of connective is the internal preview, which functions like Siri, among other nav-bots, when she offers you verbal directions.

Driving down an unfamiliar road at 50 miles per hour, the last thing you want to do is make quick swerving motions or airbag-inducing breaking to make a right turn. No, you want to know what's coming and when in order not to create a chain-reaction accident. Similarly, internal previews tell listeners what's coming in order that they can experience your speech in a smooth, navigable way. In your introduction, for example, providing a clear and concise statement of your specific purpose and central idea (a preview of what's to come) function as the navigational center of your speech. In our house building analogy, previewing your speech in the introduction is the major hallway that leads to each of the three or four rooms; without it, we're going to be lost and confused.

Internal Summaries

Fourth, and finally, (yup, you caught us signposting), speakers who are really attuned to listeners often offer internal summaries—sort of the opposite of the internal preview. That is, you're reminding your audience of the key points you've just discussed and reinforcing the relationships among them. Especially if you're enumerating several points, it's helpful to provide a quick summary of where you've been. Conclusions in particular provide a great place to remind your listeners of your central idea (by way of a review of what you've covered) so that they can take away the critical points of your speech. But you can also use internal summaries to break up key breaks in the body of your speech. Something along the lines of, "so you can see that there are three causes to the problem, x, y and z..." Again, such summary work provides important navigational information as we move down the end of that road or hallway.

Even a master storyteller like Quentin Tarantino uses the full resources of organization. In *Pulp Fiction* he even goes so far as to preview for us what's coming by using the really old filmic technique of featuring typed letters on a blank screen, just like the early silent films. In doing so, Tarantino pays homage to his film predecessors as well as helping us navigate his often densely layered films. Similarly, as speakers, we too pay our respects to our rhetorical elders by employing their tried and true organizational strategies even as we also help our listeners find their way in our speeches.

> Connectives [Flip Learning chat]

> Chapter 7 Quiz [Flip Learning quiz]

8 Research: Going Deep and Getting Closer

8.1 Google. The End.

It's really tempting in a chapter dedicated to the subject of research to write:

> Google. The end.

We are very well aware of the fact that this little Internet startup out in Silicon Valley has revolutionized the way we understand our world and our place in it. Its remarkable algorithms help us find everything from an obscure hamlet on the other side of the world to information about a great-great-great-grandmother. So good are those algorithms—and a really interesting topic for an informative speech might be learning exactly what an algorithm is or how it works—that you might start getting advertising on your Gmail ac-

Episode 8: The Case of the Occult Archivist [Flip Learning video series]

The gang goes to the library to research their speeches, where Kay unearths a disturbing secret...

count that reflects a recent Google search you performed. So yeah, it's a little spooky to get advertisements on hotels in London immediately after you were "Googling" travel in England or using Gmail to tell a friend about an upcoming trip. All that crazy John Connor talk about the machines taking over from *Terminator I* turns out to have a few grains of truth to it.

But, dare we say it, Google does have its limits—even as it attempts to scan every book that's ever been published, its Praying Mantis–looking cars prowl our local streets, and its glasses change how and what we see. These limits will become more obvious in this chapter, but it's enough for now to simply state that Google hasn't colonized the entire information world—not yet anyway. But as we noted in an earlier chapter, it's a perfectly smart thing to do a bit of "Googling" in finding a speech topic or in researching one. We just don't want you to end there.

8.2 Supporting Material, or Research

If you were to survey a bunch of public speaking textbooks written

Research...Across History! [Flip Learning animation series]
Things sure have changed over the years.

in the past few decades, you'd notice that many include a chapter called "Supporting Material." No, this is not a special freebie in a textbook sponsored by Lowe's or Home Depot. If you're at all like us, the whole DIY thing induces fear, loathing, and feelings of inadequacy. The term "Supporting Material" instead refers to a whole range of research that's literally meant to "support" what we're asking our audiences to do or understand. While we like the "Supporting Material" term because it plays nicely with our extended analogy of the house and its blueprint, it's also a euphemism that we'd rather avoid.

What we're really talking about when we're talking about "Supporting Material" is Research—yes, Research with a capital R. Textbook writers sort of assume that you're scared of it, hence the more friendly name "Supporting Material." But in our present and very wired world, you do it all the time and don't seem the least bit scared of doing it; to your generation the capital R is not the scarlet letter textbook writers perhaps once thought. No, you tend to embrace it—but you just might not call it research.

Using "Research" in Everyday Life

Do you remember the oh-so-interesting person you met at the AKA/APA mixer on Friday, the one your suite-mate introduced you to rather late in the evening? Once you've got his/her name we know where you're likely headed: Twitter, Instagram, Facebook, and all manner of social media to do your "research." Sure, some of your friends, should they find out, might call it "stalking" or "creeping," but let's just call it research; after all, you're doing some homework, right? Right. And potentially very consequential homework at that.

You do research in contexts other than your social life, too. Come to think of it, you do a lot of it. Many of you, perhaps new to your major or university, want to know which classes to take and which profs your peers recommend—and recommend to avoid. There are myriad websites on which you can do such research, but you choose to head over to ratemyprofessors.com. Said site features many if not all of your school's professors, conveniently listed alphabetically; numerical ratings based on a five-point Likert scale across several categories; emoticons representing euphoria (green), mild perturbation (yellow), and downright angry (red); and a comments section (the "hot" tamales are included for those more visually inclined). Such a seemingly scientific set of measures surely will help you take the right class with the right professor. Right?

But you also do research on consumer services–related websites such as Angie's List, a subscriber-supported place for reviews of mechanics, plumbers, roofers, builders, doctors, hair salons, and so forth. Similarly, websites and apps like Yelp give readers a numeric (are you seeing a trend here regarding numbers?) average for bars, restaurants, coffee shops, and a host of other categories. Netflix not only offers its subscribers access to films and television series but also provides weighted averages for reviews; so, too, Amazon. As for "research" sites like Lulu, let's not go there. In brief, we now live in a world where all manner of public services, products, transactions, and even professors get ranked—for better and worse. Even the winners on our favorite television programs are ranked by us, so it's something of a second skin for us at this point.

Beyond goods and services, though, we can also do research on those immediately around us, otherwise known as our neighbors. It's not hard to find out, for example, what your neighbors are consuming by way of public utilities—and what they're paying. You can also quickly find out how much they paid for their house and what they pay in property taxes. Such public records are now online and readily available. We can even find out, in many communities, who the "sexual offenders" and the "sexual predators" are in our area. We get an email alert, for example, when such people move within a certain circumference of our neighborhood. But we can also find this information at many .gov websites. With such immediate access to personal, economic, and criminal data of all kinds, is it any wonder that our collective fear, distrust, and general paranoia have spiked?

The Numbers Don't Lie; or Do They?

We've also noticed a concurrent trend: we tend to uncritically accept much of the "data" that we find online. After all, these data are scientific, right? And we have a collective thing for accumulating data, aggregating numbers, and calling that finding a fact, right? That sociology prof with the 2.6 ranking must be a lousy teacher, right? (And why is it that red-faced, low-ranking profs never get a tamale?) The numbers don't lie; it's just math and some division after all, right? So, too, the poorly rated Indian restaurant on Yelp must serve bad food and have crummy service, right? Similarly, that overweight plumber with way too much "cleavage" but who has three really great reviews on Angie's List must be one of the best in town, right? In our very sped-up and wired world, we want immediate access to data upon which to base our often very complex and consequential decisions— and some of our more inconsequential ones, too.

Property Taxes [Flip Learning chat]

8.3 Conducting Quality Research: Go Deep and Get Closer

But we need to take a hard look at that data to make sure that what seems right at first glance actually is right. This is what we mean when we talk about "research." As you do your research, we encourage you to go deeper and get closer. Huh?

In doing really careful research—and let's remember our ethical obligation to our audience here and always—we want to emphasize two spatial metaphors: depth and proximity. Allow us to elaborate. Perhaps you've heard the expression "you need to drill down further" or "you need to dig much deeper" or "you've just begun to scratch the surface." Each phrase is appealing to our spatial sense of depth—or our lack of it. In non-metaphorical terms we're being told to learn more about a given subject.

As public speakers, we owe it to our listeners to always give them our best. Yes, our best efforts to engage them with our delivery, but just as important, we need to engage them with the best research —the most accurate and the most complete and from the best sources. We realize in saying this that it's a very high ideal—but high ideals should always animate our public speaking ambitions. Think of it this way: you're asking listeners to do or believe something as a result of your speech (reflected in your specific purpose statement). Many, if not all, of your listeners will base those future actions and/or beliefs on the research you've done. Furthermore, if it's inaccurate, misleading, or very incomplete, notice what you've just done: you've led someone, or an entire group, astray. And that's just not cool, especially because the accurate data, the relevant data, the complete data can in most cases be discovered; it just takes a bit of time and patience. It also takes a willingness to find it.

Example: Researching a New Home Purchase

We would model that willingness to go deep and get closer with a very selfish example: the audience is you and the persuasive object is your wallet/purse.

Upon acing your public speaking class, graduating college, getting that great first job, and in many cases relocating, you determine that you'd like to buy a place of your own. As an educated consumer you've heard it said countless times that the investment most likely to return major dividends is a house/condo/apartment—in brief, a place you own and call home. But it can also be a disastrous investment, as the recent real estate meltdown demonstrated. In brief, you want to buy low and sell high—if you ever have to sell.

One of the keys to making a good investment, you deduce, is timing. And so, being a smart researcher, you begin following statistical trends using the National Association of Realtors web portals.[1] You're interested in several statistical measures: median and average prices for both new and existing homes; median and average prices of both new and existing homes from a year ago and the percentages of increase or decrease; rates of foreclosure by region of the country; and perhaps inventories of homes on the market. You also note using a financial source such as the well-respected *Wall Street Journal* or *Bloomberg's Financial News* that interest rates on both thirty- and

---

1 Visit link: https://goo.gl/gMRhKf

fifteen-year residential mortgages are at historic lows.

But you also know the classic real estate maxim that "all real estate is local." That is, it matters little what's happening in the nation overall; what matters is in your very particular region, state, side of town, and neighborhood. Let's say that in your region (the Southeast) all the indices suggest a slight uptick in the residential real estate market over the past year; specifically, new and used home prices are rising slightly, inventories are beginning to shrink, and rates of foreclosure are also decreasing— each of which suggests an improving housing market. You find corroborating data for your state and the metropolitan area in which you want to live. Furthermore, reading your local newspaper and talking with local realtors, you also discover that the same data hold true for the particular neighborhoods in which you're interested. Going one step further and using websites such as Zillow and Trulia, you can see what comparable properties are worth across different neighborhoods.

Let's say you've identified a place you're interested in purchasing, you've agreed with the seller on a price, and financing is in place. But there's one last detail: state regulations require a housing inspection, and so you hire an inspector and said person goes through every nook and cranny with a fine-tooth comb, writes her report, and everything checks out. No water damage, no termites, no structural problems in the foundation—just very minor cosmetic stuff.

What you've just done in this real estate example is to model our ideal researcher. You've done it for purely selfish economic reasons, but that's not the point; you've worked diligently from the global (the view at 30,000 feet) down to the most granular (a home inspection). In the process you've made a decision with the most accurate and most recent data you could find. Does it guarantee a great financial return? Since we don't have full and complete information, no, it doesn't: we simply can't predict the future. But the research we've done is as good as we can do with the facts at hand and provides us the information to make a more informed decision.

Public speaking isn't home purchasing; this we understand. But in another way the process of research is rather identical. Our advice is to drill down as far as you can go in the pursuit of the best and most local information. While we can't guarantee the future value of your house, we can guarantee that your audience and instructor will be most impressed by your ability to dig deep; after all, you're doing it for them and them alone.

Example: Researching Texting and Driving Laws

Let's try a second example of drilling down and getting closer. Recall that topic from Chapter 7 on texting and driving; more specifically, let's say that your newsfeed from your Internet browser (a surface-level bit of information) highlights the rather counterintuitive finding that texting and driving laws appear to be making things worse, not better. This surface-level headline has caught your attention because you've been known to occasionally text and drive.

And so you read more about this study and learn who the authors are and what institution or organization they're affiliated with (The Highway Loss Data Institute).[2] Your interest grows as you read quotations from the study's authors. You note and then highlight with your cursor the trade publication where the study was published and paste it into your search engine of choice. Following our metaphor, you're digging deeper. Much deeper. You next read an abstract of the article, the carefully worded and very compressed summary of the article's findings. And while that summary gives you more information, you want to go deeper and see how the study was performed.

---

[2] Visit link: https://goo.gl/iJVsZ6

Just how did they measure such a complex test of texting behavior? Did they use a self-report instrument? Did they rely on information provided by automobile insurance companies? Police reports? You see where we're going with this: deeper.

> Media Bias [Flip Learning chat]

> Education Statistics [Flip Learning chat]

8.4 Getting Closer with Primary and Secondary Source Materials

Primary Sources Original, first-hand accounts, created at the time of the event	Secondary Sources Second-hand accounts, interpretations or analysis of primary sources
✓ Interviews	✓ Most journal articles
✓ Diaries, letters, journals, or speeches	✓ Most published books
✓ Newspapers from the event/time	✓ Fact books
✓ Government documents or public records	✓ Encyclopedias
✓ Art, maps, photographs, film, and music	✓ Biographies
✓ Artifacts	✓ Textbooks
✓ Original research done through interviews, experiments, observations, or surveys	✓ Other works that interpret and/or discuss primary sources

At this point we need to introduce two technical terms: primary and secondary source materials. The terms are common in historical studies where scholarship often features both types: primary, or sources that originated the historical material in question (government statistics, a speech, a letter, or a diary entry); and secondary, or sources that are reporting or commenting on the primary material. Your newsfeed is a secondary source because it's reporting on a study, while the study itself is a primary source. Let's state this as plainly as possible: your speech instructor prizes the use of primary research materials. Your audience will, too. And we have a hunch that you'll feel mighty empowered, as a speaker, employing primary source material that you've discovered or cultivated.

But are we done with our research? Should we stop at the level of the published trade article on texting and driving? That depends, but for the sake of the example, let's say that after reading the article carefully you're left with several questions—and a careful reading usually will foster lots of good questions; no study answers all of them. A careful reading will also reveal something important on page 1 of many articles: the email and snail mail addresses of the authors. Thus have we arrived at our second spatial metaphor: proximity.

Personal Interviews as Primary Research

Dare we write an email to the authors to ask some questions? Surely they'll blow us off or find us naïve and uninformed; they might even be hostile. While we can't speak for all authors, of course, you'd be surprised how reaching out and "getting close" to authors can be incredibly rewarding. Sometimes email addresses are listed prominently; other times you'll want to go through a "media contacts" link. Not only do authors often appreciate that someone is reading their work and engaging their research, but guess what: advertising the fact that you've emailed, talked to, or perhaps even Skyped with the authors of the study during your speech is going to do wonders for your credibility; literally, the eyes and ears of your listeners are going to be opened by this intimate proximity you've cultivated. None of Google's remarkable algorithms can go this far down and get this close.

Sometimes, though, the expert in question isn't across the country but literally in your own backyard. It's amazing how often we overlook this, but if you're on a college campus, you are surrounded by leaders in a vast array of fields—from the hard sciences to the performing arts. But how would you know this? A quick tour through your university's homepage will rather quickly reveal who these experts are and on what they hold expertise. Here at Florida State, for example, we have Pulitzer Prize winners, Nobel Laureates, and countless other internationally acclaimed experts. Your campus, however big or small, will likely have them, too. Never assume that just because you happen to attend a small regional university or a community college that you don't have remarkably accomplished faculty on your campus. And, approached in the right way, these experts will be happy to talk with you. How best to make that face-to-face interview a productive one? Glad you asked.

Let's assume for the moment that your email correspondence has resulted in a time and a place for an interview (and we recommend an interview never last more than twenty to thirty minutes; folks are busy!) As a conscientious interviewer, you'll want to lay out a few more parameters via email; as with so many things, expectations are crucial to your success. So, let's list a few things to take care of ahead of that interview.

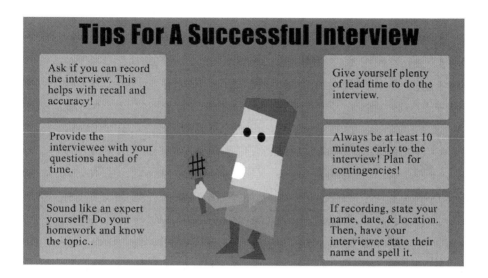

1. Ask if you can record the interview. With so many good options (whether smartphone, laptop, or digital recording device), we encourage you to record the interview for its advantages of recall and accuracy. Always have a fully charged battery and a power cord! And always offer to send a sound file to the interviewee later as nobody likes to be misquoted. And bring a pen or pencil and paper just in case.
2. Provide the interviewee with a sense of what you'd like to ask, perhaps even going so far as giving him or her the questions ahead of time. Experts like to sound like experts, so give them a little assist here (spoiler alert: most interviewees on television know the questions in advance). This also sharpens your reading and preparation.

3. Sound like an expert yourself. That is, know the details of the article/study/issue in question. Nothing impresses like doing your homework, so do it thoroughly and carefully, and don't be bashful about showing it off. Experts dig other experts. Your expertise will also be vital in asking relevant follow-up questions.
4. Give yourself plenty of lead time to do the interview; don't wait until just days before to set it up. Sure, sometimes the last minute is unavoidable because of busy schedules, but always aim for early; this way, if you need to follow up, you have time.
5. And, speaking of early, always, always, *always* be at least ten minutes early to the interview. There's nothing worse than showing up late to your own date, so to speak, so be considerate of other people's time and know how to navigate your way to the agreed-upon place. Assume that parking will be impossible, the elevator won't work, and the main entrance will be closed for renovation. In brief, plan for contingencies!
6. Finally, and if you're recording the interview, state your name, the date, and the location of the interview, then have the interviewee state his or her name and spell it. Documentation is very important even as we often overlook it in the hectic and busy moment.

These six protocols will go a long way toward facilitating a productive session. The same six protocols also hold true, save perhaps number five, for a phone interview. Since it's often hard to meet face-to-face on relatively short notice, phone interviews or even Skype sessions can also be a very productive means to obtain deep and proximate information.

But do you have to go this far? Certainly not, but if you're aiming for excellence, why not go as deep and get as close as is reasonably possible? Why settle for the surface and the secondary when you often have the opportunity to go deep with the primary sources?

At this point we should probably take a step back and inquire about the Big Pink Elephant that just snuck into the room: what are the best primary and secondary sources for doing such high-quality, in-depth research? The answer, as with so many things rhetorical, is: it depends. But let's start with the view at 30,000 feet.

> Significant Digits [Flip Learning chat]

8.5 Stepping Back: An "Aerial View" of Primary Research

Because that view is so expansive, and therefore expensive, the federal government is one of the few, if only, organizations with the ability and resources to do the kind of research that captures this view accurately. One of our favorite sources for such high-altitude work is the federal census, which is conducted every ten years.[3] The massive data sets that come out of this on-the-ground research are truly extraordinary. And if we look across many censuses, we begin to get some very important big-picture looks at where the country is moving—demographically, economically, geographically, and politically among other variables.

Similarly, each branch of the federal government employs a huge staff of researchers to get up-to-the-minute data on its citizens—including, yes, spying data in the efforts to ostensibly thwart terrorism. Think of it this way: if it's potentially important, the federal government is studying it. Measuring it. Modeling it. Keeping an eye on it. Why? So that the country can make informed decisions on whatever it is.

That same federal census gives breakout information for each of the fifty states.[4] So as we descend from the macro and majestic slopes of big data to smaller and more discrete data, we can begin to see how our state fits into the national picture. Does your home state spend more or less on K–12 education than the national average? What are its incarceration rates compared to those of the country or the states next door? What about rates of sexually transmitted disease? Population flows? Housing values? Number of registered voters? Percentage of residents older than sixty-five? Tobacco use?

Descending further, we can also get remarkably detailed data even at the county, city, and municipality levels.[5] Perhaps we should think of the federal government's incredible research apparatus this way: as the ultimate audience analysis assignment. While we're tasked with knowing something about eighteen to twenty-five peo-

---

3   Visit link: https://goo.gl/o1EFPi

4   Visit link: https://goo.gl/KdYWcP

5   Visit link: https://goo.gl/EbyATb

ple in our public speaking class at one moment in time, the federal government wants to know important things about its more than three hundred million residents over time. Whether you find that to be smart public policy planning or too much Big Brother government surveillance, the information is readily available; it's the best that money can buy—and it's your money. So go ahead and use it.

So yes, the federal government and its many branches command our attention for several reasons: its research is very recent; its research is very comprehensive; its research is not hyper-partisan and it tries to be impartial; its research asks lots of good questions that matter; it's free; and it's all fairly easy to access via the Internet. We should add that most of the government's research is presented in a coherent visual manner.

Are the Numbers Always Right? The Case of Colin Powell

But is it always right? We should ask Colin Powell.

During his days in office, Republicans, Democrats, and Independents held the four-star general, Chairman of the Joint Chiefs of Staff, and secretary of state in very high esteem. He was a career-long member of the military from humble and immigrant origins; he served patriotically and with distinction under multiple administrations; and he spoke with a tempered pragmatism. And so when his boss, former President George W. Bush, asked him to make the United States' case against Iraq and its dictator, Saddam

Colin Powell's 2003 speech to the U.N.

Hussein, before the United Nations on February 5, 2003, a skeptical world listened intently. The stakes could not have been much higher: the United States claimed Hussein was hiding chemical, biological, and perhaps even nuclear weapons from United Nations inspection teams. Further, these weapons might be funneled to terrorist organizations such as Al Qaeda, who'd attacked the United States just a year and a half earlier. Instead of airplanes, the next attack might come from the air we breathe.

Powell employed some of the deepest and most proximate evidence in the world: evidence unearthed by the Central Intelligence Agency's high-tech spying efforts and evidence provided by Iraqi dissidents who'd once been involved in the country's weapons programs. Perhaps not surprisingly, Americans were inclined to believe Powell's case—if for no other reason than who was making it. International opinion, on the other hand, was decidedly more skeptical; many claimed that Powell's case wasn't the least bit persuasive.[6]

Not long after the speech, the United States was at war with Iraq—without authorization from the UN. The United States never found the so-called weapons of mass destruction. Why? Because they no longer existed; the CIA and the Iraqi experts had been wrong. The evidence was bad; the research shoddy. Powell had been wrong—and badly. Lives were sacrificed and billions were spent on evidence that simply wasn't true.

But what does Colin Powell's embarrassing and high-stakes failure at the UN have to do with us and public speaking? After all, no lives or massive expenditures are likely riding on our evidence. True enough, but we would highlight the vital disposition at the center of the research endeavor: trust. Because we haven't done the studies ourselves, we simply have to trust others to have done the job

---

6   You can watch that speech here: https://goo.gl/uGZN8X. You can also find a transcript of Powell's address here: https://goo.gl/6UtdtZ.

well. Powell trusted the CIA. We trust the texting and driving study in the Highway Loss Data Institute. Granted, ours (or Powell's) is not a blind trust, but even the most discerning experts have to surrender, at some point, to whether they trust the authors or not.

Library Databases

In addition to the incredible resources of the federal government, you can also take advantage of the many proprietary databases, including ProQuest databases, to which your library likely subscribes. Based on our research, ProQuest databases are on par with the federal government in terms of taking information from the census and packaging it into great statistical summaries. Specifically, ProQuest's "Statistical Abstract of the United States" is a remarkable database of very useful statistical information across thirty-one separate categories. To locate the database simply search for Congressional ProQuest in your library's A–Z listing of databases. If your university subscribes to it, click on the "statistical" link in the lower left-hand corner and you'll quickly be in business.

Filtering Out the Partisan Noise

Let's discuss the term "hyper-partisan" for a moment. In our present age of the 24/7 news cycle, real-time political news, countless blogs, and billions of tweets and status updates whirring constantly, the partisan noise can get really loud. Often we just want to know, what are the facts? Who is right? Who isn't telling us the whole truth? Who is just making stuff up? These are quaint questions for some, but we haven't given up on finding answers to them; we hope you don't either.

Perhaps like us you've gotten the email forward from some crazed relative or friend who is convinced that Politician X is a communist, is not an American citizen, cheats on her husband, is an atheist, has never paid income taxes, spits on babies, burns the American flag at night, and has begun to grow red horns. Yes, we're exaggerating—but, sadly in many cases, not by much. Because we'd like to remain on civil terms with said crazed person, while also trying to educate, we head over to FactCheck.org where we can get accurate answers to our political questions. This award-winning site is run by the Annenberg Center for Public Policy at the University of Pennsylvania. We particularly like the site's "viral spiral" tab to get the latest updates on email threads that often end up in our inbox. Another great fact-checking resource is PolitiFact. The site's "Truth-o-Meter" is often featured on broadcast news to help us adjudicate claims from all sides of a given issue (and while they've had an occasional miss, this is generally a reliable source). You've heard the expression "If it's too good to be true, it probably is." The reverse also holds true: "If it's too bad to be true, it probably isn't either." Word.

There are many other fact-checking websites, including one of our favorites, Snopes.com. In our very congested, noisy, and partisan public sphere, such websites serve a vital democratic function; we encourage you to take advantage of them as you do your research. Alas, we also understand that your fact-checked email reply to the be-crazed will likely be met with something along the lines of "That's just a communist front organization financed by Bill Gates and George Soros," but keep trying; they're worth saving.

Go Local

In addition to information gathered by the federal government, institutional experts, proprietary databases like ProQuest, and fact checking done by universities and newspapers, we recommend several additional sources for credible information. In keeping with our counsel from other chapters, go local and consult your local or even campus newspaper. If a problem or event involving a particular person or issue is taking place or has taken place in your community, how is the newspaper and/or television website reporting it? Does that reporter still write for the paper? If so, drop him a note and see if you can get more specifics since that reporter can likely turn you on to other sources. Sure, it takes more time than a few mouse clicks on Google, but your audience and your instructor will greatly appreciate your efforts to get the best information from the most informed sources.

Befriend a Reference Librarian

We would be remiss at this point if we didn't put in a good word for libraries and librarians. Thus far we've simply assumed that you can go it alone when it comes to how you research a subject. And there's good reason for that: with a decent Internet connection and the right device, you're really good at locating stuff. But it's never a bad idea to enlist a trained professional in your quest to find the best information in the best source materials. If your library is like ours it seems to be more of a chic coffee lounge these days than a place to find research materials. But you won't have to look too hard to find helpful reference librarians. Don't be bashful about using their expertise. We'd have to write an entirely new and lengthy book to detail all the ways in which reference librarians have aided our research. Pop culture has given them a bad name as nerdy folks who are constantly ssshhh'ing hip and talkative patrons, but librarians really function as the beating heart of the research university. Find them. Solicit them. Take their advice. You won't be sorry.

> Mapping the Populace [Flip Learning chat]

8.6 Know Thyself and "Staying Woke"

Despite all these potentially great primary and secondary sources, a lot of research—there's that word again—shows us something terribly important—and a bit depressing—about human nature and the process of finding information and data that support our speech's specific purpose: we almost always favor information and data that support what we already believe. In other words, we let our attitudes, values, and beliefs drive what we seek out and how we evaluate it instead of the other way around. If your grandfather watches a lot of Fox News, there's a good chance it's because its programming confirms what he already believes; we love it, after all, when our deepest beliefs get reinforced by ostensibly credible sources. Similarly, you might have a penchant for listening to your local National Public Radio station because its stories comport with your views of the world.

The sagely Socrates famously admonished his interlocutors to "know thyself." We would add to this Socratic maxim a complementary bit of counsel from his contemporary, the well-respected sophist Protagoras of Abdera, who resembles a furry Matthew McConaughey. If you've heard the aphorism "man is the measure of all things," you've been exposed to Protagorean thinking. But he also had this to say to his public speaking students: "on any given issue there are at least two sides (a weaker and a stronger side) that oppose each other." Known as the two-logoi fragment, sophists taught their students to argue on both sides of an issue in order to master the art of invention—and less to deceive audiences.[7]

We'll be the first to admit that we like finding research that happens to support our point of view on a given topic. But we would

---

[7] For a fine book on Protagoras and his contribution to rhetoric, see Edward Schiappa's *Protagoras and Logos: A Study in Greek Philosophy and Rhetoric*, 2nd ed., (Columbia, SC: University of South Carolina Press, 2003).

do well in our digital age to remember the sage wisdom of Socrates and Protagoras. If you don't "know thyself," if you're hopelessly oblivious to your own biases, you will not be very good at discovering arguments and evidence for the "weaker" side. More to the public speaking point, if you happen to research only the side of the issue with which you happen to agree, you're setting yourself up for potential rhetorical failure.

If you've been reading or watching much news coverage of the aftermath of the 2016 presidential election you've no doubt come across a bunch of stories on "fake news." In our present moment when fake and real news look so much alike, especially online, it's critically important that we stay woke when it comes to sorting out which is which.

Because most of you get your news from online sources, via Facebook, Twitter, Instagram and other social media platforms, it's relatively easy for the fakers/posers/clickbaiters to tempt you; real stories and fake stories actually look and sound very much alike. In a newspaper, fake news rarely if ever happens because editors don't allow it. But on social media, where there's often no editor or filter to help us, lies and distortions and downright phony stuff proliferates.

How can we spot fake news? First, beware of sensationalist content. If a "news" story claims in bold headlines that the 2012 school shooting in Newtown, Connecticut never happened (a story that many believe, sadly) be very wary. The Internet traffics in conspiracy theories, and while some might contain a kernel of truth, most are just that: far-fetched theories. Second, be aware of the URL; does it end with .com.co? If so, you might be on a fake news site. Many borrow from legitimate news sources such as *The Washington Post* by using this little trick: washingtonpost.com.co. Don't fall for it. Third, does the article cite real names from real experts? If the article has lots of unattributed quotes, again, be very suspicious. Like your speech where you'll want to name names to enhance your credibility, so too does good journalism feature attributed quotes from experts. Next, can you click on an "about us" section of the web page? Who are these folks peddling this story? A quick Google search of the name should reveal whether the outfit is legit or janky. Fifth, be on the lookout for "sponsored content." While these stories, again, might look like the real thing, they are ads strategically placed to get your attention—and your clicks. Similarly, many of these fake news sites use doctored images to claim that something happened, when in fact it didn't. One useful way to check on the legitimacy of images is to right click on the photograph in question. You should then see several options, one of which is "Search Google for Image," which is a default setting on the Google Chrome Internet browser.

Perhaps most important of all when it comes to spotting and identifying fake news is to, yes, know thyself. In other words, is the story just too good to be true? Does the story align a little bit too well with your beliefs? I got an object lesson in fake news a few years back when a friend posted on Facebook an "article" that claimed that President Obama was seeking to outlaw certain types of handguns. Having my BS-meter triggered, I went over to Snopes.com and sure enough, the "article" was indeed a fake. I then proceeded to post the Snopes link below her original post and said, "Marsha, this story is a fake"; surely, I thought, this is being a good cyber citizen. Her reply was fascinating: "But wouldn't it be great if it was true?"

In less than 10 words Marsha captured the essence of fake news' rhetorical power: it appeals to our egos, our basic beliefs about how the world should work. Having already decided that President Obama was anti-gun, Marsha was determined to have her belief validated—even if the story wasn't true. Accuracy, in other words, was beside the point. Your great uncle Jethro still believes that the moon landing was a government hoax shot in a Hollywood studio. Right. I can almost guarantee you that Snopes refutations, however factual, won't dent his beliefs.

We saw oodles of fake news stories during the 2016 presidential campaign for a really good reason: it fundamentally appeals to peoples' basic beliefs and yes, prejudices. With some sexy graphics, compelling images and bold headlines, a hardcore right winger has no trouble at all believing that Hillary Clinton killed her former lover, Vince Foster—among others. And then proceeds to share that story with all of her "friends." At this point, sadly, facts are beside the point; we're trying to reinforce our prejudices, however ill-informed.

So yes, know thyself.

Also understand the fundamental ethical terrain you've entered. If during your speech you use a fake source, a phony news story, in the act of attempted persuasion, you're imperiling the beliefs of your listeners. Using sketchy data to influence anyone is an ethical lapse. Our highest ambition should always be to use evidence that has been carefully vetted, critically analyzed, and always sourced. Okay, stepping down from my soapbox, but you see how important sourcing our speeches is. I'm always going to try and persuade my friend Marsha with the best evidence I can find. You work on Uncle Jethro.

Research Opposing Arguments

The best speakers always know in intimate detail the other side's arguments. Protagoras and other sophists trained their students to be able to argue well on any side of an issue—not because they were philosophical nihilists but because they were rhetorical relativists: in a world where we just don't know what tomorrow might bring, public speakers need to be able to argue with great dexterity and to be able to see and understand the strengths and weaknesses of public arguments. Protagoras taught in many places including Ath-

The Bouleuterion in Priene

ens, where in the fifth century BCE direct Democracy held sway: if you were an Athenian citizen, you could vote on public policies; you didn't elect a representative to do it for you. As such, to be able to speak to the large outdoor assembly or to adjudicate evidences among many speakers, you had to be able to parse arguments, understanding premises, assumptions, and unstated conclusions. But if you already had your mind made up, if you were unwilling to listen to the other side, you weren't being a very good citizen.

Similarly, we hope you'll take on something of a patriotic Athenian sensibility when it comes to doing your research. Especially when it comes to your persuasive speech, evidence and research often don't speak with just one voice. What should the United States do about eleven million undocumented illegal immigrants, many of whom have given birth to children here? Should corporations be afforded the same rights as individual citizens? Should the government regulate firearms? If so, which ones and how? Should marijuana be legalized for recreational as well as medical use? These are big and very complex issues and no one side has a monopoly on the answers.

But if as researchers we close our eyes and ears to the other side's research and evidence, we're doing potentially grave damage to our future speech. How? Just to take the most obvious example: how are you going to create a refutative design (see Chapter 7) if you have no other side to refute? Moreover, if you don't acknowledge that there is another side to the issue, you might alienate audience members who don't hold the same position as you do.

So let's get very pragmatic about all this Protagorean talk and political theory: we encourage you to actively seek out research that doesn't agree with your side of the issue. If you're anti–capital punishment and want to give a speech on said topic, that's fine. But what are the pro–capital punishment arguments and how might you refute them? Fortunately in our day and age, it's not hard to find polarized and informed opinions on almost any subject. Uninformed ones, too. But the point is to go and seek them out. Who knows, you might end up—and should be open to— changing your mind, which is one of the functions of good research, right?

8.7 Transforming Research into Supporting Material

You're right: research done well is hard and time-consuming. But the rewards are many—especially when you get to present it to an audience. You're now the expert and there are not many better public speaking experiences than presenting your hard-won research on an important topic before an audience that you're seeking to influence. But all that research doesn't easily translate itself into rhetorically powerful speech material; in fact if we're not careful all that research can confuse an audience. It can also induce a good bit of mouth-breathing, so let's take a close look at this all-important job of translating research into compelling speech material.

Part of the trick of transforming all that good research into good supporting material for your speech is to find patterns or clusters of data and argument. Protagoras's "at least two sides" might actually have three or four sides, and these sides will become apparent once we begin looking for larger patterns. Once you can see the general contours, though, let's move closer; specifically, let's look for several things: statements that summarize research findings; statistics that crystallize the weight of the arguments; and examples that put a human face and story on impersonal data.

Summarizing Research Findings

In summarizing research findings, you can quote directly from the article or you can paraphrase; but in either case you'll want to introduce the summary material by noting the specifics of the study.

For example, you might state, "According to Rosenbaum in a 2017 issue of the *Journal of Pediatric Rehabilitation Medicine*, he found that...." There's a good bit of rhetorical work done in just this brief statement: you specify the author, the date is of recent vintage, and the scholarly source has been duly noted. Again, don't be bashful about advertising your hard work; it will accrue to the persuasiveness of your argument and it will reflect well on your credibility. If you're going to paraphrase Rosenbaum be very careful that you don't overstate his findings. Scholars and scientists are usually pretty skilled at making sure they don't claim more than their evidence supports, so pay careful attention to how findings are phrased. If you're quoting directly, double check your wording to ensure you get the phrasing correct.

Always advertise your hard work in tracking down research. Let's say, for example, that you're going to quote from the interview you conducted with Professor Walters in the psychology department. Rather than simply quoting the professor, be sure to mention the fact that you're getting this vital research from an interview you conducted with him. Letting your audience know that you went to the trouble to secure this interview will go a long way in bolstering whatever case you're making. It also speaks directly to your concern for the esteem in which you hold your listeners. The same holds true for a Skype conversation or an email exchange: such primary sources do an enormous amount of rhetorical work.

Translating Statistics

One of the easiest ways to transform an attentive audience into a prostrated mass of mouth-breathers is to bludgeon them with statistics. Statistics needs to be used with great caution, and they need to be translated. Perhaps you've heard the expression "the numbers speak for themselves." Well, we've yet to meet a number with such expressive powers! All numbers need context to be understood, and part of your job as skilled public speakers is to provide the contextualizing.

Let's say we're doing a speech on sexual assaults and how to prevent them. We first need to demonstrate that there's a problem and we find a credible recent study that reveals that more than 700 such assaults happen every day. That startling number can be further "disaggregated"—or made more rhetorically compelling. For example, we could state, "Every two minutes, a sexual assault happens in the United States, and nearly 50 percent of the victims are under the age of 18, according to Katherine Hull, a spokeswoman for the Rape, Abuse and Incest National Network." The source is duly noted, but just as important is the manner by which the statistic has been made more local, much closer to home. A skilled speaker might take this statistic a step deeper: "During the course of my speech three sexual assaults will take place in the United States—and by the time class is over, that number will exceed the number of us here today." Again, note how we descend from the abstract (700 sexual assaults every day) to the very local.

Large numbers in particular need to be translated because nobody has seen a billion or a trillion dollars. One very effective rhetorical strategy used by conservative groups to highlight how much money our federal government spends is to have a rolling ticker in the background during staged events. The rate at which that ticker turns, calibrated to our yearly debt-to-income ratio, was a masterful ploy in making a visual argument about the enormity of deficit spending. Similarly if you head over to www.census.gov, look at their "Population Clock" in the upper left. Kind of sobering to see the world's population change before our eyes.

Several years ago one of my students at Penn State University delivered a powerful speech on the Jewish Holocaust in which more than six million Jews were systematically murdered by Nazi Germany. He wanted to put a more tangible face on that number of murdered Jews. And so he took to translating that statistic in a most memorable way: he used the local football stadium. That is, most Penn State students were familiar with the massive Beaver Stadium, home to Penn State football, and which then seated 93,000 people. You could hear audible gasps when he did the math for his listeners: Beaver Stadium would need to be emptied and filled more than sixty-four times to reach six million. Nearly twenty years on and we still haven't forgotten that student's remarkable translation of that otherwise person-less statistic.

Using Statistics Ethically

Perhaps you've heard the popular expression "The figures don't lie, but the liars figure." It was a favorite of my engineer grandfather, but it, too, is misleading. Skilled public speakers are never content with just a number; they want to go deeper to understand the full context of the number. Recently in our local newspaper a prominent physicist penned an editorial in support of the Common Core, an effort to replace the state tests of No Child Left Behind for a national standard to grade students. Watch how he strategically parses what appears to be a numerical fact: "Think Florida's bar is already high enough? Think again: Florida says that 51% of its eighth-graders are proficient in math (earning an FCAT [Florida Comprehensive Assessment Test] score of 3 or higher). Massachusetts—the reigning national champion in K–12 achievement—says that 55 percent of its eighth[-]graders are proficient in math." Paul Cottle concludes, "Seems like Florida is doing OK, right?"

If we stopped here, it would be logical to conclude that Florida and Massachusetts aren't too far apart in terms of student proficiency in math, right? Only four percentage points separate the two states, after all. And Floridians might feel really good that they are so close to the number one state, right? Moreover, those blue state liberals up there probably spend a lot more money educating students than "we" do, right?

Watch what Cottle does next: "There is a common yardstick— the National Assessment of Educational Progress, or NAEP. NAEP says that, in 2011, 51 percent of Massachusetts eighth-graders— but only 28 percent of Florida's eighth-graders—were proficient in math."[8] Instead of a four percent gap, we're now at a twenty-three percent gap in math proficiency. Whoa....what just happened!? "That's because Florida's FCAT eighth-grade math proficiency bar is too low." In other words, in comparing the two states, we're actually comparing an apple to an orange, not an apple to an apple. In brief, Massachusetts's math proficiency exams are just plain harder than Florida's. Common Core, by comparison, would measure apples to apples and thus be a more accurate measure of students across states. (Have a look at your own state and how it compares to others.[9])

You see what just happened here: if we don't do our homework on the surface-level statistics, we're going to completely mislead an audience. And even though we haven't done it intentionally, our failure to drill down and understand the critical differences across state

---

8 For Cottle's editorial, see https://goo.gl/aECt1G.

9 Visit link: https://goo.gl/jvn1A8

math tests would send the wrong message to our listeners. And a terribly erroneous one, too, one that might get passed along to others that Florida is doing just fine in educating its middle schoolers. The point is: be skeptical, go deeper, try to find apples-to-apple facts, and always there's Socrates imploring us to Know Thyself.

Finally, and as we've seen in other chapters, the best teachers and the most skilled persuaders typically have the best examples. And these examples have human faces. Better yet if they're human faces with a compelling story. Take, for example, the complex issue of teenaged orphans seeking adoption. A hard sell, right? Not if you have a powerful story and a big medium; have a look.[10] After his story aired on ABC's *Evening News*, fifteen-year-old Davion Only received more than ten thousand inquiries about a possible adoption. Why? Sure the mass medium mattered, but far more important was what he embodied. In brief, he was not an abstraction—adopting orphans—but a fully human and sympathetic young man desperately seeking a home and a family. Similarly, your audience seeks the compelling part that stands for the more abstract whole (synecdoche), whatever your subject. Aristotle famously talked about the persuasive power of speech that "brings before the eyes"; he understood that three-dimensional rhetoric, not two-dimensional abstraction, moved listeners. So as you seek to translate your research into human terms, never forget the power of embodied examples.

Never forget, too, that you have exceptionally powerful research just a few mouse clicks away; moreover, your instructor fully expects you to take advantage of computational muscle and your creative imagination to navigate complex subjects. Google and many other search engines offer us an entry point into the research world, but remember: such portals are but surfaces in a world of great depth

---

10   Visit link: https://goo.gl/2JvxiV

and complexity—a world where "facts" rarely speak for themselves and where "liars" often figure.

Gender Gap [Flip Learning chat]

Chapter 8 Quiz [Flip Learning quiz]

9 Goddesses, Courtship, Persuasion

9.1 Social movements need faces. And voices.

On February 17, 2018, the gun reform movement in the United States got a face, a voice, and even a slogan. Speaking to a large gathering on the steps of the Broward County Courthouse—the seat of local power in her community—18-year-old Emma Gonzalez, a senior at Marjory Stoneman Douglas High School in Parkland, Florida, delivered an impassioned 11-minute speech that quickly went viral.[1] Almost overnight, the self-identifying bisexual daughter of Cuban immigrants went from having almost no followers on Twitter to more than 300,000. At a town-hall meeting hosted by CNN on February 21, Emma was clearly the star of the show. And, if clapping back at

---

1 Visit link: https://goo.gl/i1Sz2n

Emma González speaking at the 2018 March for Our Lives in Washington, D.C.

someone is a measure of their influence and popularity, well, this high school senior is now at the crucible of the always contentious gun control debate in the United States.

Speechmaking, as we know, has consequences—and this speech Emma gave on February 17, just three days after so many of her peers were murdered, catapulted her into the nation's conscience.

Why?

We would do well to note several things about her powerful address. First, the speech is clearly written—and with good reason: with emotions running VERY high, Emma opted to write almost word-for-word what she wanted to say. Smart move. We quit counting the number of times she wipes away the tears from her eyes, but it's in the dozens. Her script allows her to stay on message, to pause, to gather herself as she gains strength as the speech unfolds. She's also confident enough to go off script as the moment invites. So with the nation's cameras rolling, and with emotions extremely raw, Emma Gonzalez stuck to her script.

At an argumentative level, she clearly has one message for her listeners to take home: let the "kids" do it this time; the adults have done nothing but offer the perennial "thoughts and prayers." Further the National Rifle Association, on her account, has bought off the politicians in order to inure them from public opinion. She hopes to change public opinion. We think she (and her peers) did.

The gun debate in the United States seems to invite argument by analogy—a mode of argument that depends on one critical thing: are the two things being compared alike. We've seen them all: gun ownership is like driving a car (cars don't kill people, drivers do); gun ownership is like a pencil (pencils don't write bad essays, people do); other countries don't have mass shootings like the United States does. The list of analogies grows ever longer, and Emma invokes several countries that have very strict gun laws and far fewer mass shootings than the United States. Her unstated premise is that our country is analogous to those countries, and therefore mass shootings would decrease with stricter gun laws.

Re-framing is a critical resource for any policy speaker, and she makes skilled use of it at the 6:00 minute mark when engaging the issue of mental health. The NRA, among many pro-gun groups, likes to argue that mass shootings are often a function of one thing: a mentally ill person having access to guns. In other words, guns aren't the problem in such a scenario but the inability to prevent certain people from obtaining them. But Emma carefully reframes the issue from mental health to a wide range of culpable actors, transitioning eventually to the NRA, whose money funds many politicians. The loudest applause line in the entire speech happens at the 7:15 mark when she calls them out by name.

The speech ends with chorus-like chants of "we call BS," with Emma leading those chants. We would commend her judgment in using the television-friendly "BS" rather than the barnyard term it stands for. First, broadcast AND cable news can show the rousing final minute of her speech to any and all audiences rather than having to edit it out; second, that rhetorical move reflects well on this young person's credibility. In a moment of great drama and emotion, it wouldn't be hard to utter the full expletive. Emma's restraint, her PG-13 sensibility, shows us who's still in control.

Does her powerful address win the gun control day? Of course not. We need to know more about the specific policies she criticizes—from the President's Executive Order to Iowa Senator Chuck Grassley's bill. Are all members of the NRA villains who are indifferent to kids getting shot up? I hope not, since Thanksgiving Dinner at my place could get really awkward. How do we prevent mentally ill people from getting guns? How does a gun seller know if someone is mentally ill? And, by the way, what exactly constitutes a "mental illness." How are the mentally ill flagged before the purchase happens? What about medical privacy laws? We would also do well to educate ourselves on guns and ammunition and accessories of all sorts—from semi-automatic and fully automatic weapons to "bump" stocks, hollow point bullets and high capacity magazines. And always there's the 2nd Amendment...what has the Supreme Court said in its 2008 *Heller* decision? What is a well-regulated militia? What of muskets vs. AR-15s?

The country is now having this conversation. Emma Gonzalez's powerful rhetoric is helping to drive that conversation. We would do well to engage her and her eloquent peers who have lived through this traumatic and defining moment.

9.2 The "Persuasion Economy"

You and I live in a persuasion economy. Sure, we've often heard that we live in an "information economy," but we beg to differ: we make economic decisions based largely on someone's efforts at persuasion. Whether it's the advertising campaign featuring near-naked models erotically munching cheeseburgers in slow motion set to a beat or

Episode 9: Head in the Clouds [Flip Learning video series]
When the subject turns to logic, Calvin suddenly becomes a model student. But at what cost?

a good friend encouraging us to attend a film at the local cineplex, that hum you hear in our economy is the sound of persuasion.

But economics is just one important part of our larger culture's infatuation with all things persuasive. How did you get that improbable date? Yup, persuasion. How did you end up in that exceptional professor's already full class? Yup, persuasion. How did you get that job with ESPN? Yup, persuasion. How did you become a parishioner at St. Paul AME? Yup, more persuasion. And last but certainly not least, how did you end up at your present university? Yeah, lots of persuasion.

Know that our world, peopled by persuasion, is not that unique: our intellectual forebears in ancient Athens were so enthralled with the mysteries and importance of

Pompeiian fresco of Peitho (left)

Goddesses, Courtship, Persuasion   221

persuasion that they created a goddess in its honor: Peitho. She was dedicated as a civic divinity associated with persuasion in the legislative and judicial areas. Just as interesting, she was also often seen in the intimate circle of Aphrodite, the goddess of love, beauty, and procreation. Makes sense, no? Just as an inspired orator can put us under her spell, so can inspired beauty put us under its many charms. In fact, the great rhetorical theorist Kenneth Burke would much later understand the rhetorical art as one of "courtship."[2]

Persuasion vs. Force

Theorists from many disciplines and from The Beginning have studied persuasion; that study is still going strong today. We have a hunch that the many mysteries of persuasion will be studied for as long as enlightened humans walk the planet. Why? For one simple reason: persuasion's opposite is force—the use of physical and other material means to coerce agreement. None of us wants to live in a world where force is our go-to persuader; no, we'd like to live in a world where persuasion gets accomplished through less insidious methods. Reason, argument, negotiation, give-and-take, full disclosure, weighing evidence—these methods represent a world in which persuasion is indeed elevated to a lofty ideal—to a goddess in Athens, Lady Liberty in the United States.

In other words, persuasion is very dangerous to a world of static truth, one leader, rampant militarism, and smothering fear. It's hardly surprising that my good friend Ilya, who grew up in what was then the Soviet Union, never took a course in persuasive public speaking; that would've been far too dangerous in his closed world

---

[2] R. G. A. Buxton, *Persuasion in Greek Tragedy: A Study of Peitho* (Cambridge, UK: Cambridge University Press, 2010); Kenneth Burke, *A Rhetoric of Motives* (Berkeley, CA: University of California Press, 1969).

of authority and obedience. Similarly, Athens's arch rival back in the fifth and fourth centuries BCE, Sparta, didn't much value the rhetorical arts. No, the military barracks and gym, not the rostrum and assemblies, were favored by the fierce long-haired warriors of Laconia—the root term for our English "laconic," or terse in speech. If you've seen the film *300*, you might remember that our heroic warrior, King Leonidas, wasn't having too many verbal battles about how to defeat the dreaded Persians and Xerxes. No, it was all commands, obedience, and lots and lots of abs.

One of the very first extended treatments of persuasion and rhetoric was presented in the Athenian theater in 423 BCE. That play, "The Clouds," by comic playwright Aristophanes, features the dangers of teaching persuasion to a population of free people. While the play occasionally revels in the low comedy of flatulence and feces, Aristophanes understood clearly that arguments learned by free citizens of Athens were going to shake things up. A lot. Let's just say the comedic drama doesn't end well (spoiler alert) when Socrates' school is burned to the ground.[3] So much for reasoned speech in the supposed cradle of democracy.

Scene from Aristophanes's comedy, *The Clouds*

A bit closer to home, can you recall that loud argument you had with your folks when you wanted to go out with good friends your sophomore year of high school, and you kept pleading for a reason why you couldn't go? The answer, at least in my house, was "just because." Authoritarian, yes—and anti-rhetorical, too! I can still hear myself plead-

---

3   Aristophanes, *Lysistrata/The Acharnians/The Clouds*, transl. by Alan H. Sommerstein (New York: Penguin, 1973), 112-74.

Goddesses, Courtship, Persuasion   223

ing, "What do you mean, 'just because'??"

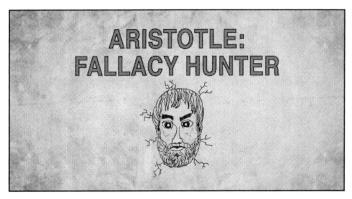

The Fallacy Hunter [Flip Learning animation series]
Aristotle simply will not tolerate bad logic.

9.3 Defining Persuasion

In this chapter our aim is to take some of the wisdom gleaned from the behavioral social scientists, as well as from the ancient and more modern humanists, to help inform your abilities as would-be persuaders. As a persuasive speaker you can navigate with great dexterity our information economy; you might have a bit of success in other areas as well. But we would also remind you that the preceding eight chapters are full of persuasive counsel, not just this one chapter labeled "persuasion." After all, topics like research, organization, delivery, style, and audience analysis all have one aim: to influence listeners in order to fulfill your specific purpose statement. So please know that our aim in public speaking is always to influence listeners in a preferred manner.

Note that we used the term "influence" in the preceding sentence; we like it because it captures more of the subtlety that occurs in many rhetorical acts. Stated differently, the word "persuasion" can be a bit daunting. Why? Because often when we hear the word we think that we have to change somebody's mind; in other words, our would-be persuadee has to do a complete 180 when it comes to our aim. And that, as we all know, can be very intimidating. When a good friend wants to do x, and we're trying to persuade them to do y, persuasion is usually very trying. Often futile.

But if we tinker a bit with our definition of persuasion, we begin to see that it's far more nuanced— and less daunting. Here's our preferred definition: a verbal and/or nonverbal process in which attitudes, values, and beliefs are formed, reformed, or reinforced.

Sure, we know that the speaker who looks like he just came out of the swamps after a month of noodling or a seventy-two-hour *Breaking Bad* bender isn't going to be very persuasive. And we also know from Chapter 6 that a well-timed silence can do remarkable rhetorical things. But let's also look carefully at those three closing terms: form, reform, and reinforce.

Reforming Attitudes, Values, and Beliefs

To "reform" someone is to engage in the sort of persuasion that we've already described: it means to change someone's mind, and this is by far the hardest sort of persuasion.

Why? Simply because people have egos and those egos have committed to a belief or course of action. Even trying to persuade a friend to accompany you to Starbucks instead of working out can be a major undertaking. Now try persuading that same person that their view on capital punishment needs reforming! Or gun control. Or Holy Communion. Or global warming. You see where we're going with this: asking a person to change his or her mind about something near and dear, big and complex, in a six- or seven-minute speech is going to be very hard. Depending on the topic, it can also be very insulting: trying to persuade an audience to become an atheist in seven minutes is likely to backfire, injuring that all-important and fragile thing we call ethos, or your expertise and character. No, we have to be more realistic about our persuasive ambitions.

Here's an idea: if you'd like to engage a hot-button topic such as capital punishment, where it seems mandatory to have a strong opinion one way or another, perhaps the better rhetorical strategy is to simply request a hearing from your listeners. Asking for a hearing, amid the very loud cultural shouting on controversial subjects, respects your audience's beliefs, even as it asks them to reconsider the evidence upon which those beliefs are held.

Let's say, for example, that a quick survey of your classmates reveals that fourteen out of eighteen believe that capital punishment should remain legal; furthermore, most of them hold that opinion very strongly. As a realist you quickly conclude that a specific purpose statement aimed at reforming these beliefs will likely be impossible. How about this specific purpose instead: to persuade my audience to consider new evidence that reveals problems with capital punishment.

The new evidence will likely take the form of DNA testing, which has exonerated scores of prisoners sentenced to death for murders they in fact didn't commit; it might also include evidence of race as well as class.

As a dedicated reformer, you might also consider "nibbling away" at the very large category called capital punishment. How so? A careful reading of the recent literature reveals that DNA is in the news but so is mental ability. Why is it ethical and legal for certain states to execute a low-medium IQ inmate but not a low IQ one? A few points on a test determine life or death? The point is many big, loud, controversial, and entrenched subjects are best approached from the edges rather than straight on. Persuasion researchers call this general strategy the "Foot-in-the-Door" approach in which a slightly open door can lead to a more fully open one. Many lawmakers, for example, realize that the U.S. Supreme Court won't be over-

"Foot-in-the-Door" Approach

turning *Roe v. Wade* anytime soon. As such, they're nibbling at the edges of abortion rights through laws involving licensing of abortion clinics, doctor staffing at hospitals, and the length of pregnancies. Very important acts of persuasion often work incrementally rather than all at once. If you've changed (reformed) your mind about an important public issue, maybe even a private one, we're guessing that it happened slowly and over time rather than in a dramatic conversion where lightning struck and you suddenly saw the light. The Supernatural might work in this spectacular persuasive manner but we mere mortals tend to be much more plodding.

Reinforcing and Forming Attitudes, Values, and Beliefs

Let's take a look at our two other terms. Often when we're asked to take a survey we'll see a numerical scale; on one end are the terms "strongly disagree" and "disagree" and on the other end are "strongly agree" and "agree." What this scaled instrument suggests is that we have intensities of agreement or disagreement; our attitudes, values, and beliefs exist on a continuum of low to high. Perhaps you are very intense when it comes to animal rights: you think we should absolutely outlaw shelters whose policy is to euthanize unadopted animals. But on many other topics your intensity isn't nearly as strong. For example, you might know something about high-capacity ammunition clips for assault rifles and that gun control advocates want them banned. You tend to agree, but you aren't an expert and therefore you want to hear more. In a word, there's room for persua-

sion; you can be nudged into the "strongly agree" camp. This type of persuasion is called reinforcing, and while still a challenge, it's usually much less daunting than reforming a person's existing attitudes, values, or beliefs.

What about "forming"? This term in our definition refers to the fact that oftentimes we don't have an opinion about a given subject. Why? Perhaps because it's a brand-new issue, or we simply haven't heard about it before. This isn't to suggest that the topic is obscure or unimportant; it's just that the world is a dynamic place and things change. Almost daily, for example, the scientific world poses new issues and challenges for us. Whether it's end-of-life care, new pharmaceuticals, new therapies and diseases, or even new benchmarks for what is "normal," the medical sciences are always evolving. One of the most important issues that states are now debating, for example, is "Right-to-Die" legislation. Should other states adopt Oregon's example and allow its citizens to end life on their own terms? Another new and fascinating scientific subject is called Epigenesis, or the study of how historical traumas can actually be passed along genetically to offspring. Whether it's a traumatic event like the Holocaust, the genocide of the Killing Fields in Cambodia, or the Middle Passage and slavery, such trauma, new research suggests, can actually be encoded in one's DNA—and inherited. Fields as diverse as foreign policy and education policy are also dynamic. Do you think every high school student in the United States should have to successfully complete the Common Core? What about standardized testing to measure academic competencies? Should the United States really be negotiating with state sponsors of terrorism such as Iran and North Korea? Public opinion on these subjects is in flux precisely because situations change; new knowledge is obtained; and new arguments are advanced. But you also have new and important issues right at home on your campus and in your community; we don't have to jet around the world to encounter such topics.

We encourage our students to look carefully at "new" subjects, or subjects that have recently engendered local, regional, national, and even international debate. Why? Not simply because they happen to be the most recent thing to hit our newsfeed. Our first sources of information on a new subject tend to have relatively more persuasive force. Makes sense, right? If we don't have a clue about something, that first person who makes a persuasive case isn't yet competing with other voices; we don't yet know the second side, to invoke the great Sophist Protagoras. Little wonder that there's a perennial race for products to be "first to market." That first smartphone, that first wireless speaker, that first solar-powered gadget—sure, being new has enormous persuasive as well as monetary advantages. We also have a thing for new pop stars, new politicians, new sports stars, and always new films and television series.

But one note of caution when it comes to "forming": relatively new subjects have inherent risks precisely because they are new, and, as such, they don't often come with a large body of research and supporting materials. Telling your audience as much is a perfectly fine thing to do; after all, we like candor, even if it's candor that tempers our optimism.

So as you can see, persuasion, the study of how influence

works, isn't simply converting a no to a yes, a vote for x to a vote for y, a like to a dislike, an agnostic to a Catholic; it also embodies forming and reinforcing. One thing persuasion is not, though, is a science. And we think that's a good thing since a science of persuasion would mean that you and I, as audience members, are simply mindless bots whose buttons can be strategically pushed whenever and wherever a persuader desires. One of the constants in persuasion-themed textbooks, in fact, is that there are few constants when it comes to how to influence others.

Topics for Persuasive Speaking

To summarize, then, what sorts of topics make for compelling persuasive speeches? Over many years of working with students on this very question, we decided to create a flow chart that captures some of our thinking on the matter. Take a look.

You can easily discern my biases about persuasive speech topics; they should be: recent, important to you and your listeners, challenging, amenable to action, and conducive to the assignment. But, you might ask, that's fine and all, but where do I FIND these topics? Again, current events provide a great place to start, but we'd also encourage you to head on over to your state legislature's web pages.

Come again...

Yeah, one of the absolute best places to find compelling persuasive speech topics is in the legislative assemblies of your home or adopted state. Here in Florida, for example, we annually have hundreds of bills up for debate in our House and Senate. One that generated a great deal of buzz on our campus in 2015 and 2016 was known as the campus carry bill—a law that would've allowed concealed carry permit holders to carry handguns on campus. As you might imagine,

Flow Chart Advice for Choosing a Persuasive Speech Topic

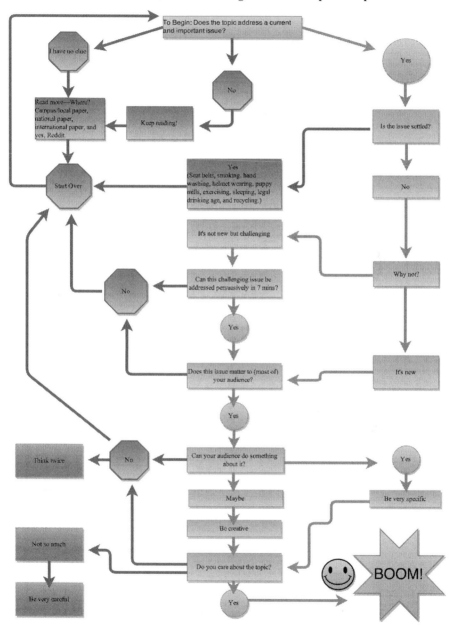

such a bill engendered very intense debate. But beyond the specifics of that proposed piece of legislation, note how it fits nicely with our flow chart: it's new (very), it matters (a lot), we can do something about it (lobbying), and we can do a 7-minute speech on either side. We'd encourage you to take a careful look at proposed laws in your state that affect college students. Such proposals are aimed at you and your classmates; as such, they might matter in very important ways. Moreover, navigate the links to find audio and video of debate on the bills; such debate can provide very important context and research for your own speech.

Whatever topic you ultimately choose for your persuasive speech, please note one important disclaimer on our flow chart: it's "advice." You might come up with a great topic and specific purpose using a very different process. That's fine. This flow chart is simply meant as one possibility when it comes to generating ideas for persuasive speeches.

> Hotly Debated Issues [Flip Learning chat]

9.4 Ethos

One of the first thinkers who tried to make a science of persuasion was Aristotle, who famously divided persuasive speech into three components: ethos (credibility), pathos (emotional appeals), and logos (logical appeals). While he might have had the first formalized word on speechmaking and persuasiveness, he certainly hasn't been the last as communication scholars continue to fine-tune our understanding of this complex practice. Let's take a look at each of the three components, or what Aristotle called "artistic" proofs.

Expertise and Credibility

Ethos has been conceptualized to mean two fairly different things: expertise and trustworthiness. The former refers to our perceived knowledge on a given subject; the latter has to do with character and personal integrity. As you can see, the two don't necessarily go together. Do you know someone who has great expertise but zero trustworthiness? Yeah, we do, too. Or perhaps you know someone who has tremendous personal integrity, someone you'd let protect your wallet but simply has little expertise. If both are valued, though, in the process of persuasive speechmaking, how might we get more of each?

Researchers offer us a good deal of counsel.[4] We know, for example, that our perceived expertise will increase with our experience with the subject, whether through education, occupation, or amount of experience. Let's recall our advice in Chapter 4 for a moment: selecting a topic related to your major, your work experience, or a hobby can jack up your ethos in a jiffy. But don't forget: you have to advertise that expertise to your classmates; at this point, we just don't know you very well.

You'll also want to be very specific when it comes to citing your sources (see Chapter 8). Researchers have consistently found that naming your high-credibility sources explicitly during your speech enhances both perceived expertise and trustworthiness. It's not good enough to say simply that "expert sources confirm that..." No, you'll want to name names and cite journals and periodicals—and don't forget the date: recency matters.

---

4   See, for example, Daniel J. O'Keefe, *Persuasion: Theory & Research*, 2nd ed., (Thousand Oaks, Sage, 2002), Chapter Eight.

Delivery and Credibility

Of course you recall our counsel on delivery (see Chapter 3): practice, practice, and then practice some more—always under "game-day" circumstances if you can find or create them. There are several reasons to do this, one of which is that "vocal nonfluencies" will detract from your perceived expertise. Another way to say this is that when you trip over your words and/or use frequent vocal fillers such "you know," "uhhmmm," and "like," audiences subtract from your expertise—but, interestingly, not your trustworthiness. Perhaps you can recall a recent conversation you had with a good friend about that person's specific expertise. We had one recently with an accomplished sound engineer, and over the course of our entire conversation he didn't miss a beat, so to speak; the words came easily, naturally, almost seeming to pour out of him. His expertise didn't allow for awkward pausing or uncertain fillers. No doubt you've experienced something similar. In brief, then, minimizing those extraneous sounds will go a long way toward adding to your expertise. Please, don't pull a Shane Victorino and have your credibility mocked before the entire world.[5]

Along somewhat similar lines, speech rates do matter in establishing credibility and trustworthiness, but only if they're really slow or really fast. Slow speakers, recently embodied to great rhetorical effect by the hard-shell Comcast couple known as the Slowskys, sound disinterested, bored with their own words—or worse yet, transfixed by their brilliance. Fast speakers—and most of us tend toward the fast rather than the slow when we speak publicly—are simply hard to hear and hard to understand. And when that deadly combination happens, as listeners we reach furtively for the phone

---

5   Visit link: https://goo.gl/zfUQvv

or the inexorable slide toward mouth-breathing occurs.

"Speaking Against Type"

What else have researchers found that adds to your ethos? Here's an interesting one: when a speaker advocates a position contrary to the audience's expectations, both perceived expertise and trustworthiness spike.[6] We might call this finding "speaking against type," or speaking against one's own perceived interests. So when former secretary of state Colin Powell endorsed then senator Barack Obama, that raised eyebrows and added to the former general's already high ethos. Why? Because Powell is a lifelong Republican and he was willing to cross party lines to endorse a Democrat. Similarly, in 2012 when Minnesota Vikings punter Chris Kluwe wrote a scathing (okay, obscene) and very public letter in defense of gay rights and same-sex marriage, his credibility spiked in part because a professional football player violated the expectation that "masculine jocks" would or could articulate a compelling defense of gay rights.[7]

Here's how this might work in your speech class: say you're giving a persuasive speech in which you argue for a ban on assault rifles. Research suggests that if you advertise that you're in fact a member of the National Rifle Association (NRA), your perceived expertise and trustworthiness both increase since the NRA typically opposes any and all gun-control measures. Or let's say that you participate in a varsity sport at your university; furthermore, you deliver a persuasive speech on the need to desegregate athletes on campus: no more special dorms, special labs, special cafeterias, and so forth. You see what's happening here: speaking against one's appar-

---

6   O'Keefe, *Persuasion: Theory & Research*, 187-90.

7   Visit link: https://goo.gl/2YkWjB

ent self-interest, and thus violating audience expectations, can be a powerful rhetorical thing, and we immediately see you in a different and more credible light. Have you ever noticed that politicians love to run against politics in Washington, D.C. (or pick your statehouse)? Sure, this is an attempt to enact the principle that speaking-against-type usually engenders.

"Liking" and Credibility

A final factor we should consider when it comes to understanding ethos involves a perceived relationship between speaker and audience; that is, when audiences like a speaker, that speaker's perceived trustworthiness increases. Note that expertise doesn't increase, but your good feelings about a speaker lead you to trust him, which can lead to all kinds of persuasive effects. But this begs a larger question: what leads you to "like" a speaker, especially someone you don't really know well? We'll let you answer that question.

That all-important variable called "liking" holds potentially enormous cash value when it comes to product endorsement advertising. We see it all day, every day. What in the world does Snoop Dogg know about Chrysler cars?[8] Presumably nothing. Sure, he has former CEO Lee Iacocca lending a persuasive hand, but seriously, Snoop? Former NFL quarterback Peyton Manning also scores very high on the "likable" scale, so he, too, can sell cars, among many other products. The remarkable Williams sisters of professional tennis fame . . . what do they know about smartphones in general and the iPhone in particular? Ashton Kutcher and Nikon cameras? Seriously? And what exactly does Beyoncé know about satellite television providers? That's not the point; research says we like them and therefore trust

---

8   Visit link: https://goo.gl/zfNznE

their judgment when it comes to the products they pitch. Whom do you like and therefore trust when it comes to product endorsements?

But when celebrities fall from favor, you'll also note a corresponding drop-off in commercial endorsements. Anyone seen Tiger Woods in anything but a Nike golf ad of late? Years later and the tag line "Go ahead, be a Tiger" is still cringe-inducing. Anybody hear from Seinfeld's Kramer recently? Is Mel Gibson selling anything other than perhaps anger management seminars? What about Lance Armstrong? Any takers on the next Bill Cosby show?

Advertisers can really strike gold on the ethos front, though, when they combine liking (and thus trustworthiness) with expertise. I don't know that we really value Michael Jordan's expertise on underwear, but when it comes to basketball shoes, his Air Jordans set the standard—even long after his retirement, and after the Crying Jordan meme went viral.[9] When celebrity chef and television star Rachael Ray sells balsamic vinegar or extra virgin olive oil, she speaks with very high ethos, as does much-loved professional golfer Paula Creamer when she sells Bridgestone golf balls. As for The Most Interesting Man in the World, Dos Equis beer has used parody to play up expertise and likability—to great pop culture effect.

However we choose to conceptualize ethos, we should never forget that Aristotle called it "often the controlling factor" when it comes to persuasion.[10] And this caused the learned Macedonian grave concern since it took the focus off of messages and put it onto speakers. We don't need to review recent world history to know that a cult of personality can have devastating consequences—in business, in politics, in religion, almost everywhere we look. For more

---

9   Visit link: https://goo.gl/cF15Q3

10 Aristotle, *On Rhetoric*, transl. by George A. Kennedy (New York: Oxford University Press, 1991).

than two thousand years and counting, perceived expertise, trustworthiness, and likability remain at the very heart of influence in our personality-driven world.

> The "Controlling Factor" [Flip Learning chat]

9.5 Pathos

The middle leg of Aristotle's Holy Trinity of artistic proofs is pathos, or appeals to emotion. From observing Athenians in the Agora and the Assembly, Aristotle witnessed an all-too-common sight: audiences' judgments were swayed by their emotional states. In observing as much, Aristotle certainly didn't discover anything new, but he did see that pathos held dramatic possibilities for the orator. If listeners could be persuaded to take action under the influence of fear, for example, how could that fear be rhetorically created? For Aristotle's fellow teacher, Gorgias, this was part of the "magic" of invention—using these invisible things we call words communicated with sounds to create material realities such as tears, laughter, anguish, and so forth.[11] Magical, indeed. Humbling, too. Why? Well, it doesn't take a Ph.D. in ethics to realize that a speaker's ability to create emotional reactions in listeners can have profound consequences—negative and positive.

---

11 See, for example, Gorgias's *Encomium of Helen*, https://goo.gl/Fm2q1B.

Persuasion and Proximity

Aristotle's great innovation when it came to understanding pathos, though, was in theorizing how emotional reactions can be created. Specifically, Aristotle claimed that proximity in both time and space was absolutely essential to create feelings of anger, fear, happiness, confidence, and many other emotional states.[12] Think about it: when a loved one dies, feelings of sadness can be overwhelming, but over time the intensity of those feelings typically subsides. Or you've had a verbal argument with a roommate and you're very angry; that anger, too, will likely diminish with time. Aristotle's theorizing on emotion is captured in the common colloquialism, "time heals all wounds." The closer in time, the more intense we're likely to feel something and vice versa. And we all know intensely felt emotions alter our judgment—sometimes profoundly and in regrettable ways.

Example: "Shutnik's Gallery"

But what about space? What was Aristotle referring to? Have a look at this video.[13] What you're watching is former President Ronald Reagan's 1982 State of the Union address. At this particular point in a long speech, Reagan singles out Lenny Skutnik, who just days prior had heroically rescued a woman from the icy waters of the Potomac River following an airplane crash. A seemingly simple rhetorical gesture, notice what former President Reagan is doing: he's bringing to life Aristotle on emotion; he's not merely talking about acts of heroism, but that heroic man (and his wife) happens to be in the

---

12   Craig R. Smith, *Rhetoric and Human Consciousness: A History*, 4th ed., (Long Grove, IL: Waveland 2013), 75.

13   Visit link: https://goo.gl/nwoLiu

presidential box with former First Lady Nancy Reagan and is visible to the entire world! Even thirty-plus years removed, you can feel the swelling emotions of pride and patriotism in the House chamber.

So profoundly moving and memorable was the former president's tribute to Lenny Skutnik that every State of the Union address since employs a "Skutnik's gallery," heroes for the world to learn about—but also to see. The rhetorical tactic has even trickled down into statehouses as governors employ the same Aristotelian proof to great effect. We Americans love our heroes and presidents are eager to show them off at opportune moments when the entire nation is watching. Want to see and really feel courage? Sure, don't just talk about it but bring in wounded American veterans who served valiantly in Iraq and Afghanistan.

Example: Boys and Girls Clubs

Let's make Aristotle a bit more practical since most of us won't be delivering State of the Union addresses. As a board member and volunteer with our local Boys and Girls Clubs, I found myself often frustrated by the community's unwillingness to volunteer their time in our clubs. Donations were great but important and lasting changes happened when kids and volunteers interacted face-to-face. But to whatever audience I spoke, whether a large group or even one-to-one, I got lots of nods of enthusiastic approval—but very little participation. Statistics didn't seem to matter. Compelling arguments didn't seem to matter. Personal appeals didn't seem to matter. Even guilt, a most powerful emotion, didn't seem to do it.

But Franklin, Tony, Deon'Shaye, and Ashley did.

Yup, I had an Aristotle epiphany: bring the kids with me to speaking events; let folks see the kids and interact with them; make

Indiana University dance marathon

the Boys and Girls Clubs real, not a rhetorical abstraction. Of course you can guess the results: suddenly audience members started showing up at the clubs; they inquired about Franklin, Tony, Deon'Shaye, and Ashley; and they told their friends about the organization and the kids they'd met. Nothing had changed about my appeal to get involved—except for the presence of four club members, and that changed everything.

There are countless other examples of the persuasive power of proximity. If your university is involved in Dance Marathon, perhaps you know that in those late, late hours when fatigue and delirium have set in, organizers bring in the young children for whom you're dancing and raising money. The emotional intensity of that immediacy has coaxed many a dancer to the finish line.

Using Emotion and Proximity in Your Speeches

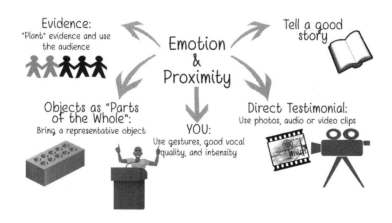

How, though, can we incorporate Aristotle's emphasis on emotion and proximity to our persuasive advantage? There are several possibilities. First, as homo narrans, you know that we all love a good story, and one of the many virtues of storytelling is that an abstraction suddenly takes on immediacy; stories bring to life and before our eyes characters and drama that can have enormous emotional power.

Direct Testimonials

Second, is there a way by which we can see or hear directly from a person in the story? To this day I enjoy putting civil rights movement activists on speaker phone in the middle of class to talk with my students about a key moment, issue, or person. You probably won't want to do this live during a speech, but you can certainly record video and/or audio. That persuasive speech you're delivering on adopting a pet from a local humane society? You're going to get a lot more persuasive if you can show us some pictures and/or video of cats and dogs housed at the shelter awaiting adoption. After all, it's easy to say "no" to text or the verbal, but cute pictures of cuddly (and needy) animals are VERY hard to resist. And as for animals who give hugs . . . automobile maker Nissan scored big with this Super Bowl commercial in 2010 as it tried to figure out how to sell a small electric car to a nation hooked on big gas-guzzling vehicles.[14]

Even though we know Mr. Suburbia Professional would be sushi for Polly Polar Bear in the real world, that's not the point. We feel great empathy for this erstwhile ursine killer because we can see his "bear hug." Funny how the hot-button issue of global warming can be rendered warm and fuzzy with something warm and fuzzy, no?

ABC news and its weekly "Person of the Week" feature em-

---

14   Visit link: https://goo.gl/dGQeWX

ployed the direct testimonial to profound emotional effect in highlighting the death of a young athlete. Aaron's three gifts in the form of organ donations allow his mom to "hear" from her dead son. Months later and we still haven't forgotten this powerful appeal to the cause of organ donation.[15]

Objects as "Parts of the Whole"

Third, think creatively about bringing an object with you that represents something of the larger whole. "How-to" speeches basically require this, but persuasive speeches can be enhanced greatly by seemingly small tokens. For example, I often bring to one lecture in particular a brick; students immediately start inquiring as to why I'm bringing an old, worn-out brick to class. I allow the curiosity to build before revealing well into the lecture that this brick is no ordinary brick; it's a brick from a historically important building, since gone to rubble. The brick functions as a synecdoche even as it brings that larger building right into our little lecture hall. Students are eager to touch it and handle it with great care, as if it's a sacred object—which it's become in a brief amount of time.

Evidence and Audience Adaptation

Fourth, always seek to invent creative ways to "plant" your evidence. As we mentioned in an earlier chapter, evidence that remains merely statistical can seem awfully distant, even boring. But when that same evidence gets embodied by real people in the room listening to your speech, things change —and quickly. Thirty percent takes on a whole new meaning when it gets dramatized through Robert, Ariel,

---

15   Visit link: https://goo.gl/HKrFTG

Emmett, Janine, Caroline, Carlo, and Cindy; things suddenly get a whole lot more immediate and personal when they get embodied. Always take care, though, not to put your fellow students in an awkward situation; explicitly named examples in such cases as students with eating disorders or who have been the victim of sexual abuse can backfire badly.

You, the Agent of Persuasion

Finally, never overlook the most valuable resource for Aristotle's all-important concern with emotion and immediacy: yourself. It's sometimes easy to overlook the fact that the most proximate and immediate thing in a speech is the speaker—her voice, his gestures, her vocal quality, his intensity. Embodying the emotion you seek to foster isn't hard when you have the right topic and make the right preparations. You want righteous anger? Show righteous anger. You want uplifting confidence? Show uplifting confidence. Done well and convincingly, audiences will follow. And so do it well and convincingly—and always do it with a careful eye toward your listeners' best interests; after all, you're affecting their judgment.

> Nearness in Space and Time [Flip Learning chat]

9.6 Logos

The third and final leg of Aristotle's artistic proofs is "logos," or the use of well-reasoned speech to influence listeners. To argue well and with good evidence represented the highest and best form of persuasion for Aristotle and his many students. To this day we still hold up this argumentative ideal as the very heart of good citizenship, the essence of legal and social justice, and all manner of practical decisions that we make on a daily basis. Buzz words such as "critical thinking" and "critical literacy" also lie at the very heart of many universities' educational mission—modern code for Aristotelian logos.

You'll also see reasoned speech paired with its opposite, force, not infrequently. That is, when reasoned speech fails, force, war, fighting, cold wars, and stare downs often happen. In our uniquely American story, the Civil War (1861-1865) was brought about by slavery; it was also brought about by a brutal beating/caning in the sacrosanct High Chamber of reasoned speech: the U.S. Senate. When South Carolina Representative Preston Brooks put a vicious beat-down on Massachusetts Senator, Charles Sumner, the war was on; it just took a few more years to formalize. Reasoned speech has also been known to fail in much lighter contexts—like a college football game. Here's a GIF of an Alabama fan that quickly went viral in which civil discourse has clearly failed between rivals.[16] Launching oneself into hostile scrums, with or without designer boots, is never going to end well.

Furthermore, for Aristotle and for us, we need reasoned speech to, yes, steer clear of hostile scrums, but also help us navigate an uncertain world where countless arguments contend for our assent. Think of it this way: if we lived in a certain world, one where daily life functioned with the predictability of a rising and setting sun, we wouldn't have any decisions to make—since there would be no debate about those decisions. But we don't live in Pyongyang; we live in a complex, unpredictable, and contingent world where arguments vie for our allegiance. So, too, in democratic Athens where public policy needed to be adjudicated by all citizens and where justice had

---

16   Visit link: https://goo.gl/M1ZhZU

to be daily determined in the law courts by jurors.

If you read Book I of *On Rhetoric* carefully you'll note pretty quickly that Aristotle had a serious Greek Jones for reasoned speechmaking, even calling it the "heart" of persuasion.[17] Compared to ethos and pathos, logos represents his ideal. Why? Appeals to credibility and emotion, as we've seen, can easily lead listeners astray—sometimes far astray. We don't need to be hair-splitting logicians to see the logical problem of handsome pirates selling us rum, "death panels" rationing health care, talking dogs selling fill-in-the-blank, "brown" immigrants taking all the jobs and/or behaving lawlessly, or a long-dead man selling us cell phone service. In other words, well-reasoned speechmaking asks for the best from speakers—and the best from listeners; it assumes that each of us is capable of making judgments about often complex arguments advanced by often uncertain evidence. Unlike ethos and pathos, reasoning requires a process—a process that can quickly prove difficult, especially when we're listening to a speech rather than reading (and perhaps re-reading) the written word.

Inductive and Deductive Reasoning

Let's take a look at some building blocks of logos, which Aristotle split into two broad types: inductive and deductive reasoning. Both types of reasoning are constructed with premises, discursive forms that offer a contestable or uncontestable statement. Induction is a form of reasoning in which particular premises add up to general conclusions, whereas in deduction general premises work to more specific conclusions.

Think of inductive reasoning as CSI (Crime Scene Investiga-

---

17   Aristotle, *On Rhetoric*, Book 1.

tion) logic: individual clues lead to other individual clues, which lead eventually to a general conclusion. Pull out any specific evidences, and the trail goes cold. But note, too, that oftentimes to get from one clue to another, deduction (or a generalization) is needed. For example, before there was reliable DNA evidence, serial killer Ted Bundy's victims often had bite marks on their bodies, which were distinguished by a very unusual tooth pattern. Would it be reasonable to conclude that any of his future victims might also have bite marks since biting is an atypical pattern of behavior? Indeed, and that is how several cases, that on the surface seemed unrelated, were connected.

More recently—and also in Florida where we seem to have a thing for the lurid and sensational— young mother Casey Anthony was tried for murdering her infant daughter, Caylee. The prosecution had several bits of evidence, including the fact that Casey was seen at several parties not long after reporting the disappearance of her daughter. Such behavior, they argued, was clearly a sign of guilt since no innocent mother would party after such a devastating loss. You see how deduction works: innocent people don't party in the immediate aftermath of their child's disappearance (general); Casey Anthony is shown in this picture here, here, and here celebrating just days after reporting a disappearance (specific); therefore, Casey Anthony is likely guilty of murder (conclusion).

Similarly, and more infamously, perhaps you remember or have heard about the so-called Trial of the Century involving O. J. Simpson and the 1994 murder of his wife, Nicole Brown Simpson, and Ron Goldman. At a key moment in the trial Simpson's defense attorney, Johnny Cochran, famously declared, "If the gloves don't fit, you must acquit." A memorable phrase to be sure. But look closer and let's see deduction at work. A bloody glove is found at O. J.'s house shortly after the murders, a possible sign of his guilt. But did that glove belong to him? To be the owner of gloves, they must fit your

Ted Bundy, Casey Anthony, and O.J. Simpson (left to right)

hands (general); the gloves didn't fit O. J.'s hand (specific); therefore, the bloody glove didn't belong to O. J. and he's likely innocent.

On a much lighter note, Direct TV has enjoyed a string of successes with its memorable commercials featuring bizarre inductive logic.[18] Watching cable television leads to a host of strange consequences, each of which leads eventually to the need to switch to a satellite provider. Compelling logic? No, Aristotle would likely be horrified, but the attempt at the logical inductive form is certainly memorable.

Aristotle's classic deductive form of reasoning, what he termed a demonstrative syllogism, is one you've likely encountered:

- Major Premise (general):
    All men (A) are mortal (B).

- Minor Premise (specific):
    Socrates (C) is a man (A).

- Conclusion:
    Socrates (C) is mortal (B).

---

18   Visit link: https://goo.gl/k18Fcr

If you've spied out some mathematics here beyond the very old-school sexism, you're not mistaken; the law of transitivity is front and center:

> If A = B, and C = A, then C = B.

Now we don't mean to terrify you with equations; we realize some of you are humanities majors precisely because you fled the horrors of seeing the alphabet intruding into the world of numbers. But in staking out how logic works, Aristotle borrows from the laws of mathematics. Don't fret, though, as most of us use some version of this logic all the time. You sports fans, we've seen you argue like this:

> Major premise:
> Any team can be beaten by any other team.

> Minor premise:
> Team A beat Team B.

> Minor premise:
> "We" beat Team A.

> Conclusion:
> Therefore "we'll" also beat Team B.

You sports fans can also see the problems with this logic since the laws of transitivity don't apply to how well a team plays on any given day and the myriad contingencies of injuries, travel, and so forth. And don't even get us started on the whole "we" business.

In other words—and this is a very crucial "in other words"—Aristotle was also one of the first to admit that we don't live our public lives in a demonstrative syllogism world; sports teams are comprised of fallible human beings not programmable blue cyborgs. No, we live in an uncertain and therefore probable world wherein we need public rhetoric to help us navigate it. Therefore, we're likely to get some stuff wrong—sometimes badly so (thus: Vietnam, *Plessy v. Ferguson*, New Coca-Cola, frosted tips for men, and pick your season of *American Idol*).

This whole conversation about syllogisms, cyborgs, and hair-care products might seem a long way from your public speaking class, so let's get back to argument basics here. At the risk of oversimplifying the critically important area called reasoning, don't overlook what you're doing whenever you deliver a persuasive speech: you're advancing a claim, with evidence, to reach a warranted conclusion—three important things. Just as you'd give a close friend good reasons why she should take Professor X rather than Professor Y for Introduction to Public Speaking, so, too, you'll want to offer good reasons why we should study abroad, how going vegan will benefit our health, why weed/chronic/skunk/nugs/cryp/sticky-icky for recreational purposes should be legalized, why ethanol is an inefficient public investment, why the legal drinking age should be lowered, or how the SAT discriminates along class lines.

All that careful and painstaking research you did needs to speak directly to why your audience should act on your specific purpose statement. And if your evidence/research doesn't speak directly to your claim, well, *South Park* might mock you, just as it did O.J.'s former defense attorney many years ago, with the unforgettable

South Park's parody "Chewbacca Defense" legal strategy

"Chewbacca Defense."[19] Amy Schumer does her own Chewbacca Defense, though with Pudding Pops and cake.[20]

Logos and Your Specific Purpose

Let's linger for a moment over that vegan topic, especially because we have a thing for red meat; this is going to be a tough sell, in other words. Here's a key question: do you want your audience to actually become vegan, or do you want to persuade them that a vegan diet is healthier than a meat-based one? The former is decidedly more challenging since we're talking about taking action rather than altering attitudes. But either way, you have to be very clear about your intent in your specific purpose statement. Many times we've observed that persuasive speeches quickly run off the rails because students aren't clear about what they want their listeners to do as a result of the speech. So be very clear about your intent. Once you've settled on a purpose, what's next? We think you'd be wise to offer up a definition: just what is vegan? It's not vegetarian, nor is it macrobiotic, so be specific (we prefer this one: no vegan food comes from something with eyes).

Now we're ready for those good reasons, but you've got a pesky little issue remaining: you have to be very specific about the phrase "health benefits." Almost all persuasive efforts hinge on the meaning of a key term or phrase, so you're going to want to be very specific here. Let's say your research suggests three such benefits: increased energy, lower incidence of certain cancers, and reduced risks of cardiovascular disease. Each of your three good reasons speaks directly to an important cultural value: the desire for a long and healthy

---

19   Visit link: https://goo.gl/SR3qkR

20   Visit link: https://goo.gl/JAj18t

life. Please note that if you threw in a fourth good reason about the cheaper cost of a vegan diet, you'd be off topic and therefore illogical (Chewbacca) by your own definition.

"Foot in the Door" Strategy

At this point are we done? If you're asking us to become vegan, let's take a cue from the social scientists who study persuasion for a living: let's try the "foot in the door" or incremental approach to changing someone's eating habits since a radical conversion overnight isn't likely. Since you the speaker are presumably vegan, how about a call to action: join me for lunch tomorrow at the Union. Or how about this: try one meal, say breakfast, in the next few days, and then a second, perhaps lunch a few days later. Or ask your audience to consider adding "meatless Mondays" to its calendar. Or pass around some of those awesome kale chips you made. In other words, you're opening the door just a little bit, inviting your listeners to take small steps on the way to what could amount to a very major change in a person's life. It's always wise to remember that when you're trying to persuade, you're intruding—yes, trespassing—on another person's world; do so gently—and always with good reasons.

Shark Tank [Flip Learning chat]

9.7 Five Types of Inference

Let's turn for a moment to the all-important, yet difficult task of judging the quality of our arguments. Even if we aren't making Chewbacca arguments, how do we know whether we're making compelling arguments, ones that are logically valid? Glad you asked. One

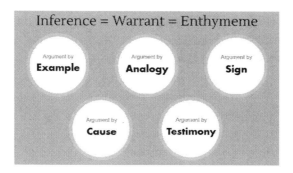

of the country's leading argument theorists, David Zarefsky, helps us make sense of this very important subject.[21] Borrowing from British logician Stephen Toulmin, who in turn borrowed from Aristotle, Zarefsky posits that whenever we make a claim, supported by evidence, we're implicitly arguing that a relationship exists between the claim and evidence; this relationship is what Zarefsky calls an inference (what Toulmin called a warrant and what Aristotle called an enthymeme), and there are five general types of inference: by example, by analogy, by signs, by cause, and by testimony. Let's have a more detailed look at each type.

Argument by Example

When we argue by example, we're implicitly claiming that the specific instance (our example) is typical for the more general claim. In other words, the specific instances are in fact representative of the general. Let's say during your visit to campus as a high school senior you noted that everyone you came in contact with was friendly. You conclude that your university is a friendly place. Is that conclusion warranted? Similarly, you notice that four of your communication

---

21 David Zarefsky, *Public Speaking: Strategies for Success*, 6th ed., (Boston: Allyn and Bacon, 2011), 176-205.

major friends each have gotten jobs upon graduating; therefore you conclude that communication majors will quickly get jobs. A logical conclusion? Zarefsky advises us that whenever we argue by example, be sure to ask these questions: Are there enough examples? Are your examples representative? Are your examples ambiguous?

Argument by Analogy

Second, and for whatever reason, we love to argue by analogy in which we compare two situations, implicitly claiming that the situations are identical or nearly so. Whether the analogy involves gun deaths, the legal drinking age, socialized medicine, or legalizing drugs we often claim something will occur because of an apparently similar situation observed elsewhere. Will the number of deaths caused by handguns really go down in the United States with fewer legal firearms? Japan's experience with such laws suggests that in fact they will. Notice what you're doing here: you're claiming that Japan and the United States are similar. Can we really compare Europe with the United States when it comes to lowering the drinking age and DUI fatalities? Is Denmark analogous to the United States?

If it's not countries and laws, it seems like some loud-mouth politician who doesn't know his or her history is always claiming that an opponent is like Hitler, Stalin, Idi Amin, or pick your genocidal tyrant. In fact, the *Oxford English Dictionary* recently recognized a new phrase, Godwin's Law, which states, "As an online discussion grows longer, the probability of a comparison involving Nazis or Hitler approaches 100%." Similarly, the louder and longer public speeches and debates rage, the more likely someone is to drop the Hitler/Nazi analogy. We would do well to remember that Hitler's evil was sui generis, literally "of its own kind." Sportswriters hard up for news love to gin up controversy and interest by comparing Athlete Y to Athlete X, Team A to Team B, or claim that a talented college shooting guard might be "the next Michael Jordan." The point is: be very careful when comparing like to like. Sometimes situations and people aren't very like at all. Folk wisdom captures our caution well: "be careful when comparing apples to oranges."

Argument by Signs

Next up, the argument by signs, where the presence of one thing stands for the presence of another. Like its cousin, reasoning by analogy, we have a penchant for connecting one sign (often observable) with another (not observable). "What's wrong with Jillian? I saw her crying earlier today." Notice the inference: tears are a sign of something being wrong. Jillian, by the way, might be just fine; her tears were in fact tears of joy. Nations are forever concerned about enemies' troop deployments and artillery movement. Why? Such movements can be signs of impending aggression. Oftentimes we hear during a brutally cold spell, "Well, so much for global warming." In other words, cold temperatures are a sign that the planet is not heating up. When former President Obama appeared to bow before a Saudi leader, some pundits read this as a sign of his (and thus our) weakness.

You and I are adept sign readers; we're forever on the lookout for those telltale indicators: "Dude, she isn't into you; she hasn't looked over here all night." When a Hollywood power couple comes to the same event in separate cars, uh oh: Brad and Angie are having serious problems (yikes, Brad and Angie were!). Or they could've just had scheduling problems with the babysitter. Other signs are more certain: when Angie and previous beau Billy Bob Thornton (seriously?) were practically swallowing each other on the red carpet, yeah, there might be something going on between the two. In any case, whenever we argue by signs we should always carefully interrogate what are the signs of what.

Argument by Cause

Whereas signs stand as something like synonyms for each other, causal inferences implicitly connect an effect to a cause. Going back to our vegan example, notice that we're arguing that changing just one variable (our diets) will cause beneficial health effects. Natural scientists as well as social scientists often argue in a causal manner, trying to isolate variables for their effects. Perhaps you'd like to deliver a speech on the dangers of violent video games to young people. As evidence, you offer up studies that show more aggressive behavior in video game–playing audiences compared to non-video-game-playing audiences. Great, but is gaming the sole "cause" of the relatively more aggressive behavior? You see what we're driving at: we have to be cautious when attributing causes to certain effects and vice versa. Sometimes seeing a black cat and experiencing bad luck is mere coincidence.

Conservative commentator Jack Posobiec invited a pretty hilarious tweet-storm after he tweeted out the following: "There's never been a terrorist attack at a Nascar race. Nascar fans are all armed. Draw your own conclusion." Posobiec, as many very quickly noted, was making a really bad causal inference: that the presence of guns deters terrorists and terrorism. Have a look at some of the really funny responses.[22]

Argument by Testimony

Speaking of scientists, fifth on the inference list is argument by testimony, wherein we borrow from the expertise (yes, ethos) of others to help make our persuasive case. Advocates of certain causes often

---

22   Visit link: https://goo.gl/Ad9cVn

marshal experts to their case for them—whether the expert happens to be an economist, an historian, or a chemist. Often during presidential campaigns, candidates will argue that X "number of economists claim that my plan will reduce the national debt." Even better (per our earlier argument about expectations) if those same economists are non-partisan or even from the "other" political party.

Expertise, though, can be a bit slippery: is a former three-star general the best person to be advocating for more defense spending? After all, they work in the defense industry, right? How many times have we seen Sean Penn trying to save the world? Terrific actor, and well intended, but what does he know about the politics of Haiti or the logistics of disaster assistance? Experts can also be wrong—very wrong. Remember our example about the CIA and the Iraq War? We might also ask former presidential candidate Mitt Romney about his expert team of well-paid pollsters who had him winning rather convincingly in 2012—even late on election night.

Each of the foregoing five types of reasoning suggest one thing: we need to proceed cautiously when it comes to connecting our claims and evidence. Even reasoning that looks compelling on the surface can turn out to be suspect or even—gasp!—wrong. But even when we proceed with caution, we can sometimes still get it wrong. Why? Because the world is an unpredictable place and nobody has all of the evidence. But in helping you become better debaters and logicians, we also want you to be aware of several fallacies—bad arguments—that many folks from all walks of public life make. For you more visual learners, we have included a link to Ali Almossawi's *An Illustrated Book of Bad Arguments*.[23] There's also a great compilation of fallacies here.[24]

---

23   Visit link: https://goo.gl/wvCHnv

24   Visit link: https://goo.gl/zQrnQF

The world of logos, the world of argument, reasoning, and debate, is great fun even as it's also very challenging. Inferential chains of reasoning, unstated premises, unspoken inferences, and leaps in logic are at the very heart of our technological, legal, political, theological, and even personal worlds. What sets us apart from other animals, so says Aristotle, is our ability to reason, to abstract, and to theorize. Unlike Chewbacca, we symbol-using animals will continue in our quest for the logos, even as we'll inevitably make mistakes along its many paths.

Storytelling and Persuasion

We should close this chapter on influence by discussing a type of speechmaking on which Aristotle had little to say: storytelling. The griot, the raconteur, the stand-up comedian, the really good attorney, that amazing history teacher, that captivating imam/priest/rabbi/minister, each relies on a hard-won ability to tell stories; they have a talent that paints vivid and compelling pictures with words. Of course they can tell the story with just the right tone of voice: an inflection here, a pause there, a hand gesture in this direction, a turn of the head in that direction. But their talent is fundamentally about creating a dramatic scene, bringing characters to life, and sequencing key details in just the right way.

As listeners we're addicted to stories, storytelling and storytellers, and it starts when we're children just learning basic sounds and then words. Many of us, in fact, insisted on bed-time storytelling! It's no surprise that the storytellers over at *The Moth* are garnering big and interested audiences for stories of all kinds. We also know that a good story well told can change the world. But how can we change the audience seated right in front of us?

Glad you asked.

Here's what the experts who study what's called "narrative persuasion" have to say about persuasion and storytelling. First, and similar to what we learned about humor in Chapter 3, the story needs to be well integrated with your specific purpose. To tell a story, in other words, just for the story's sake won't lead to influence; in fact, it might do just the opposite. Audiences tend to get immersed most fully in stories that ring true with their lives and experiences (so back to audience analysis, again!). Researchers have also found that the more visual the story, the more persuasive it can be. And here we can once again hook up with our friend, Aristotle, who argued that an ability "to bring before the eyes" of an audience is rhetorically very powerful. In other words, even as we're hearing a story with our ears, we're seeing it with our imagination. Good stories can also be far more memorable than evidence presented in lifeless statistics or character-less data. Finally, persuasion scholars have repeatedly noted a very important detail: it's VERY hard to argue with a well-told story. Our ability to resist a good story, in other words, is negligible. It's not hard to come up with counter arguments, especially on a subject we know a lot about. It's a whole lot more difficult to come up with counter stories, different narratives that can rebut a point of view.[25]

Note, then, where this research leads us: back to the ethics of speechmaking. If indeed we are "suckers for a good story," stories that we'll also tend to remember, know that as a speaker you have a few obligations: if it's historical, tell it accurately, and since stories always stand in for some larger claim, make sure that claim is clearly communicated. And last, let's be clear about the power of a good story: it can easily deflect audience attention away from being

---

25 Helen Bilandzic and Rick Busselle, "Narrative Persuasion," in *The SAGE Handbook of Persuasion*, 2nd ed., eds., James Price Dillard and Lijiang Shen (Thousand Oaks, CA: SAGE, 2013), 200-219.

critical to being unusually receptive. As our sophistic friend Gorgias reminds us, speech does indeed mesmerize—through sounds and stories. While the goddess Peitho was something of a minor deity in Gorgias' Athens, she was decidedly not worshipped by the Athenians' arch rival, Sparta. Peitho remains a force here in twenty-first century America. And we should celebrate that rhetorical vitality, if for no other reason than it privileges a culture of reasoned speech and open debate, not one of brute force, the barracks and authoritarian Truth.

Analogies in Politics [Flip Learning chat]

Chapter 9 Quiz [Flip Learning quiz]

10

Seeing and Believing in a Visual World

10.1 Visual Aids and Crutches

Trust us: we've been there.

You begin the lecture as an audience member with high expectations, good energy and a commitment to really learning the material. But ten minutes into the lecture and the only thing you're engaged with is deep, gimlet-eyed mouth-breathing.

What happened?

PowerPoint happened.

When Eye-Candy Overpowers the Speaker

In an age of high-tech projection, snazzy visual software packages, and an eye toward information exchange efficiency, the public

Episode 10: Please Stand By {Flip Learning video series}
Everyone comes out to Calvin's first art show, where technical difficulties lead to a surprising revelation.

speaker, it seems, is increasingly obsolete. While we're not quite as vehement as Katrin Park, we understand where she's coming from.[1] Instead, as audience members we're left to passively spectate slide after slide, chocked full of information that we're supposed to write down and then regurgitate for the next exam/quiz/assignment. Even the really accomplished user of PowerPoint or Prezi often becomes something of a carni-barker, entertaining us with the next hand-held mouse click as we watch something swoosh-swerve-explode-jiggle-twerk or whistle onto a projected screen. What was once eye-candy has increasingly become eye-gouging.

Now before you start throwing rocks at that high-tech and expensive visual apparatus, we should emphasize that we're not anti-visual. Used intelligently and with careful preparation, visual materials can add enormously to our speeches. Remember that informative speech on the Mountain Pine Beetle? We simply can't do that speech well without at least seeing the furry critter. Or that anatomy lesson we're offering; we can't do it well, either, without seeing what

---

1 Visit link: https://goo.gl/hJkAq3

we're talking about. So, yes, visual aids matter to public speaking.

You Are Your Own Best Visual Aid

But we would also remind you: you are your own best visual aid. Even in our high-tech world.

Come again? Yeah, when you get up in front of your peers never forget that the most important visual information you offer is your own body and appearance. Moreover, when there's a disagreement or contradiction between your body and your words, we almost always believe the body. We can't tell you how many times a speech has crashed and burned because speakers haven't taken a visual inventory of what they looked like. Those unwashed sweats, greasy ball cap, moth-eaten flip flops and oleaginous countenance are communicating vital visual information to your audience. And unless you're trying to make a point about sloppy dress, you're really doing enormous damage to that non-negotiable thing we call character, or ethos. If you can't care enough to care about how you look, your audience is going to be very underwhelmed. In certain contexts, they might even be hostile.

Take, for example, a very important international event that occurred back in 2005. Former Vice President Dick Cheney represented the United States at the 60th anniversary of the liberation of Auschwitz—a Nazi death camp where more than a million Jews were executed during World War II. Held outdoors in southern Poland in the middle of winter, the world's assembled dignitaries dressed the part—except for Cheney. As you can see here, the former Vice President really blew it. As the columnist notes, Cheney "was dressed in the kind of attire one typically wears to operate a snow blower."[2]

Just to be "fair and balanced" about sartorial choices in the executive branch of the federal government, Kim Kardashian was not the first to "break the Internet" over a revealing photograph. No, former President Obama beat Kanye's wife by a few months when he appeared at a summer press conference in 2014. In. A. Light. Tan. Suit.[3] Given the loud and immediate social media outrage over the former president's choice of colors, you would have thought the U.S. just surrendered to North Korea. Many could not abide a sitting president wearing such "informal" colors in the White House briefing room. The former president's team responded by saying it was one of his favorite suits—and that he looked forward to wearing it for the upcoming State of the Union Address! So whether it's Donald Trump's hair or Hillary's pantsuits, we pay very close attention to how our leaders dress when they speak to and for the nation.

Audience Expectations

We don't expect *Downton Abbey* formality when you deliver your speech, but we do have expectations, as does your audience. We want most of all to be taken seriously. A simple question should suffice when it comes to your appearance: does my appearance enhance the message and specific purpose I'm trying to convey?

So if you're giving a speech on golf etiquette, sure, dress like a golfer. If you're giving a speech on how to dress for a job interview, go ahead and dress the part. If you're giving a speech on tourist destinations in your region, fine, look like a tourist. We don't think

---

[2] Robin Givhan, "Dick Cheney, Dressing Down," *Washington Post*, January 28, 2005, C01 (https://goo.gl/rnqEQp).

[3] Visit link: https://goo.gl/5fP4go

you need to head to the Theatre Department to "play the part" with props, but we do want you to be very aware of the many non-verbal messages you're sending. And, yes, be aware of how to use those non-verbals to your advantage.

How to PowerPoint [Flip Learning animation series]
A few tips on how (not) to use a presentation in your speech.

Simplifying with Visuals [Flip Learning chat]

10.2 Visual Aids and Strategic Rhetorical Effect

Let's return to the more traditional themes of visual aids—and how and when to use them for strategic rhetorical effect.

A Note of Caution: Drawing the Eye Away

Researchers have shown us over many years that visual aids, designed well and used well, can do several things: they can increase interest in our speeches; they can boost our credibility; they can make our speeches easier to listen to; and, they can make our speeches far more memorable.[4] In other words, when we can use visual aids, sure, let's use them.

But we would add a note of caution at the outset: for a short speech in your public speaking class, you really don't need a full-blown PowerPoint or Prezi presentation (and your teacher may not allow it). Save these sorts of visual and text-heavy graphic presentations for the business meeting, formal lecture, or detailed public presentation where in fact they are the norm. We should always remember that when we include a visual aid, this functions to move the viewer's attention from us to something else. And we always need to be cautious when doing that. As public speakers in training, we want your audience's attention to be on you, not some inanimate object—however eye-fetching.

New and Widespread Use of Visual Rhetoric

Now back when I was in your seat, when VCRs and Atari Pong were going to change the world and rot our collective minds, our public speaking texts usually had a very brief section on visual aids. Why? Simply because they were typically very cumbersome to use. Cueing up a VCR tape on a massive movable cart with a TV and VCR, cables and long extension cords, etc., between speakers is really torturous. Overhead projectors were heavy and loud and needed special transparencies. Don't even think about setting up a slide projector; that could take weeks. So you can see why emphasis on the visual and public speaking wasn't a major deal a few years back.

---

4   William J. Seiler, "The Effects of Visual Materials on Attitudes, Credibility, and Retention," *Speech Monographs* 38 (1971): 331–34; William J. Seiler, "The Conjunctive Influence of Source Credibility and the Use of Visual Materials on Communicative Effectiveness," *Southern Speech Communication Journal* 37 (1971): 174–85.

Today, though, with our excellent and fairly widespread classroom projection technologies, smart boards, portable computers, easily accessed wi-fi and Bluetooth, and Storage "clouds," the opportunity to be visual rhetoricians has never been better. And guess what? It's only going to improve as the technologies improve and new visual possibilities are created. In the not-too-distant future you'll likely be able to project large images from your smartphone, in 3D, and without a screen.

10.3 Types of Visual Aids

There are many different types of visual aids; they include charts, tables, graphs, maps, photographs, film and video, physical objects, a drawing or sketch, and of course people.

Charts

A chart typically involves arranging words and/or numbers based on a fairly obvious organizing principle; often times those words and numbers are graphically illustrated. On the following page is an example of a color-coded chart involving a Body Mass Index for both men and women.

With the proper projection this graph is fairly straightforward to interpret: the x and y axes progress from lighter to heavier and from shorter to taller; and, the categories also follow a logic from underweight to obese. Note, too, how the yellow reassures while the red suggests a warning:

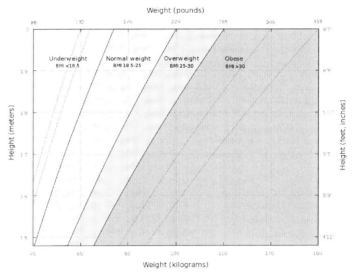

Body Mass Index chart

The "Flowchart"

But there are many types of charts; one of our favorites is the classical "flowchart" which organizes information based typically on directional logic provided by yes and no.

Graphs

A second type of visual aid is a graph, often featuring an x and a y axis, which measures a relationship between the variables represented on those axes. Let's say that in a speech you're giving on education spending, you're interested in showing your listeners what percentage of Americans have high school diplomas, some college education, or at least a Bachelor's degree, and how that's changed over the past 70 years.

From a relatively uneducated populace in 1940, your listeners can readily see (and thus understand) the growth in educational attainment.⁵ And please note the sourcing on the graph, per our discussion in Chapter 8.

The Pie Graph

Of course graphs don't always have to feature variables mapped on an x and y axis; you can always create the ever-popular pie chart, which typically show proportions via proportions and color. Ever wonder how our federal government allocates all of its $4.2 trillion 2017 budget? Well, glad you asked; here it is, represented graphically with this pie.⁶

We particularly like this pie chart for its graphic representation of a common student predicament.⁷ Of course all of you ace public speaking students constitute that thin piece of blueberry pie; this we already know!

Maps

And then there are maps. Wow, are there ever a lot of maps these days. With software sophistication, satellite technologies, and data assembling/tracking functions on the rise, we can represent so many different variables on world maps, national maps, state maps, county maps, even maps down to the municipality level. Come to think of it, we can "see" you at the local watering hole if you enable the right software on your smartphone. Google, of course, has pioneered mapping with its Google Earth applications; suddenly we can see in a few mouse clicks most of the inhabited planet—including the cracks

---

5   Scroll down to Educational Attainment graph: https://goo.gl/JczXbo

6   Visit link to view the 2017 federal budget pie chart: https://goo.gl/CEUVEa

7   View first pie chart image: https://goo.gl/kcDAZd

in your driveway. Unless you're willing to go completely off the grid, you're going to be visible. Check out this map over at metrocosm.com.[8] It tracks immigration to the United States over nearly 200 years of world history.

Mapping the Elections

On the following page, for example, is the national map we saw the morning after the 2016 presidential election; the red states indicate a majority of voters voted for Donald Trump, while the blue states represent a majority of votes for Secretary of State Hillary Clinton.[9]

Interesting map to be sure. We can easily see, even at a glance, that Trump carried a contiguous section of the country from eastern Washington all the way to the Outer Banks of North Carolina. As much as this map might tell us, it also obscures a lot, too. So, let's get a bit more granular if we can, seeing how counties within states voted.

Just taking a quick look at this map, it seems incomprehensible that Hillary Clinton received more than 200 electoral votes—and that she won the popular vote by more nearly three million votes. We should remember, though, what exactly we're looking at: county results, not populations in those counties. If we wanted to drill down further we could, given that election results are in fact tallied by county. What was the vote tally in your home county? How did that change from 2012? Did your red state go blue back in 1996? What about 1984?

---

8   Visit link: https://goo.gl/WmjL17

9   Visit link: https://goo.gl/CJGich

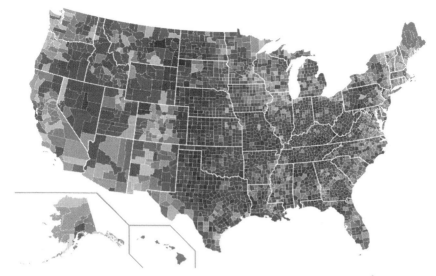

Results by county of the 2016 presidential election

Maps Over Time [Flip Learning chat]

Photographing the Presidency [Flip Learning chat]

10.4 Visuals in a Digital Age

As we noted in Chapter 8, the federal government of the United States keeps remarkably detailed statistics and information on its citizens. Demographers employed by the U. S. Census Bureau continue to innovate in sharing that information with us. Have a look at their very sophisticated data visualization center and see what other possibilities exist as to how to represent factual data.[10] In our digital

---

10   Visit link: https://goo.gl/9DTXhi

world, visually framing data is limited only by your imagination; the hardware, software and information awaits your creativity. And let there be no mistake: compelling visuals can be incredibly persuasive.

To sample from only one advertising campaign, Verizon has leveraged mapping technologies and clever visuals to sell its cell phone services to millions of customers. Here's just one of their ads from a campaign attuned to the rhetorical power of maps.[11]

Using Photographs

Of course there are other visual aids that we could employ in our speeches, ones that don't necessarily rely on new technology. A well-placed (or projected) photograph can be very important, especially if you're perhaps commemorating someone we don't know; we're always curious, it seems, to match a portrait with a biography. If the photograph comes from a website, we'd encourage you to download said image to a flash or hard drive simply because websites don't load at vital moments, the campus wi-fi always goes bad at the wrong time—and sometimes pictures get taken down. In a relatively small, intimate setting you can perhaps get away with an 11 x 14 image; larger crowds and room will of course require much bigger images. If students err, they tend to err on the side of too small. So please be aware that even in confined settings it's hard to see detail.

That mistake can easily be compounded with this one: realizing that some folks in your audience are squinting and/or having trouble seeing your photograph, you do the polite thing: you pass around the photograph so that everyone can see it. Uhhmmmm, you've just, inadvertently, created a potential problem: when your audience should be listening intently to you, instead they're star-

---

[11] Visit link: https://goo.gl/FVoryo

ing at your visual aid. This mistake, of course, can be made with any visual aid, not just a photograph. If an object goes around the room during a speech, same problem: it's very hard to listen well and engage this visual. If you need for your classmates to each see/handle the visual aid/object, please make sure that happens after your speech rather than during it. You simply don't want to compete with their attention, nor do you want to sacrifice the precious time you've been given to speak.

Film and Video

Film and video can definitely make a speech pop, especially if the clip in question is short and speaks directly to the point. Generally speaking, if the clip lasts any more than a minute, it's too long. Ideally it's 20-40 seconds so that we can hear from you. If you can do a dry run with the technology just ahead of your speech, great; the last thing you want to have happen is for the clip not to function and a key (perhaps essential) detail is lost. Remember when we were discussing Bill Clinton and the wrong speech getting loaded into his Teleprompter? He averted a major crisis by virtue of his experience and skills as a speechmaker, but it also shows that even the best technology can fail.

Planning for Contingencies

Here's what we recommend: if you're using technology to assist you with your speech, be able to answer this question in the affirmative: can I still give a good speech without it? Our experience, through a lot of trial and many errors, is that technology will often fail. And it will fail for a number of reasons over which you have absolutely no control. Yeah we know: your alarm didn't go off in your dorm room because the power surged at 4 a.m. You can't know that....until it's too late. Similarly you can't know that the bulb in the projector will go out; the university's servers will freeze or they're scheduled for maintenance; your operating system won't talk or sync with another operating system; the audio refuses to work; the tech responsible for that room has gone home for the day; you can't log on because your login and password on this machine can only be verified with a text and your phone just ran out of juice; somebody just spilled his coffee all over your thumb drive; and on the list goes. Each one has happened to me or somebody I know. I bet you could make this list a lot longer.

10.5 Common Mistakes

Let's move to a different subject since this one gives me night sweats. Keep in mind I'm not trying to talk you out of using a high-tech (or a low-tech) visual aid. We just need always to plan for contingencies. Even when those visuals are working, even when the technology hums like the Enterprise after a Spock tune-up, we should avoid a few common mistakes:

> 1. Don't leave your visual up for too long; use it only for as long as you need it. If you keep that photograph up for the entire speech, guess what: some in your audience will become rather infatuated with it by speech's end. If you want to show your listeners that Mountain Pine Beetle (and you should), and you're speaking in a rather large lecture hall, be careful: if you project him up there behind you for too long it will look like he's about to ingest you for a snack.
>
>> However, if you're going to inform us about how to critique a piece of art, for example, by all means, leave that picture up through your speech so that you can

refer to it as needed.

2. Be careful about becoming enamored with your visual aid: speakers often aren't aware of the fact that they spend a lot of time looking at it. And talking to it. Trust me: it's easy to do and I occasionally still do it. We should be keeping steady eye contact with our listeners, not talking intently to Mr. Beetle.

3. Be very strategic about when in your speech to incorporate a visual aid. The ancient Greeks developed a concept called "*kairos*," or the fitting time or moment in a speech. Build some suspense leading up to revealing your visual; make your listeners curious to see just what it is you're about to share with them. Don't overplay or overstay your welcome, of course, but taking your time in revealing a key visual can function rhetorically to enhance that kairotic moment. Bottom line, use discretion when it comes to when and how long you display visual aids.

> As for what that key visual is, you know our list of "verboten" objects from an earlier chapter. Be very attuned as to what you can and can't bring to your particular campus. And please keep in mind that not everybody in your class will share your enlightened sensibilities about sex toys, Internet porn, hunting knives, feral cats, and so forth. As always, if you have questions about the appropriateness of topics, objects, photographs, and strategies, yes, please consult with your instructor well ahead of time. Some things we just don't want to see.

4. If you're going to project any text during your speech please make sure it's large enough for all to see, and double and triple check the spelling. The last thing you want to do is embarrass yourself with a spelling error or a grammatical gaffe. Leaving the "l" out of "public speaking," as more than one author has done, is just hard to live down!

The Power of Well-Timed and Creative Visuals

To close, then, absolutely: think hard and creatively about the ways in which a visual aid can enhance your speech; some speeches really cry out for it. It's hard, for example, to give a "how to" speech without the essentials right in front of you and your audience. Done well, visuals have a rhetorical power that no words, however eloquently delivered, can match. Is it any wonder, then, that Aristotle praised speakers who could "bring before the eyes" abstract concepts?[12] Nearly 2,400 years ago, he understood that seeing can be believing. Whether or not the sagely Macedonian was also a "Belieber," we know for a fact that he was a True Believer when it came to the power that well-timed and creative visuals can have on audiences.

"Weather Fails" [Flip Learning chat]

Chapter 10 Quiz [Flip Learning quiz]

---

12   Sara Newman, "Aristotle's Notion of 'Bringing-Before-the-Eyes': Its Contributions to Aristotelian and Contemporary Conceptualizations of Metaphor, Style, and Audience," *Rhetorica* 20 (2002): 1– 23.

11 Speaking on Special Occasions

11.1 Speech, Meaningfulness, and Special Occasions

Our lives are punctuated and defined by transformative life events: graduating from high school and college, landing our first "real" job, getting married, formal entries into adulthood such as bar/bat mitzvahs, and Quinceañeras, achievements and awards related to our work or play, and yes, death and dying. You might note that nearly all of these events are often accompanied, even defined, by speechmaking. And while we recognize that you will definitely be giving informative and persuasive speeches throughout your life and in various contexts, perhaps the majority of your speechmaking will take place on these "special occasions." If you've participated in any of the aforementioned events, you understand the power of speech to punctuate that event. A great eulogy, a memorable toast, or an inspiring commencement speech—each often adds critical layers of

Episode 11: So Long [Flip Learning video series]
The semester is over, and the gang all say goodbye in their own ways.

meaning to such life events.

So important are these moments of speech that Aristotle gave them their own genre: what he called epideictic speaking, or speeches of praise and blame. These days we won't do much speechmaking with the sole aim to blame—or throw major shade—but we certainly do a whole lot of speaking to praise. Whether this tendency to praise is the rhetorical equivalent of giving every kid a trophy or just the hallmark of a culture generous with compliments, suffice it to say that we have a large appetite for celebrating and ritual—both of which get enacted and performed in speeches. Think of the most recent Academy Awards, Video Music Awards (VMA), Country Music Awards (CMA), Adult Video News Awards (AVN), or Emmys, for example, and you'll note how we equate accomplishment and success with speechmaking. Giving thanks and doing it well are indeed staples of the genre. Our culture, as with many others, also punctuates the finality of death with speechmaking, as if to speak back to that ultimate void of silence.

In brief, we like our life events and the rituals associated with them to be solemnized, remembered, and understood by public speaking. In this chapter we take up four special occasions: the speech of thanks, a speech of introduction, a wedding toast, and a eulogy. There are, of course, many other forms of address that commemorate and praise—perhaps the most prominent being a commencement speech—but these four represent genres of speechmaking that you are likely to be called upon, sometimes unexpectedly, to deliver. Understanding the dynamics of each occasion and its attendant expectations will help us navigate the important moment with rhetorical finesse; it will also speak to our character in important ways.

Praiseworthy Virtues

So let's think about this for a moment: what does our culture deem worthy of praise? What sorts of accomplishments should we honor with speech? Sure, we realize that American culture in particular can be partial to the superficial: the "hot bod" featured in Take Your Pick of the Day website is beyond ubiquitous as is the pricey swag sported by celebrity X doing over-the-top thing Y.

Perhaps we might borrow from Aristotle's list circa 330 BCE to get us started. His list of the virtues (*kalon*) includes the following, in this order: justice, manly courage, self-control, magnificence, magnanimity, liberality, gentleness, prudence, and wisdom. Furthermore, Aristotle claims that "the greatest virtues are necessarily those most useful to others."[1] Save for gendering courage, (for we know in our enlightened age that neither sex holds a monopoly on the virtues) the list has aged pretty well.

Here's another list of virtues, perhaps more widely recognized than Aristotle's pre-Christian inventory: the famous beatitudes from the *Sermon on the Mount* single out for praise the poor in spirit, the

---

1   Aristotle, *On Rhetoric*, transl. George A. Kennedy (New York: Oxford University Press, 1991), Book one, chapter nine.

meek, those who mourn, those eager for righteousness, the merciful, those pure in heart, peacemakers, and those who are persecuted for the sake of righteousness. While the two lists feature important differences, there are also unmistakable similarities, especially in being kind/generous/just to others.

Other faith and intellectual traditions also have lists of virtues—virtues that can speak eloquently to audiences in the twenty-first century just as they spoke with great meaning to previous generations.

Our "Saints" of Praise

Rosa Parks, Mother Teresa, Nelson Mandela, and Steve Jobs (left to right)

It's also a useful exercise in inventorying virtue to examine closely what and whom we single out for praise among our more recent "saints." When Rosa Parks, mother to the American civil rights movement, passed away in 2005 she was praised for her quiet courage, fr shunning publicity, and for an unstinting thirst for justice. Similarly when Mother Teresa died in 1997, she was lauded for her compassion and care for the world's most needy. Perhaps a more secular saint, South Africa's Nelson Mandela has been praised for his pursuit of peace, forgiveness, and reconciliation and for an otherworldly patience in the face of oppression. With a little bit of rhetorical creativity, we also have room in our pantheon of saints for entrepreneurs and innovators such as Apple's Steve Jobs, who died in 2011. In an ad campaign that might very well have been autobiographical, Apple (with Jobs doing the initial voiceover) memorably praised "the crazy ones" who took a risk and changed the world.[2] Entertainers (Michael Jackson, Heath Ledger, Kurt Cobain, Elliot Smith, Phillip Seymour Hoffman, Prince Rogers Nelson, and David Bowie, among many others) are also commonly singled out by American culture for mass eulogizing.

So yes, even in our postmodern world of irony, excess, fluid identities, cynicism, mash-ups, twerking, tweeting, doxxing, gaslighting, and the Kardashians, we still have room for the virtuous. Perhaps especially in our postmodern age are we nostalgic for the verities of virtue. We think you'll find that speeches that highlight virtue(s) will be received favorably—especially when those virtues belong to people other than the speaker!

Master of Ceremonies [Flip Learning animation series]
The original MC, Gorgias, of Leontini, provides advice on how to bring down the house.

---

2   Visit link: https://goo.gl/kAhouy

> Commencement Address at USC [Flip Learning chat]

> Your Favorite "Special Occasion" Speech [Flip Learning chat]

> David Foster Wallace's Graduation Speech [Flip Learning chat]

11.2 Speeches of Thanks/Acceptance

Which brings us to winning awards and the opportunity for big and loud self-aggrandizement. We'd counsel with one word: don't. The mere fact that you're winning an award—however big or small—calls attention to your achievement and typically doesn't need an exclamation-point-for-self. Frankly we admire award winners who, to borrow a football analogy, look like they've scored a touchdown before and act accordingly. Recall, too, that Muhammad Ali's boasts about being "the greatest" were always stated before the fight; afterward it was all humility and praise for his opponent.

As talented students eager to make your mark on the world, perhaps you will win some honors or awards over the course of your life. And while we're rooting for you to win a lot of them, we're also rooting for you to deliver an excellent speech of thanks.

Podium Preparation

So how should we proceed as we make our way to the podium to receive that trophy/plaque/check/framed object? First things first: if you know you're in the running for an award, don't be so humble that you avoid preparing. Speaking from experience on this one, I can tell you that it's very intimidating to speak even coherently before eight hundred people after receiving a major award without the least bit of foreknowledge. I hadn't been told that I'd won a major service award back in 2007, and so I showed up to the ceremony ready to congratulate another nominee. I was both thrilled and then kind of horrified to see my name on the program that day—and very quickly set about to figure out what to say before a large crowd and with television cameras rolling. Let's just say that it didn't go so well, even for someone who's pretty heavily invested in public speaking!

Once you're at the podium, there are no hard and fast rules about delivering a brief speech of thanks. But we'd note three key elements: brevity, humility, appreciation. If this speech lasts more than a few minutes—unless it's a very formal induction ceremony and speaking expectations are firmly in place—you've spoken for too long. Moreover, if you pull out a carefully typed acceptance speech at the lectern, this might prompt the following thought in your audience: "Can you believe so-and-so was so presumptuous that he typed up his acceptance speech...wow!" Or some such snarky comment. You see what we're driving at here: speeches of thanks should be a bit "underdone." Nobody likes the chest-thumping braggart going multisyllabic and extended metaphor at an awards ceremony.

Speech Themes (a.k.a. "Be Humble")

So here's what we recommend by way of themes: be humble (we love self-deprecating humor, save for our president); recognize and thank the people/committee adjudicating the award (be humble); recognize and thank the person/people/group that nominated you (be humble); and recognize and praise the person/ideal for whom/which the award is given (be humble); and, if appropriate, recognize the people instrumental in helping you accomplish the achievement for which you are being honored (we don't want you to suffer any

awkward post-award regret for failing to thank your significant other). And please smile. We've witnessed many an acceptance speech in which the award winner appeared sullen, bored, or dyspeptic because they simply didn't smile. So go ahead and flash us your gleaming grill; you've just won an award and you're happy about it! Remember what we said back in Chapter 2, that big ole smile—a Duchenne Smile—does a ton of rhetorical work for you and for us.

A favorite acceptance speech was delivered in a remarkably impromptu way by actor Tom Hanks upon receiving the Best Actor Oscar for his role in the moving drama *Philadelphia*. Watch how he graciously thanks many, humbles himself, and still manages to powerfully address those who've died from AIDS, people living as HIV-positive, and gay Americans in an emotion-packed mere three minutes.[3]

Emma Stone accepting the award for Best Actress at the 2017 Oscars

One of the most talked-about speeches of acceptance we've ever heard, one still making the rounds on the sports talk show circuit, involves iconic athlete and pitchman Michael Jordan. Upon his induction into the basketball

---

3   Visit link: https://goo.gl/Gjfaic

284   Public Speaking in the 21st Century

Hall of Fame, Jordan made the appropriate rhetorical gesture in terms of offering thanks, but listen to whom he thanks and for what ends.[4] For an athlete famous for settling scores and seeking out motivation to fuel his own unrivaled excellence (rendered metaphorically as a "log on the fire"), it's hardly a surprise that Jordan tallied up the list for all the world to see and hear. But on your account, does his "Airness" deliver enough humility for this particular occasion?

11.3 Speeches of Introduction

Just because you're not winning the award doesn't mean a speech of introduction isn't important; in fact, we've seen some important occasions largely ruined by speakers who didn't take this rhetorical job seriously enough. By definition, these speeches introduce, but depending on the occasion you might be introducing the next speaker (often the "featured" one), you might be introducing an award's description, you might be announcing a winner, or you might be doing some combination of all three.

There are several important rhetorical moves with a good introduction. First, and recall our earlier emphasis on humility, this event that's about to happen by virtue of your introduction—it's not about you. Think of yourself as the proverbial "wing" woman or man; your job is to help make the event and person really shine. As a reward, if you do it well, you get to bask in the other person's glow. But first things first: make absolutely 100% certain that you know how to pronounce the person's name correctly. You'd be amazed how often this little, but monumentally important, detail gets overlooked—and how terribly embarrassing it is for everybody at the event. The conscientious speaker always double checks with the person she is

---

4   Visit link: https://goo.gl/jEQWFH

introducing to get the pronunciation just right. If you don't think the stakes can be enormous when it comes to pronunciation, just ask the Nike executive who botched Golden State Warrior's point guard, Stephen Curry's name. Curry was being courted by the Oregon-based athletic colossus for a potential 9-figure shoe deal—that's right, 9 figures—when an executive repeatedly called him Steph-on rather than Steph-en. It didn't help any when a PowerPoint presentation, again, intending to persuade Curry to join their team, featured a slide of then-Oklahoma City Thunder star Kevin Durant rather than Curry. Suffice it to say that Curry did NOT sign with Nike.[5]

Seve Ballesteros and Stephen Curry (left to right)

Pratfalls in Pronunciation

The charismatic and immensely talented Spanish golfer Severiano

---

5   Visit link: https://goo.gl/DZdsWE

Ballesteros had a difficult name to pronounce, especially for the non-golfer who didn't know of his many exploits. At an awards event in London, he was introduced as "Ballerina Sevesteros." Seve (Sev-ee), as he was known by his peers, could only laugh at the awful butchering of his name. As you no doubt are aware, some folks have last names that are just plain hard to pronounce, or they have surnames that, on the wrong lips, could sound profane. How do you pronounce, for example, these not uncommon, and very perilous, last names: Boehner, Pusey, and Phuc? Good question…better find out before we get to the speaking dais and better yet, make sure we have a phonetic spelling in our notes so we get it right.

Funnyman David Letterman was sure to generate big laughs whenever he talked about Dick Assman. Similarly, ESPN announcers used to revel in announcing in what place NASCAR driver Dick Trickle finished. Yup, names can be kind of funny, but let's make sure we can pronounce them accurately lest the laugh be on us.

Contextualizing the Speech

Now that we've nailed down the speaker's name, we need to do some contextualizing work; that is, for what purposes is the speaker speaking or the award being given? You'll want to carefully define the event/award and then make the important connection to the speaker/awardee. So, for example, if you're introducing the winner of a civil rights–themed award, tell us first about the award in question and what it honors; then connect the specifics of the award to the winner. Never assume that the audience will simply understand that connection because someone is winning an award. Make the aims of the award and the awardee's achievement explicit. Again, be sure that you have the details right when it comes to the awardee's biography.

Similarly, if you're introducing a speaker at an event, and

not for winning an award, highlight the speaker's credibility and achievements without going too granular. Frankly, we don't need to know a speaker's life story or every item on his résumé. Rather, pick a few important details, perhaps in consultation with the speaker, that function to establish the speaker's bona fides. In addition, if you have a relationship with the speaker, perhaps you might use a bit of your time to tell a revealing anecdote that prepares an artful segue to the speaker/speech/occasion; never forget, regardless of the rhetorical occasion, your audience as homo narrans.

11.4 The Wedding Toast

One of the enduring rhetorical staples of ceremonial speaking involves the wedding toast. While Owen Wilson and Vince Vaughn turned the wedding reception upside down in their film *Wedding Crashers*, an enduring theme of that same event is the speech/toast offered by the maid of honor and the best man. So ritualized has the practice become that to leave it out would somehow compromise the entire event; we need, it seems, spoken validation of this new union by those best positioned to give it. Chances are you might be asked to deliver such a speech for a best friend, a brother or sister, or even a re-marrying mom or dad. Adding to the stakes of this important moment and speech is the fact that nearly all weddings these days are professionally filmed for posterity—to say nothing of the vernacular video that is then quickly uploaded to YouTube, Facebook, and Twitter. Notable wedding toasts are well into six-figure viewings on YouTube, so the rhetorical stakes can be global! What, then, does this important genre require of us?

As with all things public speaking, careful preparation is key. To "wing" this address under the influence of Dom, Jack, Mr. Beam, Tito, OE800 or your spirit of choice will just result in a slurring, embarrassing mess—one that no film editor, regardless of talent and software, can fix. So back to our counsel in Chapter 2 and high communication apprehension: do not avoid preparing, especially when alcohol may be involved! We do not want to see your rhetorical disaster on *Tosh.0*.

Authentic Introductions

Once you have the microphone in hand—and please know that there's a really good chance that said microphone will cut out in mid-speech—you first need to introduce yourself and your relation to the bride and groom. Never forget that this roomful of folks likely won't know who you are, and because of that they don't know your relationship to the couple getting married. Audiences especially love to hear about "first meetings," so you might begin with a story about how you met—and what that meeting foreshadowed about your future friendship. Before you do that, though, be sure to scope out where you're going to be giving this important little speech. Is there a place for some notecards if you need to peek at them? If not, make sure you have clear, brief notes that you can hold in one hand and refer to with ease. And don't be afraid to gesture naturally, even while holding said notes. Writing out the speech word-for-word isn't always the best option, however well done, for most informal receptions; better to go for the key word or phrase outline. Remember that listeners aren't expecting oratorical perfection at this event; they are, though, expecting rhetoric that enacts the authenticity of a warm and enduring friendship. So no worries on perfection; nobody expects it.

Don't Forget the Purpose

You also don't want to forget your purpose: not just to lift a glass but to offer "good reasons" as to why that glass should be lifted enthusiastically; in a word, you're offering your personal stamp of approval on this union. Now there are a lot of different, fun, and creative ways to do this, but here are some suggestions that are as old as the genre. First, this is a splendid occasion for storytelling, particularly stories that go back a ways and how your relationship started, how it grew, and how a new person (the bride or groom) changed that relationship. In brief, and by way of organization, this is an excellent opportunity for imposing a chronological design on what might initially appear to you as scattered anecdotes. Try to avoid the random telling of stories and aim for moving listeners from a past to a present.

Choose Your Stories Wisely

Now what those stories are is your call. Audiences seem to have a penchant for ones that are a bit embarrassing, ones that are unusually revelatory, ones where an emotional bond is revealed, and ones that disclose that love, in word and in deed, binds this couple together. As this suggests, there's a lot of rhetorical work to do in only a handful of minutes (anything longer and people will start looking longingly at their booze and/or watches). Now about those embarrassing or revelatory stories, let's remember that grandma and grandpa might be in the audience; mom and dad will likely be there, too, to say nothing of the attending clergy. So that really hilarious story involving either public nudity, drunk-texting, bodily fluids, posting bail, or all of the above, should probably remain your shared secret. The Greeks called it propriety and the Romans called it decorum, and it is far more decorous of you to shade stories toward the G or PG-13 crowd than the NC-17 or, God forbid, XXX. Don't forget:

you are likely being filmed. And grandmas can be very unforgiving—sometimes downright spiteful when it comes to their brood.

One of the last stories you might tell, one that begins the important transition to the actual toast, involves the couple rather than your relationship to just the groom or the bride. That is, is there a story that captures—think synecdoche here: the part stands for the whole—the unique relationship that you're celebrating? Is there a moment that typifies the changes in both bride and groom made possible by their union? You see what we're driving at: a memorable story helps validate, consecrate, and celebrate in this very public ceremony the vows a couple has just exchanged. "In sickness and in health, for richer and for poorer" is heavy stuff; your speech gives added authority and evidence to that commitment.

Speaking of film and posterity at the wedding reception, here are two really fine examples of a groomsman and a matron of honor doing justice to this important life event.[6]

11.5 The Eulogy

Former President Obama speaking about Sandy Hook

Eulogies, literally good words (eu-logos), have been with us from the beginning it seems. Just as a marriage ceremony and reception represent a beginning performed with speech, so too does death require its own closing ceremony marked by speaking. In fact, one of the earliest surviving

---

6   Visit links: https://goo.gl/CkJUSm & https://goo.gl/Cp9epT

Statues of Pericles and Abraham Lincoln (left to right)

and complete speech texts is Pericles' fifth century BCE funeral speech for Athenian soldiers killed in the ongoing war with Sparta. As recorded by the historian Thucydides, the Athenian general and political leader delivered his immortal funeral oration to commemorate his fallen countrymen and the glory of Athens. Lincoln would do much the same, albeit in a much shorter speech, nearly 2,300 years later at Gettysburg. To this day and into the foreseeable future, Americans remember Pearl Harbor and 9/11 with speeches commemorating the dead even as we rehearse and celebrate what it means to be Americans. Individual deaths, particularly of those deemed too young to die such as Emmett Till, John F. Kennedy, Martin Luther King Jr., Princess Diana, Whitney Houston, and Cory Monteith, cry out for discourse that helps us make sense of the senseless.

As with most things public speaking, though, even death doesn't prescribe a single approach to speechmaking; context and culture matter in very important ways even in the highly ritualized practice of mourning the dead. An Irish wake is not a Mennonite burial service is not a four-hour home-going service at the African Methodist Episcopal church. Different cultures, different religious denominations, and different ethnic groups simply do death and mourning very differently; "sitting Shiva" in Judaism is radically different from the chanting and musical cadences of the black church.

Challenges in Delivery: Raw Emotion

One of the principal challenges in delivering a eulogy is that the moment is typically so fraught with emotion. Whether the death in question was expected or not, whether you're eulogizing a long life well lived or a short life lived recklessly, a number of emotions will likely be present, and perhaps they will be very raw. As such, a manuscript speech may very well be in order. That is, a eulogy presents a fitting moment for a speech that is delivered via the written word rather than being extemporized. This isn't to say that really fine eulogies can't be delivered from a keyword outline or from no outline at all, but we'd encourage you to think hard about delivering such a speech from a manuscript. And remember: you can always go "off script" depending on the rhetorical needs of the moment.

Disguising the "Teleprompter"

Let's talk about that manuscript for a moment. Have you noticed that our presidents usually speak from a very carefully prepared manuscript, especially on important occasions? They usually disguise the fact that they're reading (we generally don't like folks to read to us) by looking left, looking right, and in general looking to most of us as if they're speaking extemporaneously. Often they're not; they're using a teleprompter, a screen that scrolls their speech, word for word. The rhetorical stakes are simply too high for presidents to botch a phrase, give a bumbling answer, or even think off the top of their heads. As a result, presidents become really good fakers at sounding extemporaneous even as they're reading verbatim from a carefully prepared manuscript.

One of the more remarkable televised speech performances involves former president Bill Clinton. Specifically, as he started to speak to the nation live and in prime time on September 22, 1993, on the vital issue of national health insurance, Clinton noticed to his absolute shock and then horror that the wrong speech had been loaded into the teleprompter! Fortunately for the president he had a hard copy of the address at the lectern, but you can still see him doing some pretty well-concealed improvising.[7] You also note that Clinton doesn't sound as if he's reading to the country; rather, he's giving a formal talk that "sounds" extemporaneous. Our guess is that he rehearsed the reading of this important address many times to get the sound just so.

You'll want to do the same if you're delivering a speech from a manuscript. Tripping over words, looking extensively at your manuscript, losing your place—these are just a few of the land mines of delivering a speech in this manner. But those perils are balanced by the fact that a manuscript allows you the opportunity for eloquence, to say something profound and memorable in a stylized manner. Lincoln did not extemporize the Gettysburg Address, nor are many, if any, of those fabulous TED Talks not carefully scripted (and note how the term "Talk" suggests an informality that's just a bit of a fib). So sure, in preparing to deliver a speech with a manuscript you have some unique opportunities, ones of which we hope you take full advantage of.

Pro Tips for Flawless Manuscript Delivery

By way of delivering that manuscript flawlessly, here's what we recommend:

1. Try to find a place to put your manuscript; to have to hold it can distract your audience and can distract you as well.

---

7   Visit link: https://goo.gl/3HrV6X

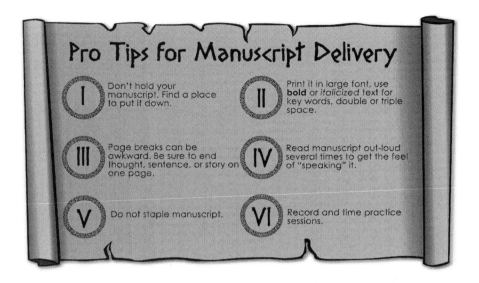

2. When you print out the speech, think seriously about increasing the font size to 14 or even 16, not because you're farsighted but because it makes reading that much easier. Using bold and *italicized* text for key words or points you'd like to emphasize is also a handy trick, and don't be afraid to write in speaking cues (e.g., "pause") to enhance your delivery. And always double or triple space!
3. Page breaks can be awkward when it comes to reading a speech. Be sure to end a sentence, thought, or story on one page and start a new one on the following page. Such page breaks are vital to a seamless delivery.
4. We encourage you not to staple the manuscript. Why? Because you end up with a bunched-up mess by the close of the manuscript and it becomes progressively harder to read it. Simply turn over each completed page and start a new pile. This also prevents you from getting pages mixed up and out of order–one caveat here, just make sure you have your speech pages in order before approaching the

podium.
5. Read the manuscript out loud (at minimum) several times to get the feel for the words and to see where you need to pause. Don't just read the manuscript silently in your head; do the full articulation. Get the feel of "speaking" it. Make edits to get the sound just right.
6. Finally, record and time your practice sessions so that you can hear yourself and hear how the pacing works. Recall that the sound we're aiming for is extemporaneous, not someone badly reading *The Night Before Christmas*. As this suggests, to get that sound sonorous will require no small amount of practice.

Singling Out the Right Attributes

Now that we've got the manuscript delivery preparations sorted out, let's get back to the actual content of that eulogy. By definition those "good words" function as a form of praise, so we need to figure out what attributes we'd like to single out for praise. We encourage you to work inductively in figuring this out; that is, because a eulogy should be radically particular, what stories best embody a particular virtue? Let the stories drive the virtue and not the other way around.

As this suggests, a eulogy is perhaps the most likely genre of speaking for storytelling. And whether those stories are told chronologically, topically, or both, they should cohere around a virtue or set of virtues. Note, though, that these virtues can be VERY broadly defined; we don't have to hew just to Aristotle or to the New Testament to define them for us. Neither one mentions dealing with life's complexities and heartbreak with a sense of humor. Neither one mentions a willingness to listen to a needy friend. Nor does either one praise an ability to tell a friend or family member rather emphatically to "get their stuff together." Virtue, like speechmaking, is particular to a given culture.

Turning Vice into Virtue

Regarding this last "virtue," Aristotle gives his reader several suggestions for turning a potential vice into a virtue: "and when praising one should always take each of the attendant terms in the best sense, for example, one should call an irascible and excitable person 'straightforward' and an arrogant person 'high-minded' and 'imposing.'"[8] Notice what Aristotle is counseling here: if you're having a tough time figuring out what to praise, extend the logic and form a virtuous trait. At a recent close friend's funeral, for example, a husband spoke about his wife of thirty-five years; just the fact that he could give a speech under such sad circumstances was remarkable to us, but what he said had us laughing and thinking about ancient Greek rhetoric. That is, Mickey claimed that his wife was "just a bit of a control freak" and proceeded to provide really funny examples of how that control manifested itself over many years of marriage and raising a family. "Control" in this case was transformed by a loving husband into the virtue of devotion to family.

So was your great-uncle Harold sort of tight with money? Did he get the proverbial "alligator arms" when it came to reaching for his wallet? Or did he simply claim to have, yet again, forgotten his wallet? Well, you can transform "tight" into "exceedingly generous" with what he left behind, right? Similarly, it doesn't take a rhetorical genius to transform "living recklessly" into a "thrill-seeking adventurer," does it? So even a person's "weaknesses" or eccentricities can be made virtuous with careful attention to the magic of invention. We don't think you're lying as much as giving the most favorable

---

8   Aristotle, *On Rhetoric*, Book one, chapter nine.

interpretation possible; and if we can't be generous in death, when can we?

Maintaining the Correct Context

But whether the virtues need a bit of fine-tuning or not, let's remember that audiences love to hear stories in the context of celebrating a life. And let those stories function as examples of a life well lived. We would encourage you to limit your eulogizing and storytelling to that person and his or her life. Some speakers have gotten into trouble by shading an epideictic speech into a political one. Even with speakers who lived a very public and/or political life, it's probably best to leave the controversial stuff out; we can do legacy talk in the future. Let's mourn and celebrate rather than politicize and score points.

Speechmaking: The Importance of Emotion

We should close this chapter by spending just a bit of time on emotion. One of Aristotle's most important contributions to rhetorical theory, at least for us, is how he understood emotion. That is, he claimed that the degree to which people felt emotion, any emotion, was directly related to space and time. In other words, the reason why you're feeling such profound sadness at a funeral is because a death very recently happened (time), and you were close to the deceased (space). You've heard the expression "time heals all wounds." That folk wisdom is a direct descendant from Aristotle, who saw firsthand just how important emotion could be to speechmaking. After all, we don't make the same judgment when we're angry as opposed to when we're calm.

But the person usually asked to deliver a eulogy often was very close to the deceased; as such, emotions can overwhelm our ability to speak. And if you don't think you can deliver a eulogy people will understand; perhaps a friend or family member can deliver your carefully crafted words for you. But if you do want to deliver a eulogy, work hard at concentrating your energies on that manuscript, the words themselves, rather than the audience, the occasion, and of course the lost loved one. We've found that by focusing deeply, almost obsessively, on the text of our remarks, we can get through even extremely emotional situations. But again it takes practice.

And if you do find yourself quite literally "choking up" with emotion, your audience gets it; in fact they're likely experiencing it right then and there, too. But after gathering yourself, do your best to turn your concentrated energies back to that manuscript; in it, as opposed to a keyword outline, can be your mental focus and your emotional comfort at a difficult moment. Watch and listen as Kevin Costner focuses intensely on his manuscript during his moving eulogy to his friend and co-star Whitney Houston, all while delivering his address with just the right pacing. Note, too, how Costner helps listeners understand that Houston's greatness and her tragic demise sprung from the same source.[9]

The speech of introduction, the speech of thanks, the wedding toast, and the eulogy are only four of the most common forms of commemorative speaking. You've heard others, including the commencement speech, perhaps the motivational speech; no doubt you've also heard many speeches called apologia in which a public figure offers an apology. In a day and age in which we don't do much "public blame," the apologia functions rhetorically as our act of contrition. Instead of blaming others, the apologia asks speakers to look in the mirror—and when done well, to seek forgiveness. From Bill Clinton to Tiger Woods and Lance Armstrong, we want our celebrities, our athletes, our politicians, and even our clergy to seek public

---

9 Visit link: https://goo.gl/GBhMAi

forgiveness when they blow it.

We hope you'll never have to offer a public apology. But you will likely find yourself in the role of eulogizer, toast-er, thank-er, and introducer, and hopefully honoree. Prepared carefully and delivered well, such speaking roles allow important cultural occasions to be both celebrated and memorable.

> Senator John McCain's Eulogy [Flip Learning chat]

> A Son's Eulogy {Flip Learning chat]

> Chapter 11 Quiz [Flip Learning quiz]

12 Seeing and Hearing the Magic

12.1 Models of Public Speaking Excellence

In this our final chapter of *Public Speaking in the 21st Century*, we wanted to provide our readers with some models of excellence across the informative, persuasive and special occasion speeches. We realize that we run a certain risk in showcasing these speeches and speakers: namely, that these represent the only possibilities of rhetorical excellence. We would remind you, though, that these are samples; as such, they represent possibilities—nothing more. The last thing we want you to do is to slavishly mimic what you're seeing and hearing, but we do want you to get a feel for what's possible. We should also highlight the fact that they're featured here because we selected them, not The Omnipotent G/god of Public Speech who has authored many public speaking books. As such, they represent our biases and predispositions. As such, they'll also change as we expe-

Episode 12: The Impossible [Flip Learning video series]
Class is out for the semester, but TA Robert's work is never done.

rience more speakers and speeches.

The principles that we've highlighted and explained in *Public Speaking in the 21st Century* provide you with a template for thinking strategically and intelligently about your speechmaking. In saying as much, we'd remind you that a shiny new Lamborghini and an old clunky Ford share four wheels and a combustion engine. In other words, crafting the eloquent, the exquisite, the beautiful and the sublime are possible only once you've carefully grasped the foundations. And those foundations will often lead speakers in different directions. A "paint-by-the-numbers" approach to public speaking greatness simply doesn't exist. And despite Plato and Aristotle's search, it never will. But those moments of insight, those flashes of brilliance, those bursts of creative energy, facilitate the magic of invention—the elusive magic that Gorgias glimpsed and described more than 2,400 years ago, and the same magic that animates our public discourse in a Democratic society.

12.2 Speech Samples

Informative Speeches

Social Media [Flip Learning speech sample]

Audio Professionals [Flip Learning speech sample]

Epilepsy [Flip Learning speech sample]

Pacifism [Flip Learning speech sample]

Panic Attacks [Flip Learning speech sample]

The Life of Samuel Morse [Flip Learning speech sample]

Persuasive Speeches

Participate in UNICEF's Clean Water Campaign [Flip Learning speech sample]

Make Computer Science a Priority [Flip Learning speech sample]

End the Death Penalty [Flip Learning speech sample]

Take a Philosophy Class [Flip Learning speech sample]

Special Occasion Speeches

Ode to Sebastian [Flip Learning speech sample]

Graduation [Flip Learning speech sample]

My Bed [Flip Learning speech sample]

A Tribute to Old Friends [Flip Learning speech sample]

Credits

6 NPR logo via Wikimedia Commons (PD); **6** Ted Talks logo via Wikimedia Commons (PD); **6** Shark Tank logo via Wikimedia Commons (PD); **10** Image via Wikimedia Commons; **16** Image via Wikimedia Commons; **25** LeBron James image by Keith Allison via Flickr (CC BY-SA 2.0); **25** Stephen Curry image via Flickr (CC BY-SA 2.0); **25** Michael Jordan image by Basketballphoto.com via Wikimedia Commons; **26** Joshua Bell image by Alexander Böhm via Wikimedia Commons (CC BY-SA 4.0); **26** Bill Russell image via Wikimedia Commons (PD); **27** Winston Churchill image via Wikimedia Commons; **27** Warren Buffett image by Fortune Live Media via Flickr (CC BY-SA 2.0); **27** Rihanna image by celebrityabc via Flickr; **27** Adele image by marcen27 via Wikimedia Commons (CC BY 2.0); **37** Image via Pixabay; **42** Image by Kevin Rushforth via Wikimedia Commons (CC BY-SA 3.0); **46** Image via Wikimedia Commons (PD); **47** Gary McCord image by Keith Allison via Flickr (CC BY-SA 2.0); **47** Samantha Bee image by Montclair Film via Flickr (CC BY 2.0); **47** Stephen Colbert image by Montclair Films via Wikimedia Commons (CC BY 2.0); **48** Image by Eric Draper via Wikimedia Commons; **58** Julian Knowle image by pfctdayelise via Wikimedia Commons (CC BY-SA 2.0); **58** Beavis and Butthead by methodshop.com image via Flickr (CC BY-SA 2.0); **61** Image by Southbank Centre via Flickr; **64** Malcolm X image by Herman Hiller (World Telegram staff photographer) via Wikimedia Commons; **64** Elizabeth Cady Stanton image via Wikimedia Commons (PD-US); **67** Jesse Jackson image by Elvert Barnes via Flickr (CC BY-SA 2.0); **67** J.K. Rowling image via Wikimedia Commons (PD); **79** Image by Steve Clarkson via Wikimedia Commons (PD); **79** Image via Wikimedia Commons (PD); **81** Image by Simon Fraser University–University Communications via Flickr (CC BY 2.0); **84** Image via Wikimedia Commons (PD); **85** Image by Blausen.com staff ("Medical gallery of Blausen Medical 2014," *WikiJournal of Medicine* 1 (2014): 10) via Wikimedia Commons (CC BY 3.0); **86** Image by Jim Bowen via Flickr (CC BY 2.0); **104** IUD image by Sarahmirk via Wikimedia Commons (CC BY-SA 4.0); **104** Tesla image adapted from original logo by Tesla Motors via Wikimedia Commons; **109** Kim Jong-un sketch by User P388388 via Wikimedia Commons (CC BY-SA 4.0); **109** Miley Cyrus image by Mass Communications Specialist 3rd Class Casey J. Hopkins via Wikimedia Commons; **119** Barack Obama image via Barack Obama Presidential Library (PD); **119** Kanye West image by Marcus Linder via Flickr (CC BY-SA 2.0); **119** Taylor Swift image by Eva Rinaldi via Flickr (CC BY-SA 2.0); **121** Lemon image by Nick Youngson via Picserver.org (CC BY-SA 3.0); **121** Lemonade image via Pixabay; **123** Abraham Lincoln image via Wikimedia Commons (PD-US); **123** Edward Everett image via Wikimedia Commons (PD-US); **133** Image via Wikimedia Commons (PD); **134** Image via Wikimedia Commons (PD); **138** Walter White image by jaroh (SrilArt) via Flickr (CC BY-SA 2.0); **138** Tyrion Lannister image by Duncan Hull and art by akse_p19 via Flickr (CC BY 2.0); **154** Image by Gage Skidmore via Wikimedia Commons (CC BY-SA 3.0); **157** Image via Pixabay; **160** Image by Warren K. Leffler (*U.S. News & World Report*) via Wikimedia Commons; **162** Image via Wikimedia Commons (CC BY-SA 3.0); **163** Image by Ossewa via Wikimedia Commons (CC BY-SA 3.0); **165** Image by Camera Eye via Flickr (CC BY 2.0); **192** Image via Pixabay; **195** Image via Wikimedia Commons (PD); **197** Image via Wikimedia Commons (PD); **206** Image by Elelicht via Wikimedia Commons (CC BY-SA 3.0); **216** Image by Mobilus In Mobili via Flickr (CC BY-SA 2.0); **219** Image via Wikimedia Commons (PD); **221** Image via Wikimedia Commons (PD); **238** Image by Ftkrwalc via Wikipedia (CC BY-SA 3.0); **245** Ted Bundy image by the Florida Department of Corrections via Wikimedia Commons (PD); **245** Casey Anthony image by the Orange County Sheriff's Office via Wikimedia Commons (PD); **245** O.J. Simpson image by Peter K. Levy via Flickr (PD); **248** Image via FilmLoverss site; **266** Image by amfucla via Wikimedia Commons (CC BY-SA 4.0); **269** Image via Wikimedia Commons (PD); **278** Rosa Parks image via Wikimedia Commons (PD); **278** Mother Teresa image via Wikimedia Commons (PD); **278** Nelson Mandela image via Flickr (CC0); **278** Steve Jobs image by Matthew Yohe via Wikimedia Commons (CC BY-SA 3.0); **282** Image by Kamyar Adl via Flickr (CC BY 2.0); **282** Image by Disney | ABC Television Group via Flickr (CC BY-ND 2.0); **284** Seve Ballesteros image by Jonjamdar via Wikimedia Commons (CC BY-SA 3.0); **284** Stephen Curry image by Keith Allison via Flickr (CC BY-SA 2.0); **286** Image by Illuminance Studio via Flickr (CC BY 2.0); **289** Image by Lawrence Jackson via White House Archives; **290** Pericles image via Max Pixel; **290** Abraham Lincoln image by Jeff Kubina via Flickr (CC BY-SA 2.0)

Made in United States
Orlando, FL
04 September 2023